REMNANTS

Rosemarie, c. 1952.

ROSEMARIE FREENEY HARDING

REMNANTS

A Memoir of Spirit, Activism, and Mothering

WITH RACHEL ELIZABETH HARDING

DUKE UNIVERSITY PRESS   DURHAM AND LONDON   2015

© 2015 Duke University Press
All rights reserved
Printed in the United States of America on acid-free paper ∞
Typeset in Arno Pro by Westchester Book Group

Library of Congress Cataloging-in-Publication Data
Freeney Harding, Rosemarie.
Remnants : a memoir of spirit, activism, and mothering / Rosemarie Freeney
Harding,
with Rachel Elizabeth Harding.
pages cm
Includes bibliographical references and index.
ISBN 978-0-8223-5868-8 (hardcover : alk. paper)
ISBN 978-0-8223-5879-4 (pbk. : alk. paper)
ISBN 978-0-8223-7558-6 (e-book)
1. Freeney Harding, Rosemarie. 2. African American scholars—Biography.
3. African American civil rights workers—Biography. 4. Mennonite
women—Biography. 5. Civil rights movements—United States—History—
20th century. I. Harding, Rachel E., 1962– II. Title.
E185.97.F835A3 2015
323.092—dc23
[B]
2014039595

Chapter 4, "There Was a Tree in Starkville," is reprinted with permission
from *Sojourners*. Chapter 24, originally published as "Atlanta's Mennonite
House," is from *Widening the Circle: Experiments in Christian Discipleship.*
Copyright © 2011 by Herald Press, Harrisonburg, Virginia 22802. Used by
permission. Chapter 29 was originally published as "Bernice Johnson Reagon:
A Song in the Time of Dying" by the Veterans of Hope Project. Used by
permission.

Cover art: Rosemarie Freeney Harding, c. 1986. Photo courtesy estate of
Walter Lee Dozier.

CONTENTS

A gallery appears after page 143

There is no scarcity. There is no shortage. No lack of love,
of compassion, of joy in the world. There is enough.
There is more than enough.

Only fear and greed make us think otherwise.

No one need starve. There is enough land and enough food.
No one need die of thirst. There is enough water. No one
need live without mercy. There is no end to grace. And we
are all instruments of grace. The more we give it, the more
we share it, the more we use it, the more God makes. There
is no scarcity of love. There is plenty. And always more.

I

This is the universe my mother lived in. Her words. Her ways. This
is the universe she was raised in, by parents from rural Georgia who
came up in the generation after slavery. People who had lived with
many terrors but who knew terror was not God's final say. This is the
universe she taught me. Whatever I call religion is this inclusive,
Christian, indigenous, Black, southern cosmology of compassion and
connectedness. It is the poetry of my mother's life.

Mama died at the end of winter in 2004. For almost ten years, we
had been writing. Gathering up her stories—her long, sweet flashes of
brilliance, her prayers, what she remembered of her Woodlawn, Chicago childhood and the high strong laughter of her mother and aunts;

her father's gentle work-worn hands. She was giving me what she knew I would need to survive this world; and what I would need to love it. What she wanted me to tell about her, what she knew of God, the people we come from and her many magnificent companions in the movement for justice in this nation.

Lord, I have been writing Mama's story for too long. Much too long. Passing through so many sicknesses to get here—hers, my father's, my brother's, my own. But she stood there, like the mother in Lucille Clifton's poem, at the other side of the river, holding out her heart, set to throw it across when my waiting hands could finally catch it.

II

> God sent me before you to preserve for you a remnant on earth, and to keep alive for you many survivors.
> —GENESIS 45:7 (REVISED STANDARD VERSION)

Mama trained her mind toward the good. Even before she knew anything about Buddhism, or the Dalai Lama. Before she ever traveled to India. I don't know when it started. Maybe she was born that way. Or perhaps she had seen her own mother and father do it so often, her aunts, too, that it became an artless response. She would lean naturally into the side of encouragement and moral strength. And forgiveness, though she was not imprudent.

She could find a blessedness in anything. She assumed it was there and no matter how deeply hidden, her expert hand would scoop it out and show it to you.

In her counseling, she used a Japanese practice of gratefulness, Naikan/Morita Therapy. It emphasizes training our spirits toward gratitude, especially for our mothers and those others who sacrifice so much for our happiness and well-being. That appealed to her. "It works quickly," she told me. I told her she wouldn't have many clients if she kept asking people to remember what they had done to hurt their mothers and all the things their mothers had done to take care of them. "That's the opposite of how most psychotherapists make their money," I said. She laughed.

The Dalai Lama says look upon all beings as if they were our mother—the person who has loved us best, loved us most in our life; the person who has been kindest to us. Treat all beings as if they were our mother. Because, in fact, they are. Mama says the Dalai Lama said, "We have all been each other's mothers."

In my classes, Mama tells the students we have all been the good one. And we have all been the "evil" person. We have all been many things. And we yet carry those lifetimes in our cellular memory. Just as we carry all of the universe in our cellular memory. So there is no judgment of others. Just the will to do good toward them. To show kindness in this life. We all want happiness. We all want someone to be kind to us. We all want and need and have the right to joy in this life. To avoid unnecessary suffering. None of us is more worthy than the next. None of us is less worthy than the next. We are all the same in this. We have all been each other's mothers.

III

> Listen to me, house of Jacob and all the remnant of the house of Israel, a load on me from your birth, carried by me from the womb: till you grow old I am SHe, and when white hairs come, I will carry you still; I have made you and I will bear the burden, I will carry you and bring you to safety.
> —ISAIAH 46:3–4 (NEW ENGLISH BIBLE)

This book is neither autobiography nor biography. But some of both. And something else. It is Mama's and it is mine. Mostly it's a representation of the richness of my mother's creative imagination, the mystic streams of her spiritual life, and the lyricism and joy of her activism. It is also the way she modeled for me a female-centered, indigenous wisdom about the world.

There are women in communities all over this country and around the globe, I'm sure, like my mother. I have met some of them. Women with original and powerful ways of understanding life, ways that come from the struggles and pleasures of their lived experience, but that may not find much expression beyond their kitchen tables, their market stalls, or the crises in which their families inevitably turn to them for guidance. (Like Mamie Till-Mobley said, "Any trouble I've ever had in my life, it took Mama to get me out.") My mother had a few outlets for her magnificence. But not nearly, it seems to me now, enough.

Mama had an acute and gentle intelligence about navigating the world—finding the wine, the sweetness in the unexpected places. The hard places. And sharing it. Making it last. Making more. (Talk about loaves and fishes . . .) Her understanding of social justice activism situated struggle very comfortably alongside hospitality and mothering. This is a meaning of activism I have not seen widely discussed among scholars, but the women of the Southern Freedom Movement (and their families) know about it. More than anything, it is an activism based in "being family"—bringing people into the house, literally and figuratively. Making room and making welcome. Letting people know there is room for them in the vision, in the struggle, in the nation, in the family.

IV

I will gather the remnant of my sheep from all the lands, and I will bring them back to their fold and they shall be fruitful and increase. I will set shepherds over them who will care for them, and they shall fear no more, nor be dismayed, neither shall any be missing.
—JEREMIAH 23:3–4 (RSV AND NEB)

Mama joined the Mennonite Church when she was a young woman, around twenty-one. Her older sister, Alma, joined before her and Mama followed, admiringly, in Alma's footsteps. It was the Mennonites, the Movement, and her marriage to my father that sent my mother south to Atlanta in 1961.

I was born there; my brother Jonathan too. We lived in a household that streamed with progressive ideas and people—Black nationalists and pan-Africanists; African independence movement intellectuals and artists; labor organizers; Quakers and Mennonites (and a few Catholics and Southern Baptists) who were trying to live a witness of peace and racial reconciliation; student activists; our Chicago cousins; blues musicians and folk singers; painters and writers; radical publishers and co-op founders; and just plain ole good-hearted people. All kinds. Of course, the freedom movement people were the mainstay—our parents' activist friends and comrades who were like a big extended family to my brother and me.

In the houses where I was a girl, there were beautiful sepia-toned paintings by Kofi Bailey and Elizabeth Catlett Mora's Mexican-workshopped black-and-white prints. A full set of Blue Note jazz albums and folk stories and songs from Atlantic and Folkways records that my mother borrowed weekly from the library for us. Also lots of books. Black children's books were an emerging genre and my father brought home from his travels the newest titles for me and Jonathan. Black coloring books, Black comic books, biographies and histories for children with illustrations by Tom Feelings and Jacob Lawrence. Most of the books in the house were from my dad's collection of American and African American history and literature, but there was, too, a growing set of texts on comparative religion, Eastern philosophy, meditation, and the Christian contemplative tradition. People like Gerald Heard and Thomas Merton, and, of course, Howard Thurman. Later, Paramahansa Yogananda, Bawa Muhaiyaddeen, Hannah Arendt, and the Dalai Lama. These were Mama's books. Both of my parents were interested in these world teachings about peace, about centering, about the grace in our shared humanity and the transformative power of love, but for my mother, they were a special sustenance and she read them with quiet enthusiasm. The spiritual teachings were places she went and considered and remembered the way she considered and remembered Bible verses or my grandmother's counsel.

. . .

My parents met in 1959. They were among the few African Americans in the Mennonite Church of that era. Both were eloquent and perceptive public speakers who shared an interest in how the Mennonite witness of reconciliation and peacemaking could contribute to Civil Rights struggles, and what insights those struggles could offer back to the Mennonite Church. Shortly after their marriage in 1960, with support from the Mennonite Central Committee, my mother and father moved to Georgia as representatives of their denomination to the Movement and established "Mennonite House"—an interracial voluntary service unit, community gathering place, and retreat space for activists and peace church volunteers. It was the first of its kind in the region.

Before and after Mennonite House, Mama taught school and did social work, infusing her activities with an essential compassion and respect (and self-respect) that she modeled on her own mother, who learned it from her parents and grandparents—those southern generations who repeatedly transformed collective trauma into empathy and acumen. Mama surely absorbed some of that skill. People would come to her, in private moments or in public tears, and she would put her hands on them and draw out the pain so they could drop it. Or she would show them how to make something useful of it—a song, a dance, some poetry for those following behind. That's what she did with her own grief, until it weighed too heavy even for her. Then it was lifted.

All throughout my life, although I wasn't aware until much later, Mama must have been collecting and laying out teachings and experiences like a trousseau. What she read and studied, judged against what she lived, balanced with what she knew in her heart to be truthful and good. These beautiful, useful garments; worn close to her skin: the movement work; years of research on Ida B. Wells-Barnett and the history of Black women's activism; friendship with Makota Valdina Pinto, a Candomblé priestess from Bahia (Mama and Valdina each spoke slices of the other's language enough to recognize their kindred lives); visits with my father to Hopi elder Thomas Banyacya and Dhyani Ywahoo, a spiritual leader of the Cherokee nation; study with Michio Kushi; the initiations she took with Lama Zopa Rinpoche; and the Vipassana meditation and Feldenkrais training and certification. And so much more . . .

All of this spiritual and intellectual exploration was undergirded by the foundational wisdom my mom received from her mother, Ella Lee Harris Freeney, whom everybody called "Mama Freeney." And, toward the end of her life, as she reflected on it, my mother said, "It's all the same source. The way Mama Freeney and Grandma Rye and them taught us, the way they lived, is the same as these beautiful teachings from around the world, Rachel. It's all the same, baby. Everywhere we go."

It was a lifelong conversation with my mother I had. She knew that she could be accused of irrationality, but there was nothing more rational, more logical, more grounded in reality for Mama, than the way the universe loves and tends to every living being within it. That was the life model for her.

By the time I got to know her as an adult, Mama's mystic way in the world was "hidden in plain sight" like the freedom quilts and slave songs whose steal-away meanings were camouflaged. She lived, in moments, an exquisite, shamanic love for the world in open concealment. Simultaneously feeding and protecting a philosophical approach to life that connected her powerfully and intimately to her own source of supply—which was both ancestral and cosmic. Either way, it was something that reminded her, in almost everything she saw, that the universe is filled with mercy and forgiveness. And that people will always fight for justice, reach for a way to be whole in the world.

Candomblé—a lyric, poetic, ancestral religion of strength and supplication—echoed my mother's mystic attention to life, to the universe, to spirit. My first visit to a temple in Bahia in 1985, was for a *festa de Xangô*[1] at the terreiro of Olga de Alaketu. My attraction to this Afro-Indigenous Brazilian tradition was immediate, visceral, and sublime. The orixá rhythms stammering out the names of God; the smell of holy leaves; the smoke-grease flavor of old iron pans and palm oil; the insistent, inherent language of drums.

Mama taught me to know the presence of God in the kitchen; ancestors in cooking—her hand raised, shaking an affirmation out of her bones; sharp percussive claps; prayers and gestures of prayers sliding into pots of greens and chicken. We ate her tenderness. Candomblé was a religion I knew from home. Women slicing onions and cutting meat. Tending fire and telling stories. And any moment, any moment at all, they enter—the *ancianos*—coming in through the door, a window, the floorboards: rising up the helixed ladders of our own breath and blood. Telling God.

This African-based mysticism was a deep strand, a wide band, in my mother's life, as it is in my own. It is why I am drawn to study and write about Candomblé, Vodou, Santeria, and other ritual traditions of the Afro-Atlantic diaspora. It is also, I am convinced, an underappreciated resource of Black American life and culture that has a great deal to teach about who we are and what our history offers to the world. To paraphrase Alice Walker, it is often in our mother's lives and gardens (and kitchens) that the numinous, the persevering, and the creative meet.

v

And I will make her that halted a remnant, and her that was cast far off a strong nation.
—MICAH 4:7 (KING JAMES VERSION)

My mother lived forty-four years with my father. Stayed with him "through many dangers, toils, and snares." She taught him and fought him and forgave him. And loved him and taught him some more. It was a difficult union in some respects. Nevertheless, when my parents were able to work together they were an absolutely amazing pair. Both intellectually sharp and full of imagination, Mama and Daddy were capable of deeply inspired thinking and, at their best, each generously fed the other's genius.

What they created together—in workshops, in classes, in their comments and revisions of each other's writings and speeches, and in their ministry to people around them—was an offering of astounding beauty. My mother and father both loved history and people. And they shared a remarkable devotion to this country, believing profoundly in its democratic and creative potential. In the best times, I loved simply being around them. Their conversations and company fascinated me far and above anything my peers could offer and they nurtured my curiosity about the world.

My dad is past eighty now, a senior scholar of African American history whose work resonates in the DuBoisian tradition of scholarship firmly yoked to social justice activism. And his life has its own poetry, its rhythms urgent, tangled and soaring. . . . In Mama's final year, and since, he is a magnified comfort, a rock.

Mama and Daddy were both activist-scholars. While she raised my brother and me and a half dozen of my younger cousins who lived with us at different points, Mama wrote a master's thesis on Ida B. Wells-Barnett focused on the antilynching activist's biography and the progressive leadership of African American women. When we were older and in college, and as she cared for her aging mother-in-law, Mama did another master's degree in nutrition and social work, documenting the benefits of a healthy diet for the rehabilitation of juvenile offenders. In the year before she passed, she talked about doing a PhD in archaeology; she wanted to study the African burial ground in New York City. Always, my parents shared a conversation about the radical tradition in American life; and as they began to teach and write jointly about the relationship between spirituality and social activism, my mother's strengths and sagacity surfaced in more obvious ways.

VI

And the remnant that is escaped of the house of Judah shall yet again take root downward and bear fruit upward.
—2 KINGS 19:30 (KJV)

If you didn't know better, and you saw them at a public gathering, you might at first think she was a gentle helpmeet. *(Or, you might not.)* If you were lucky, or simply present long enough, you'd see her rise up in the middle of a crisis room and deftly turn the tension into a reconciling, embracing wind. She could do it subtly; or she could do it like a tornado.

My mother knew how to talk, how to debate. She was a brilliant debater. She would think of perspectives and justifications that occurred to no one else in the room until she uttered them. My grandmother, Mama Freeney, loved logic and thinking and trained all of her children to use their minds inventively and well. Mom won speech and debating contests in high school and college and she developed into a thoughtful and passionate public speaker.

Sometimes though, she sat silent in the public circle and offered her mothering and mentoring to the offended/offending parties only afterward. She knew so much about healing . . . about recognizing the underlying, unspoken wounds that catalyzed the outbursts on the surface.

A few years before Mama passed, the Veterans of Hope Project convened an activists' retreat at the Fetzer Institute in Michigan. Most of the participants were older folks from the movement days—people like Tom Feelings, Grace Boggs, Zoharah Simmons, and about twenty others. There were a few people present under thirty, but not in equal numbers to the elders. Two of the young folks, a man and a woman, were working with a film crew to document the retreat and they felt particularly alienated from the conversation and history shared by the elders. While they gathered footage and sound, they were also observing and quietly seething inside. They didn't see themselves reflected in the stories, in the planning, in the community. And on the last day (something explosive almost always happens on the last day with activists, doesn't it?), the young people from the film crew blew up and told everybody else they were hypocrites. Most of the older people were stunned. They certainly didn't see themselves that way and they wondered where the youths' seemingly sudden rage had come from.

The retreat had been coming to a close and people were talking about what it had meant to them—how rejuvenating it was to be in the company of ones who shared some of their history and some of their earnest, frustrated love for their country. The young videographers declined to join the circle, saying the gathering had no place for them—people who were not movement veterans, or professional community activists, or nonprofit administrators. They said they had thought several times to leave, and now, here at the end of the weekend, when everybody seemed to be relishing a kind of feel-good moment, they were angry and hurt because it seemed as if none of this had anything to do with them.

By the end of her statement, the young woman was turning to walk out, visibly choked up and emotionally exhausted. Mama went and got her, and stood next to her, bringing her back to the circle. My mother looked around at all of us and said the responsibility of the elders is to take care of the youth, to protect them. "No, you can't leave," Mama said, holding on to the young woman whose eyes were watering now. "Because you are part of us and none of our work means anything if our children don't know that we love them."

Mama stood there talking to the circle, holding the girl tight around the shoulder and turning the energy in the large open room from defensiveness and frustration to proof that this family we had made over the three or four days of our gathering was strong enough to mend a circle some had not even seen was ruptured.

VII

Remnant: What is left of a community after it undergoes a catastrophe.
—*THE ANCHOR BIBLE DICTIONARY*

In 1997 my mother was awarded a fellowship to the Mary I. Bunting Institute at Radcliffe College. At the time she was very sick. She had recently been diagnosed with diabetic neuropathic cachexia (a rare and debilitating neurological complication of diabetes) and was struggling to find a treatment that her sensitive body could tolerate. She wanted very badly to accept the fellowship and do a research project on the relationship between spirituality and social activism among veterans of the Southern Freedom Movement. She also needed some time and space of her own to think and to heal.

Mama originally envisioned *Remnants* as a book that could serve as a manual for people in the helping professions—social workers, community activists, teachers—giving them encouragement and creative models for grounding their work in a broadly inclusive vision of community, justice, and human relationships.

I had just finished graduate school and was taking care of my mother as her condition became more acute, so I accompanied her to Cambridge where we shared a one-bedroom apartment for almost a year. We visited medical specialists, experimented with various treatments for the wracking pain and extreme weight loss Mama was experiencing, and in the moments when she was strong enough to sit with a tape recorder, we talked—about family history; about politics; the joys and lessons of her childhood; the strangeness and meaning of her current illness; her study in India with Tibetan lamas; the plays and performance pieces she envisioned as healing ceremonies for our fractured nation; the ancestors, the orixás and God; and the Black southern mysticism that informed so much of her mother's and grandmothers' wisdom.

Remnants quickly grew from a manual into a more personal memoir, influenced by our conversations and my curiosity about the details of my mother's life, and the roots of her spirituality and her politics. We began work on a collection of essays and stories, poems and recipes, play fragments and autobiographical remembrances that connected my mother's history with stories of the many extraordinary women and men she knew from the movement days. She was trying to get well from the accumulation of burdens she carried, using the writing as a way to explore how she and other movement people had come through trauma in the past. In a way, it served that purpose. Telling her story, with support from staff and colleagues at the Bunting Institute, and restorative visits to see her family in Chicago, Mama saw her health improve remarkably by the end of the fellowship year.

Once we returned to Denver, I worked only sporadically on the project (to my everlasting chagrin). Mama wanted to finish it quickly, but I was by then helping to direct the Veterans of Hope Project and found it hard to make the time we needed to pull all the pieces together. After Mama passed, I left the day-to-day operations of the VOHP and began working in more earnest on the book.

. . .

The voice of this text is now our mixed utterance. Our dialogue. While Mama was living she would tell me stories or write a first draft of her ideas and I would stretch and mold and shape the text further along and then read it back to her to make sure it still said what she wanted it to say. She'd tell me if it was good or if I had left out something or had missed a detail or tone she wanted to emphasize. And I'd work some more and come back again. Sometimes, I'd add things that occurred to me as interesting or helpful and usually (but not always) Mama would say "Oh yes, that's good. Let's put that in too." In shaping the chapters of this book, I have employed stories I heard from Mama all my life; entries from her journals; interviews with her family members and friends; essays she and I wrote together while she was alive; and transcriptions of more than forty hours of our taped conversations (made mostly between 1997 and 1998).

Like any mother and daughter, we had our discords. We both tended toward the dramatic—although my dramas were passive-aggressive and Mama's moments of fire were strikingly lucid. And while she didn't generally interfere in my life choices as an adult (most of the time I was asking for her advice anyway), if she got a strong feeling about something she'd let me know. Sometimes to my frustration, and sometimes to my relief, her instinct was usually right.

Our family moved a dozen times before I was sixteen. Different neighborhoods, different cities. Mostly because of my father's academic itinerancy and my parents' political commitments. Mama said, "Some people moved around a lot because they were mili*tary*; we moved because we were mili*tant*." Sometimes the accommodations were only temporary anyway or the rent was too high. Through it all, Mama worked very hard to give Jonathan and me stability. She and her nephew, our cousin Charles, made all the packing and unpacking every year or two seem like fun. I was a fairly well-adjusted child, but I needed a lot of affirmation in the midst of so much unpredictability. My mother and my cousin made sure I had it. In the final seven years of her life, as I worked to claim and nurture my voice as a writer and scholar, my mother was my mightiest champion—giving support without stint and in abundance, a broad infusion of confidence and love.

But Mama needed her own space and air. All my life, she was looking for retreats—monasteries, meditation centers, places to go breathe some quiet, restore her strength, and hear herself think. While my grandparents were still living in the family home in Chicago, she would go there. Home. A respite. The family took care of her. Even so, she said later, the problems in the marriage had a constructive effect. They pushed her further into some-place infinite. She had to make an inner sanctuary where she could do the alchemy of healing her own spirit, so she could get up and keep dancing.

. . .

Through my mother's story, *Remnants* seeks to bring the indigenous wisdom of the African American community, particularly of women, into engagement with more academic understandings of intellectual produc-tion. At various points, this book is in dialogue with the work of historian of religions Charles H. Long, dramaturge George H. Bass, womanist writer and scholar Alice Walker, philosopher and mystic Howard Thurman; with the wisdom and experience of religious activists Clarence Jordan, Martin and Coretta King, Anne Braden, Will Campbell, Marion King, and His Holiness the Dalai Lama; and with the creative insights of artists Bernice Johnson Reagon and Lucille Clifton, among others. These engagements help situate *Remnants* as a resource for critical investigation of indigenous African American religious and philosophical thought in relationship to a range of other traditions.

Like Walker's *In Search of Our Mothers' Gardens*, Lucille Clifton's *Genera-tions*, and Gloria Anzaldua's *Borderlands/La Frontera*, this book contributes to and draws from the critical, ethical, philosophical, and creative meth-odologies that are, in current parlance, understood as "womanist." These are approaches that profoundly wed interdisciplinary, intellectual work to reflective insights emergent from the lived experiences of women of color. The rhythms and tones of *Remnants* are conversational; its narrative is pop-ulated with stories and poems and dreams, as well as analytical essays and autobiographical meditations. In some ways the quality of the text is like music, jazz, and old soul—you'll hear it best with your heart, the inner ear.

My hope and expectation is that the book will speak to many communi-ties and disciplines, crossing varied terrains of academia, community, and spirit. Obvious points of scholarly interest will be found in the subdisciplines of religious studies: especially African American and Afro-Atlantic religion; comparative religions; American religious history; womanist theology and ethics; public theology; Anabaptist studies; mysticism; and spirituality and social justice. In particular, *Remnants* provides helpful avenues for examin-ing a meaning of Black southern indigeneity as a cultural-religious scaffold for the 1960s freedom movement struggles and as a grassroots philosophical tradition with valuable insights about the uses of compassion in healing the experience of trauma. Scholars and students in other fields, such as history (African American social history, the Great Migration); literature (spiritual autobiography and coming-of-age narrative); sociology (family studies, social movement theory); peace studies; ethnic studies; and women's and gender studies, will also find benefit in the text.

The book will be particularly valuable to activists, teachers, students, and artists—those members of our larger society who are in especial search for ways to gather and express both informed critique and fervent hope for the transformation of our society.

.   .   .

Remnants proceeds in roughly chronological order. But it is also circular—starting from the ancestral Georgia ground and ending there as well. The book is organized in six sections, plus a foreword and afterwords. The foreword includes this preface and an opening reflection "(the light)," which introduces the mystic-spiritual element in my mother's life running throughout the narrative. The preface is my attempt to outline major elements of my mother's worldview and personal experience as well as to offer guidance about the nature of the text and help readers appreciate its somewhat unorthodox timbres. With the exception of the preface, the afterwords, and the call-and-response of the section called "The Bunting," this book is written in my mother's voice, sometimes from verbatim transcriptions of tapes and journals, sometimes from my reassembled memories of her words and ideas, often a combination of both.

The first and second sections of *Remnants*, "Ground" and "North," are animated by motifs of ancestral history and extended kin, beginning with the stories of an enslaved great-grandmother, Grandma Rye, and coursing through the family's life in early twentieth-century southwest Georgia, their move north to Chicago in the Great Migration, and Rosemarie's youth and young adulthood in a city that was an incubator of joys and possibilities as well as a place of deep segregation and constraint. This portion of the book illustrates the spiritual values my mother learned from family in examples of our death and dying rites; daily associations with extended kin and neighbors; the special tolerance for children, people in crisis, and social outcasts; the dreams, visions, and personal, mystic spirituality of her own mother and Mama's early encounters with the inexplicable, the holy. Among the chapters here are stories of angels and ghosts in the Georgia backwoods; Daddy Freeney's memories of the lynchings that sent him north in search of safety for his sons; Aunt Mary's fistfights with death and the snowstorm that paralyzed Chicago when death finally won; the yellow-flower healing teas of my mother's great-grandmother, Grandma Rye; and meditations on the battered shields and ironic beauties of blackness.

The third portion of the book, called "South," recalls Mama's years as a full-time worker in the freedom movement, her perspective as a racial reconciliation activist and the spiritual journeys she began in the aftermath of that time. It includes stories of her work as cofounder (with my father) of the first integrated social service agency in Atlanta, Georgia—Mennonite House—in 1961; recollections of their travels in the South as an "advance team" for organizations preparing to launch desegregation campaigns; and reflections on the transformative spirit and power of the movement. This section also incorporates stories of Mama's friendships with men and women who embodied a convergence of spiritual conviction and dedication to social change, such as Clarence and Florence Jordan, southern white founders of Koinonia, an interracial agricultural community in Americus, Georgia; Anne Braden, a white Kentuckian with a lifelong commitment to racial and economic justice; Howard and Sue Bailey Thurman, deeply ecumenical spiritual elders to my parents; Martin and Coretta King who lived around the corner from us in Atlanta; and Bernice Johnson Reagon, early member of the SNCC Freedom Singers[2] and founder of the women's a cappella group, Sweet Honey in the Rock.

The latter parts of *Remnants*, "The Dharamsala Notebook," "Bunting," and "The Pachamama Circle," trace Mama's immersion in the mystic traditions of Buddhism and contemplative Christianity. Here again she is drawn to reconciliation, forgiveness, and healing—the grounding values of her earliest life. In this portion of the book, she connects the practice of Insight Meditation (Vipassana) to the visionary traditions of African American folk religion; and ties Tibetan Buddhist teachings on the purpose of human life to the lessons Rosemarie learned at her own mother's side as they visited dying relatives and friends. This section examines the links among the healing of personal wounds and societal injustices; and between the search for meaning and reconciliation in Mama's life and the journeys of others who were her companions. In many ways, "Bunting" and "The Pachamama Circle" coalesce as the mystic heart of the text. In a grammar of medicine, womanist storytelling, and ritual, these sections narrate my mother's journey through a staggering, uncommon illness and recount how her effort to tell the stories of her life moved her toward renewed strength.

The AfterWords of the book are a poem and two essays I wrote in the years following my mother's death; the poem is an homage to Oyá, the Yoruba energy of storm and transformation, and to our fugitive forebears. One essay is about Mama's extraordinary engagements with my students and the other describes the experience my father and I shared of my mother's final weeks of transition. The last pronouncement of the text, "(the Call)" is Mama's—offering to all in her reach an assurance of ancestral strength and an urge to reclamation of our national identity as a place of compassion and justice.

VIII

> But now for a brief moment favor has been shown by the LORD our God, to leave us a remnant, and to give us a secure hold within his holy place, that our God may brighten our eyes and grant us a little reviving in our bondage.
> —EZRA 9:8 (RSV)

When my mother died we held two memorial services. One in Chicago at my cousin Phillip's house, which was mostly family and a few old friends. And another one, a larger one, later that spring in Denver, where people from many strands of my mother's life came to honor her with stories and songs and fellowship.

At the first memorial, the one in Chicago, my father stood up and told everyone how Mama had inspired and directed him to be the kind of teacher, writer, and pastoring presence he became. He said, "When Rose and I were first married, I sometimes spoke in a judgmental way. I had a tendency to lecture in hard, harsh tones—especially about racial justice issues; criticizing people for what they were not doing and doing wrong. My manner could be rough, even caustic at times. Rose observed me for a while, and then she took me aside and said to me, 'Vincent, you're a good speaker. But you can be very critical. People need encouragement. If you can give them that, it will inspire them to know they can change.' "

Standing there, surrounded by my aunts and cousins and family friends from way back, I announced that I had known many intelligent people in my life—growing up around universities and in the movement. I had studied at plenty of fancy schools myself—but my mother was the smartest person I knew. Categorically. She was brilliant—on multiple levels simultaneously. Creatively, emotionally, intellectually—there wasn't a problem any of us ever had that she couldn't figure out how to help us through. I mean her mind was *sharp*. Nothing got by her. Sometimes she perceived things so quickly and so keenly and so differently from anyone else, that I had to whip my head around to catch the backdraft of her genius as it sped on its way to the next sun.

Remnant: the remaining. the part leftover. the trace still perfumed; ephemeral and persisting. the buried things. coming up out of the ground like ladders.

Her dying was hard for all of us. We were weary and undone. I was not there at the very end. The ambulance beat me to the house and her heart had already stopped. But Daddy and my Aunt Sue were there and they held Mama's hands and rocked her soft and sweet from this world to the next. The emergency workers revived the heartbeat but nothing else, and then at the hospital, not even the heart would pulse on its own. Mama had gone.

We sang for her in the hospital room. Waiting the day or two until everybody could come to say good-bye. Hymns and spirituals. The old-timey church songs she loved like the blues. And the prayers from Ikeda and Bawa, from Lama Zopa and the orixás. We washed her with mint and marjoram and roses. We placed suras and Tibetan prayers on her chest, her forehead, whispered into her ears. And then, after the wires and tubes had all been released from her body and the room was quiet, we sat a while longer. Then we left.

Mama is gone, but she is not. Her hand still rests on my back when I am troubled, or sick, or frightened. She comes and she watches us. Her nieces and nephews. Her children. Our father. Her sisters. Her beloveds. All the circle of those who remember her. We are her remnants. The remaining lace, the cloth. The small rocks. This book, not perhaps what she would have made of the vestiges, is still hers. And mine. And yours . . .

RACHEL ELIZABETH HARDING

DENVER, COLORADO

Notes

1. A public ritual ceremony in honor of the orixá of fire, justice, and communal well-being.

2. The Freedom Singers were a singing group formed in 1963 by young activists in support of the Student Nonviolent Coordinating Committee.

I can't say exactly where the Light entered, where it started from. Suddenly, it was just there with me. A white light, bright enough that it should have hurt to look. But it didn't hurt. In fact, as the Light grew and enveloped everything in the room, I felt the most astonishing sense of protection, of peace. It surrounded me and I was in it, so joyfully. I don't know how long I was engulfed by this Light, this space. But when I came out of my room my family was looking at me oddly, like there was something different about me they couldn't quite name.

It was an afternoon when I was about twenty-one. I had been in my room, just resting. Aunt Mary and Mama Freeney them were in the living room. My Aunt Hettie too. Some cousins, a sister, a friend. Our house was always full of family. I had come in from work and greeted everyone awhile. Then I went into my bedroom to rest. I was just lying on the bed. Maybe dozing. And then I was in the Light.

"Baby, you alright?" they asked me when I stepped out of the room. They said my face looked different, more peaceful. I smiled, and told them I was fine. Because I was. Whatever came to me, that afternoon in my room, left me with a great sense of comfort.

The Light became a kind of touchstone in my life. It was so much love. Like an infinite compassion. At the same time it was something very precious and intimate. It awed me, really. And when I walked out of the room, everything looked different. Clear. Even later, outside the house, in my classes and at my job, everything looked sharper. It was like a heightened sense of presence. Almost a shine.

I never wanted to talk about it much, because it seemed proud to do so. Also because it wasn't the kind of experience one could easily describe.

I believe Mom and Dad and the family had already given me a foundation in forgiveness and compassion. I received such care as a child. Already, growing up, I wanted to be a nurse. I tended to my nieces and nephews whenever they were ill and Mom even sent me to check on neighbors who were not feeling well. There was a German family named Anderson that lived down the street from us and ran a cleaners. The son had horrible asthma attacks. Mrs. Anderson would call Mama Freeney for help when the attacks came and Mom would send me down the street to the pharmacy to get medicine and take it back to the Andersons' house. I'd give the boy his medicine and sit with him until he was breathing more steadily again. Mrs. Anderson would be so worried about her son, so agitated, that once someone else arrived to help, she usually left the room for a while. And I didn't mind staying.

I already had this leaning toward healing in my life. And the Light was so full of acceptance and care . . . It fed that in me, I think.

Soon after the experience in my room, I was looking for a way to go deeper. I must have associated the Light with spirituality, in some sense; even though I didn't have a language to fully articulate it then. But I held it close to my heart. And I joined my sister Alma's church, Bethel Mennonite, on the West Side of Chicago.

I had visited Bethel a few times and as I got to know more about the Mennonites, I started to see that what they believed—about nonviolence and forgiveness, for example—resonated with what I had learned in my family. But mostly, I was looking for something spiritual to connect to, and my sister Alma was a model of kindness and integrity for me. I really admired Alma; and anything she thought was good, I thought was good.

I do believe that whole experience put me on a path. And the Light stayed with me a long time. It gave me a sense of security and deep internal connectedness to God, I would say. All these journeys I've been on, these spiritual practices and traditions—from the Mennonites to Bawa Muhaiyaddeen and the Dalai Lama—the meditation, the prayers; I've been trying to sustain what the Light gave me. What it awakened and showed me. I guess that's what the definition of "spirituality" is for me: whatever sustains us like the Light sustained me for years. Is it similar to the Light? *Is it the Light?*

As I moved away from my family and struggled for years with the unexpected strains of my marriage I needed the grounding and shelter and strength of that Light. There is something in there, in that profoundly embracing energy, that allows you to come out with a kind of forgiveness, an absence of animosity. It's like the Dalai Lama says, there's nothing we can't go through. We can live through it all with compassion. I want to tell you that this Spirituality of Compassion, if we can call it that, can come through very ordinary people. Look at me. I'm not particularly intelligent; I have my failings just like anybody else. And I'm certainly not the only one who has experienced this. There are so many ways—some people go through Vipassana meditation; some say they have seen Jesus; or that they've met the Buddha. However they describe it, they've met . . . Help. Encouragement. A deep deep encouragement in this life. For me, it was the Light.

1 · Ground

2 · Rye's Rites
(poem)

her broom. the sand of her yard. the bare feet of morning. sweeping
circles in the dirt-dust. in the sun-rising. stick broom of straw. her
breath. the strength of her heart. old strength. old love humming.
sweeping a company for the sun. circles in the red dust. circles in
the new air. stick trace. straw trace. passing straw along the ground.
passing leaves along the ground. a little wind to move death.

My great-grandmother rose mornings before the household, washed
her face and hands, rinsed her mouth. She climbed down the porch
stairs to the backyard and chose between her fishing pole and her
circle broom. The broom came first.

Grandma Rye is the furthest back we know. Somebody said she was
an African. Landed in Virginia. Sold to Florida. In slavery-time she
worked for the captain of a steamer, up and down the Carolina and
Georgia coasts. She cooked. Some of her children died. Some of
them she couldn't keep. The last of them, born close on to Freedom
stayed with her. One by the captain, she named Ella; three by a man
she loved, she named Eliza, Willoughby, and Hester.

My sister Alma is a praying woman. All of my sisters are praying
women. When I am sick, Alma tells me Grandma Rye prayed for my
health. All of our health. All of our blessing. All of our coming
through. Her children, their children, their children's children.

Grandma Rye bends low and breathes on the sand. makes wind circles
on the sand of her yard. sweeps death loose from georgia red dirt.
cleanses it of venom. passes leaves over the deaths of her children. over
the loss of her children. makes lines stretch. makes prayers stretch.
passes straw over grief gone and coming. gives us a place in the world. a
long-breathed prayer in labor. a way to heal. a trace . . .

3 · Grandma Rye

My great-grandmother, Mariah Grant, cooked on an open stove that looked like a big fireplace. She had a metal tripod where the cast-iron pots hung suspended over the heat. When she made cornbread, she poured the batter right into a ring of coals. Joe Daniels said it had the best taste.

Joe Daniels and Pansy are two of my older cousins. They grew up in Leesburg, Georgia, with all the family and Grandma Rye, which is what everybody called her. What we know about Grandma Rye is that she loved fishing. Every day, well into her nineties, she walked a dirt road into the woods to a place on the Kinchafoonee Creek and sat there with her cane pole and the worms and watched the water ripple out in front of her. Her great-grandchildren took turns going along to keep Grandma Rye company. Some liked the walk and the worms and the quiet, some didn't.

Grandma Rye's fishing spot was a few miles from town and on the way she pointed out flowers and plants, stopping sometimes to pick a stem and crush a few of the leaves between her fingers. "This one is what we gave to Pamp when she had fever last month. Takes the fever right out. You'll sweat a good while, but it breaks the heat." She'd put the crushed leaves to her nose and then hold them for the child to smell. They'd walk some more, Grandma Rye pointing her finger at a patch of blue blossoms near the base of a black walnut tree or pinching a couple of dark sweet berries from a bush so the girl or boy could taste them.

She was an herbalist. She was a slave in Florida when she was young and she learned about herbs and roots there. "Florida was full of herbs," she used to say. Had more than Georgia. According to my mother, Mama Freeney, the Black folks in Lee County hardly ever got yellow fever or jaundice because Grandma Rye knew what to make to keep everybody well. "She tried to show me when I was a girl," Mama Freeney told me. "I used to go fishing with my grandma and she tried to tell me, 'This is for the scarlet fever, and this is for when babies get croup.' I listened a little but I really wasn't paying attention like I should have been. I told her, I said, 'Grandma we got doctors now, we don't need all of that anymore.'" Grandma Rye might have looked out of the side of her eye at her granddaughter and half-smiled. She'd have put whatever she had in her hand into her apron pocket and then they would have walked on.

Other than stopping to show the child a few plants and trees, there wasn't a lot of conversation when the grands and great-grands went fishing with Grandma Rye. They'd get to the pond or the creek side and find a place to sit on a large rock, or a log, or up against the trunk of a tree. The old woman would bait her hook, then she'd cast out and sit. Waiting for a draw on the line and watching the shudders on the surface of the water. There just wasn't a lot of talking. If the child got tired he might lean his head in Grandma Rye's lap and doze a while. If it started to rain and the child awoke to ask, "Are we gonna go now, Grandma Rye?" she might tell him, "No, child. This is just a light one. It'll pass," and cover his head with her apron. And rest her hand on the child's forehead. Sure enough, the rain wouldn't last long. It was just a sprinkle really. A refreshment for the tall grasses and the canopy of trees. And for her.

You had to sit with Grandma Rye as long as she felt like staying. That's the part that could make it hard. Some children don't like to be quiet that long. The more noise you make, the more disturbed the fish are. The less noise you make, the sooner they'll bite. I know this even though I never knew Grandma Rye. I was two years old when she died. She stayed in Georgia with her daughter, Ella Stewart, when the rest of the family moved north. But I always loved fishing.

Fishing must have been a way to be still. They say Grandma Rye was quiet and she was strong. She lived to be 105. Already quite old when my sisters and brothers knew her, they said she cooked and cleaned for herself practically till she died.

The stillness was something my mom loved too. Although she didn't have many chances to fish once the family moved to Chicago, Mom found other ways to get it. There was someplace inside she'd go, especially in moments of distress. When a family member was in trouble, if a difficult decision had to be made, whenever she had something on her heart, Mama Freeney would get quiet. She could be in a room full of people, and it would be clear, after a moment, that she was also someplace else at the same time. She would close her eyes, maybe make a subtle hum to herself. A softness came over her in those moments, a kind of covering . . .

I think Grandma Rye had this tendency too; the going inside and getting what she needed there to emerge a little stronger. That ability would have been essential, to come through what she came through in life. What we know about Grandma Rye is this: she loved fishing, she cooked and healed, and she had been a slave.

She could have been brought here from Africa as a small child. Some in the family heard it that way. Maybe she was born on this side of the water and it was her mother who came across in the Middle Passage. We're not certain. But this much we know: Mariah Grant was in Virginia as a young girl when somebody purchased her and carried her to Florida where she worked as a slave. She lived in Cedar Keys, and maybe in Tampa for a while as well. The man who owned her also owned a boat that sailed along the coast. My great-grandmother cooked for the man and his crew in the boat. She cooked in the kitchen of the master's household too. And when she was about eighteen years old, Mariah had a child by that master. She named her daughter Ella. Later, she had three other children by a man she loved and married: Robert Grant. That was Eliza, my grandmother; a son named Willoughby; and a daughter named Hester.

In those years, in Florida, Grandma Rye saw a lot of meanness. And she wondered about God.

In 1981, *National Geographic* magazine asked my husband to write an essay on the Underground Railroad. We decided to trace parts of the route ourselves, with our children, starting in Maryland and going through Pennsylvania, Ohio, and eventually up through Michigan into Canada. We were assigned a photographer and made our way into communities where the memories of slavery's traumas and escapes were kept among the descendants of those who had lived them.

In the midst of this, I talked to my mother about what she knew of Grandma Rye and our family's history. Mom was born around 1888 and her parents spent their early childhoods enslaved. She remembered that Grandma Rye talked of a friend who escaped from slavery in Cedar Keys, Florida. "More women than men got away," Grandma Rye had said. It was harder for the men to get away but both men and women were trying and some made it. There were white men who patrolled the roads and woods and the edges of the swamps, looking for fugitives. These were the paddy-rollers, and they beat the people they caught to death.

I asked Mama Freeney if she had ever heard of Harriet Tubman, and she told me, "Yes, I've heard of Harriet Tubman. Grandma Rye talked about her . . . but there were a lot of Harriets. Women like her, you know. And men too." People who risked their lives to get away and then came back, time and again, to rescue their children and parents and cousins and friends. "Oh Lord, yes," my mother remembered the stories. Yes, there were some, like Grandma Rye's friend, who made their way out.

My sister Alma, who is twelve years older than me, listened to our great-grandmother as a child. Grandma Rye told the youngsters gathered around her, looking up into her face, that slavery made her wonder about God. Slavery-time was so hard, she said, "The master's family had it so good and we were suffering so bad."

"We prayed a lot," Grandma Rye said. "And we thought about this God of the white folks, wondering who it was they were praying to. We thought maybe we should pray to this God as well. And we did. But times didn't get no better." Alma says that after a while Grandma Rye and the other slaves simply accepted their plight. Praying still, but not really hoping for more. But I think differently.

There is a lot of silence around Grandma Rye's spirituality in the family. We never talked about how our ancestors took on a new religion or what remained of the ways we had brought with us from Africa. But as I think about it now, so much in my mother and great-grandmother's manner in the world pointed toward rootedness, a very old strength. They were trusted women. They were healers. They were the ones others gave their money to when trying to save it for something important. Grandma Rye wouldn't return it to you until the agreed-upon time and circumstance, no matter how you insisted or cajoled. And Mama Freeney did the same. People came to them with fears and worries and angers and sadnesses and my mother and great-grandmother made those things into something else. Something lighter to carry.

I'm convinced, their spirituality had a source more profound than an anguished nineteenth-century conversion to the faith of their oppressors. And then, too, they transformed that faith once it was in their hands.

I have the feeling it wasn't a straight path from our ancestral ways to this new religion. It's still not a straight path. I think about the Native Americans, the way they were forcibly evangelized; so much taken away. Yet in their dances, like in ours, there remains a connection, an acknowledgment of the deepest and oldest aspects of their spirits. It's something in the body.

Sometimes I wish I could talk to somebody who was there when Grandma Rye was questioning the Christian God, working out the transition. Figuring out what parts were useful, what parts should be ignored; and where the connections lay between what she already knew to be true of the world, true of herself and God, and what new things the struggle (to be human) in this land was teaching her.

For Grandma Rye, perhaps it was fishing. The way to cultivate her own connection to spirit—something linked to the natural world, to the ancestral energies of Africa. Fishing allowed a contemplative space, indeed required it. A nearness to the energy of water. Maybe she even found it in the open fire; so many years of her life at the flame. Even though she had been forced there, maybe she found an affinity with the alchemy of fire: altering the properties and tastes of things into sustenance and flavor. Or it could have been the plants she knew and spoke to as she picked them to help care for someone ailing. Perhaps a combination of all of these, and something else too . . .

My family has a streak of unspoken mysticism running straight down the middle of the bloodline. It is a streak connected to healing and to justice. And in my experience, it is also connected very much to silence. The silences about those parts of my great-grandmother's religiosity that did not fit easily with acceptable Christianity; the heft of prayer and waiting inside God's presence. The wisdom about life cycles and the recognition of healing properties in the earth around us. The mystic line is also connected to laughter and the unnerving creative power that rested just under my mother's tongue in the telling of her ghost stories. My cousin Pamp and my sister Mildred say some people thought Mama Freeney was a witch. Some were even just a little bit afraid of her, because she could conjure presences so convincingly in her stories that people listening would turn around to look behind them and half-expect to actually see the invisible woman my mother was just then inviting into the room.

Mama Freeney taught us to recognize the reality of spirit in the world through those stories passed to her, in the southwest Georgia woods, by her elders like Grandma Rye. She taught the same lessons in games she played with the grandchildren—chasing them through the house in her housedresses, her mouth gumming a drone, deep and potentially frightful to little children; cornering them in closets till, in an excited mixture of elation and fear, they broke past her and ran shrieking-laughing to the other end of the house, where she followed and started pursuit all over again, until either they or she was too exhausted for another chase. My niece Jean swears Mama Freeney made the bedsheets rise without touching them.

What we know about Grandma Rye is that she is the farthest back we can go in the female line of my family. My mother's mother's mother. We know she fished and healed and survived slavery. She cooked over an open hearth and told her grands and great-grands about the people who risked death to be free. Grandma Rye was the generation that wondered about God. She took from the old ways her silences, her mystic attention to the world, her knowledge of plants and herbs and people, and fed this into the family line so that it would live there alongside the new things.

And she prayed for us. Grandma Rye prayed this to God: *Bless all the generations that follow me. The generations that come from me. My children and their children and their children's children.*

And we are here.

Southwest Georgia is where Lee, Terrell, Dougherty, Schley, and Sumter counties rub up against each other in the Flint River basin, and where creeks with names like Kinchafoonee and Muckalee snake through and spill over, as the water heads south. The face of the land when I got there was slow small hills and fields of cotton, peanuts, and corn; turpentine mills and piney woods; the clay a red juice in rain, red dust in hard sun. This is where Otis Redding and Bernice Johnson Reagon came from. Where Jimmy Carter was raised; and where a white country preacher and his wife established an interracial, radical Christian farm in the aftermath of World War II. This was also the home of the Albany Movement in the early 1960s, and the starting ground of the international affordable housing program—Habitat for Humanity. And, many years before, it was where my great-grandmother, Mariah Grant, arrived from Florida, with the children she could keep, and settled when slavery ended in a town called Leesburg.

My parents, Dock and Ella, were born there, and left. They left with most of my aunts and uncles, all of my older brothers and sisters, my maternal grandparents, and a generation of my cousins. Almost everybody, it seems, who could go, did go north. Philadelphia, New York, Detroit, and for most of my family, Chicago. I was born at the end of that journey. My sister Norma and I were the first of the northern generation of Freeneys. And while cousins and friends from Georgia visited us throughout my Illinois childhood, none of my relatives went back until the 1960s. I was the first to return.

My parents didn't talk to me about why they left Georgia. At least I don't remember much conversation about it. But the elders in the family were always protective of children and I'm sure they must have had conversations and remembrances among themselves that the younger people were spared. It was not until I had joined the Mennonite Church, married, and decided with my new husband to go to Atlanta to work full-time in the freedom movement that my mother and father began to tell me some things. They were, understandably, fearful for my safety. The state I was returning to was the same one from which—thirty-five years before—they had fled.

There was a tree, my mother said, in a place called Starkville, along a road where people passed daily going to and from their labors. It was a large tree, an old tree, and the branches spread crooked-wide in all directions. "They used to hang people there," Mom said. "They would hang a man there and then make all the Colored go and look. If you get down that way, ask somebody to show it to you." My father, too, warned me in his quiet ways. And perhaps my going south brought up more memories for him, because as he aged, he began to tell his grandchildren about some of the horrors he had witnessed.

A few years before they left Georgia, a man and all three of his sons were strung up from different limbs of that tree in Starkville and shot, their bodies left to hang as gruesome and vicious warnings to others. That man and his children became why Daddy Freeney decided to leave. This he did tell me, "I wanted my sons to live."

In spite of all of this, I think my parents were proud of me and even happy that in some sense, the family was now returning from a long exile. My daughter, Rachel, was born in Atlanta in December 1962. She and her brother, Jonathan, were two of Dock and Ella's last grandchildren, and the only ones raised in the South. When my father died, we found a calendar from 1962 on the wall of his basement workshop. All but its last page had been torn off and it hung permanently at the month his first Georgia-born grandchild came into the world.

Going south for me was thus, in some ways, a homecoming. Atlanta was a logical place for a movement-based project headquarters, a southern city that viewed itself as more progressive than some others. We traveled throughout the region on behalf of the Mennonite Church and in liaison with organizations like the Southern Christian Leadership Conference (SCLC), the Student Nonviolent Coordinating Committee (SNCC), the Congress on Racial Equality (CORE), and the Fellowship of Reconciliation (FOR). But there was something beyond the logic of an administrative deci-

Rosemarie with Martin Luther King Jr. at Shady Grove Baptist Church in Leesburg, Georgia, c. 1962. PHOTO COURTESY OF RACHEL ELIZABETH HARDING.

sion that drew us to Atlanta. Among our strongest movement connections quickly emerged the campaigns and communities of southwest Georgia.

These were connections that started forming even before we left Chicago. I met Clarence Jordan in 1961 when he came to speak at Woodlawn Mennonite Church. I was immediately struck by the soft cadences of his voice and his warm country manner. He reminded me very much of my own father and uncles. The work of racial reconciliation and justice that Clarence and others were doing at Koinonia Farm seemed both exciting and profoundly important.[1] Vincent and I kept in touch with the Koinonia community, and once we arrived in Atlanta, we made frequent visits to the farm in Americus for rest, reflection, and fellowship. Like Koinonia, we were trying to create a spiritually grounded, service-oriented interracial community, and the place we founded—Mennonite House—was a kindred spirit to Koinonia.

Another important connection was the Albany Movement. In 1961–62, SNCC and other freedom movement organizations were invited to Albany to help mobilize a citywide campaign to desegregate public facilities, register Blacks to vote, and otherwise challenge the structures of white supremacy in the city and its environs. I did a lot of behind-the-scenes organizing. Vincent and I participated in many demonstrations and we came to know members of that community very well. What I saw reminded me of my family in Chicago—from the abundant hospitality, and the familiar comfort foods, to the remarkably unassailed dignity of people struggling for their most basic democratic and human rights.

Finally, there was something about the land. I remember driving down the narrow unpaved roads toward Americus and Albany—brush and high grass on both sides, mist rising there in the early mornings. I tried to imagine what those roads might have been like when my Indian ancestors first made them, when my African ancestors walked and worked them, and when my father and uncles were building houses, courthouses, and train stations along them in Macon, Albany, and Leesburg. My father told me that he made bricks from the clay under these roads.

My relatives in Chicago—especially the older ones, my parents, aunts and uncles, who had lived into adulthood in Georgia—shared something with the southerners I was meeting now. In spite of its horrid and painful history, southwest Georgia (like the southeastern United States generally) has a sweetness. It is often vaunted, romanticized, and even sometimes derided as a conceit. But as I've experienced it, in the region itself, and in the lives of the exiled African Americans who raised me, it is true.

My older sister Mildred speaks admiringly of our aunts, our mother's sisters, who worked as domestics in the houses and hotels of Chicago's elites and in the factories of the city's industries. They carried themselves with so much grace and self-assurance. Often, it was in their tone of voice. Not too high—as it might have been if one were upset. And not too low—as if one were angry. But a modulated, gentle way of speaking. A southernness. Perhaps the tone originally developed from the mixture of African, European, and Native American pronunciations that guided the sounds of the early days of the colonial encounter. Or, maybe it began as a marker of status—gentility as leisurely language. It seems, too, that especially for

Black folk, there may have been something about the vocal timbre, the words chosen, the manner of speaking, that was protective. During slavery and in the years of viciousness that followed, one's voice tone, one's decisions about how and what to say, could literally save one's life. So there is that too—the legacy of violence in the sweetness. And some people may think it is a bad thing to preserve a quality of voice reminiscent of subservience, of persecution. But if it is reminiscent of those things, it also expresses a human creativity in oppressive circumstances; something crafted that ultimately transcends and transforms the original defensive uses.

There were lessons, indirect perhaps, in the choices my parents made about telling stories of their lives down South. I think they were conscious of the impressions left by brutal memories and they used reticence and discretion to point toward an alternative. The absence of a full reporting, in my childhood, of the southern horrors, was not so much that Mom and Dad wanted us to live in simpleminded obliviousness; rather, they wanted us to always hold a basic respect for other human beings. Even for people who might victimize us. They wanted us to be able to develop our own spirits without undue prejudice; not to be so burdened by disdain that we couldn't grow our souls. I think they understood that the terror they went through, stark as it was, was not the last word in human experience; and that there are chords deeper and more resilient than racism can ever be and they wanted to give us access there.

Going "back" south, then, I carried the memories of family and friends who had lived there and left. The stories were in me, in an embodied, visceral way. Growing up among Black Georgians, Mississippians, and Alabamans meant that I absorbed a sense of that which was horrific in the place they had gone away from. It also meant that I absorbed a sense of what was potentially healing from that same place.

. . .

As the youngest child, I lived at home after my older brothers and sisters had gone out on their own. I remember one time when I was alone in the house with Mom and Dad. From my bedroom I overheard them in the kitchen talking about their times down south. Their voices were light and warm as they talked about the people with whom they had shared good times—laughing together at the remembrance of past joys. They joked between themselves about long gone things.

I can't specifically remember anything they said, but I know that it gave me a feeling of connection with family members whom I had never known.

Some who had left the South years before my parents did—like my mother's brothers, Tom and McFall, who went to Mexico, the Philippines, and the Panama Canal. And like my father's uncle who had settled in Liberia and raised a family there although he returned to Leesburg when he was ill because he wanted to die at home.

I heard security in the delighted rising and diminishing of my parents' voices. Where they sat together at the kitchen table—maybe snapping beans together, or eating Mom's hot rolls with coffee—their mutual pleasure in reminiscence was like a soft and sturdy pillow under me. Somehow, knowing that they shared so much, that they had so much in common, so many warm confidences of family and friends and life before Chicago, was a kind of protection; another layer of relations wrapped around me like bunting.

When I went South, I took all my memories with me. The memories of violence and the things-too-terrible-to-talk-about and the memories of the people who survived them. Especially the people who survived them—my family, and so many others I knew, who had found a way (inside themselves and out) to live beautiful lives . . . anyhow. And when I got to Albany and Macon and Americus and Leesburg in early 1961, I was met by other people, other southerners, Black and white, who had also found a way—and who were working hard to make that way wider.

Note

1. Koinonia is an intentional community, founded in Americus, Georgia, in 1942 by white Southern Baptists Clarence and Florence Jordan and Martin and Mabel England. The community was deeply committed to racial and economic justice and suffered tremendous harassment and violence from the Ku Klux Klan and others who saw Koinonia Farm and its members as a threat to traditions of white supremacy.

Daddy Freeney registered for the draft in 1917. He signed up with his brother, Paul—"Buddy Paul" he called him. Daddy didn't go to the war, though. He already had two children. Maybe the army didn't take him because the war was winding down, or maybe they had reached the limit of Black men they wanted for the segregated units. Then, too, the white Georgia draft board didn't want Black men to fight. Wanted them to stay in the fields and on the tracks. Daddy's race was listed as "African" on his draft card and the card is signed with an "X," his mark.

My parents lived in Macon then and Daddy worked for the Central of Georgia Railroad. He was a fireman, keeping the coal-fired engines expertly tuned and stoked with steam. Daddy knew the engineer's precision job and did it even though he never got the title. He did construction too—made bricks and laid them for the train station. And he always farmed, always had a plot of land where he grew things. My father experimented with grafting fruits into new varieties, making new things appear. In the family, they say Daddy Freeney invented nectarines, grafting together a peach and a plum. Some white men who had heard about him and his fruit came from California. They took some samples back. Daddy had side jobs too, doing chores for white people to make extra money.

He said he'd be in a store, sweeping or whatever, and the white folks would be talking to each other as if he wasn't there. Talking about Black folks. It was a curious thing. The white people must surely have seen him. But they had learned to act as if Blacks were inconsequential.

By completely ignoring his presence, they showed that they neither feared what Blacks thought, nor cared.

So, this one particular time, shortly after the end of World War I, Daddy was working around in a store, or at the train station, and there were some white people—men and women—nearby having a conversation. "Our biggest trouble nowadays is these colored men," one of the women said. Or, maybe she said *boys*. "They're back from the war and thinking they have a right to stand up to a white person. The Germans got them all confused, making them forget their place." Now the contradictions and ironies were obvious. The Germans were nursing their own insidious racism, of course. The southern white woman nonetheless thought it was they who had "put ideas" into the heads of America's Black soldiers. Certainly, even before the war, African Americans were keenly aware of the injustices they suffered in the land of their birth and supposed citizenship. Fighting now in Europe, they were emboldened (and even further outraged) by the paradox of risking their lives on behalf of a country that degraded and terrorized them.

There were many instances of Black soldiers coming home at the end of the war—and this happened again after World War II and Vietnam—with a strong conviction that if they could fight for democracy on the other side of the world, they had a right to democracy at home. A lot of the men were refusing to genuflect to white people, not saying "Yessir" and "Yes ma'am," not stepping off the sidewalk and into the street when a white person passed by. They were challenging Jim Crow laws by refusing to sit in "Colored" sections of buses and trains, and white people were noticing. After World War I, lynchings increased in many places in the South. Those Black people who dared to "get out of their place" were often made examples to traumatize the rest of the community into something that looked like compliance.

"That's right," one of the white men agreed, "our biggest problem now is these colored who went over there and got to fraternizing with the white people." Maybe he didn't use the word "colored." Maybe he said "nigras" or even worse. They were sitting around in that Georgia afternoon talking about the fear and anxiety they had that African Americans, aided by white Germans, would threaten the basis of their way of life.

Sometimes just the act of walking around a southern town in a U.S. army uniform was cause enough for trouble. When Joe Daniels was a young boy in Leesburg at the end of the war, he saw a Black soldier ejected from a passenger train as it rolled through the town. The train didn't even stop. "He was riding in the only car they had reserved for Black people—right behind the engine where they fire up the smokestack. Right up in that smoke. That's where the Black people had to ride. The man had on a wool army suit with

Daddy Freeney in the family store at 4160 South Wentworth, 1960s. PHOTO COURTESY OF RACHEL ELIZABETH HARDING.

wrap leggings, you know, where they wrap the legs up. And they made that man jump. He wasn't bothering nobody, he was just going where he was going," Joe Daniels said. "I guess they didn't like it because he had on this uniform. He had to jump out the window and run down the tracks. I'll never forget it."

While the white folks talked around him, Daddy Freeney went about his business. Sweeping, moving crates and boxes, cleaning up. He tells the story with some humor—the absurdity of being the subject of this serious conversation, and yet essentially being a nonentity in the room. He said later, "White people are funny like that." Then, too, he told the story in a way—how should I put it?—as if to emphasize, *this is just the way things are.* He was describing the way we are expected to live. The way others expect us to be. As if we're not present. As if we don't matter. And at the same time, our outrageous, insistent living causes great fear.

6 · Joe Daniels
Getting Unruly

Joe Daniels is one of Aunt Mary and Uncle Willie Dan's children. When we were growing up, he had four brothers and sisters, but there had been others. Same in my own family. Some of the children died. Some disappeared. Joe Daniels had two older brothers—Willie B. and Wiley B.—who left home as young men. "They just never came back," Joe said. "And they never did write." In 1946, Aunt Mary and Uncle Willie Dan got news that both of the older sons had been killed. The brothers were gone then about twenty-five years, but somebody sent word.

My mother had brothers like that. Tom and McFall.[1]

They left Georgia after the first war and stayed gone. When their little sister, Aunt Bird, died in Detroit, they went to the funeral with overseas wives—Filipina or Panamanian, Alma says—and visited for a few weeks. Then, they disappeared again. Every so often there'd be a letter, which is how we knew where they were. Mom saved them in a trunk but time and dislocations have lost them now.

Some men were always leaving. Especially the young ones. As if the air was too tight or the trees noxious. Some left the state and some left the country. McFall was in the 1910 census listed as a gang laborer on a public road for the Lee County Convict Camp. Ten years later he was gone. No trace. Tom, his older brother, gone too. Mama Freeney's uncle, Willoughby Grant, went to Florida for forty-five years. And Daddy Freeney had an uncle who left for Liberia after slavery, started a family, and stayed there until it was time for him to die. Then he came home. But Willie B. and Wiley B. and Tom and McFall never did come back to Georgia and didn't stay long anyplace else inside the border. Hawaii, Panama, the Philippines, Guadalajara, Cuba—names and places we heard they might have been. Anyplace but the United States of America.

They went on ahead and we lost them. But eventually just about everybody else left too. Grandma Rye was almost a hundred when the family went north; so she stayed in Macon with her daughter Ella Stewart. I never met her but her hands are on the family yet.

. . .

Joe Daniels is tall. More than six feet. He was a tradesman like his father; a builder. And he liked to gamble. Even now, in his eighties, slowed somewhat and walking with a cane, he is a handsome man whose audaciousness and confidence lie just below a quiet surface. To hear him tell it, he's been forthright all his life. Which is part of the reason his family had to get out of Georgia. "See, I've always been strong," Joe tells us. "That's one of the reasons my parents had to leave."

Back in Leesburg, Aunt Mary and Uncle Willie Dan weren't bad off. Aunt Mary always had businesses—she sold J. E. McBrady cosmetics and household goods door to door like an Avon lady, and she had a little store in town. Uncle Willie Dan was a master carpenter and he ran a barbershop on weekends. He worked on houses and city buildings six months out of the year and farmed the other part.

"I remember one incident that happened right in front of my father's barbershop." Joe Daniels is talking at Christmas now, at my niece Nataleen's house. Remembering sixty years back. Rachel and I are there with the tape recorder catching what we can of my sisters, my older cousins, Joe. He's talking: "My father had made me a little shoeshine stand and it was right outside his barbershop. And across the street was a great big store where all the people, the sharecroppers, would come and get supplies once a month.

"Some of those people would work all year—year after year—and they'd make twenty bales of cotton. And at the time they probably could get, I don't know, maybe five hundred dollars a bale. But they would never get it. They'd work all year and they never would get out of debt. They would have these crops like peanuts and cotton but the people never would get out of debt.

"Anyway, this big store was owned by four or five brothers by the name of Cannon. I'd be sitting in front of my father's barbershop with my shoeshine box and one of the brothers would call me over, say, 'Come on, Will, I want you to shine my shoes.' He called me by my father's name, Will.

"I'd shine his shoes, but I never would say 'Yessir' and I never would say 'No sir.' Because he wasn't but twenty-one, twenty-two years old. He wasn't no old man. I said, 'Yessir' or 'No sir' to the old people. But this man was just a few years older than me. He tried to bribe me. He'd give me a dollar. That was a lot back then. They wasn't paying people that worked in the fields but a dollar a day. Work all day, from sunup to sundown and get a dollar. And here he's giving me a dollar to shine his shoes.

"Then maybe every couple of months he'd give me three dollars to wash the big windows in the store. They didn't have no squeegees or anything like that. I used a pail and a rag and I cleaned it inside and out. Three dollars for the windows. That was more than grown folks were making. Why was he giving me so much? Because I would never say 'Yessir' and 'No sir.' He was trying to get me to say it.

"That's another thing. You could grow up with them, play together and know them all your life, and as soon as they get to be eighteen or nineteen years old they want you to pay them that kind of respect. I'd say it to people my father's and mother's age: 'Yessir' and 'Yes ma'am.' But that's all I'm going to say it to. And I wouldn't do that if I didn't want to. I was kind of stubborn.

"It was hard for my parents because I could be headstrong. One time my little brother Perc and me were in a gun shop—that's a fascinating place for little kids. The white man who owned the store told me to go get a pail of water and while I was gone he asked my little brother Perc if he knew how to dance. Perc said something to the man that he didn't like and when I got back the man had my brother by the arm and was kicking him. We both ran out of the gun shop and over to my father's barbershop. And the gun-shop man followed us. He stood there in the doorway of the barbershop with his arms folded, telling my father, 'You better teach your boy how to talk to white folks.' Well, I grabbed an ax handle and ran right under his arms and started hitting that man in the butt with that ax handle. My father had to stop me. When I got home, they were trying to get a mob of people to come down for me, but nothing happened that time. But there was quite a few incidents."

Joe says his parents came north because he was getting unruly. "I was getting out of hand. I mean, I wasn't going to take all the stuff you had to take then."

. . .

Uncle Willie Dan's skills as a builder and Aunt Mary's enterprising nature ensured them a little more money and status than many, and they shared what they had. Uncle Willie Dan built a large, long wooden table with benches for the sides where his children and a coterie of friends and relatives ate together every day. They raised Jersey cows and pigs and piled sand from the creek to store white potatoes through the winter. Sweet potatoes underground in something like a teepee filled with straw. Hogs slaughtered and salted, vegetables and fruits canned. Aunt Mary had a special garden, half a block long, where she planted everything you could think of—greens, okra, corn, potatoes, cabbage, pole beans, butter beans, squash. "People could just come and get whatever they needed," Joe remembers. "We always had more than enough." And we knew how to share. It was how we survived.

Like my own father, Uncle Willie Dan had a car at a time when few folks—Black or white—owned motor vehicles. Once, Joe Daniels and his dad were driving into Albany on the state road, the dirt highway. Uncle Willie Dan's Tin Lizzy Ford passed a policeman in a Chevy, leaving him dusty and angry. When they got to town, the officer threw a Coke bottle at Uncle Willie Dan, and Joe told the policeman if he ever hit his father again he was going to kill him. And the next day, Joe Daniels came to town with his shotgun.

"You see, in the South, when a kid gets ten or eleven years old, his father buys him a shotgun. And they teach you how to hunt. You know, it starts around Thanksgiving. You go out and shoot possums and wild turkey and whatever else they have. So, the next day I took my double-barreled shotgun and went back into town. I knew I wasn't supposed to be shooting in town, but I was shooting at targets near the railroad yard. Well, the policeman didn't do nothing about it right then, but they called my Daddy and talked to him. And right behind that, it didn't take long, my mother and my sister Dorrie and my little brother, Isaac, all left. Then my sister Pansy left with her daughter, Middie Jean. The last ones to leave were us older boys and the men—my father; Jesse, who is my sister Pansy's husband; my brother Perc; and me."

Then, too, Joe was getting into what there was of a fast life in the little town. He told us about the places back up in the hills, in the woods, where Black people built their churches. The protected spaces—the churches that started as "brush harbors"—outdoor worship sites, with simple coverings, where there was privacy surrounded by the thickness of the natural world. They were out of the easy reach and sight of whites so they were good not only for worship but for other activities as well. "Every time I looked around," Joe Daniels recalled hesitatingly, "people would be gambling outside those churches. Sometimes it would be shootings right on the grounds of the church. They'd be preaching the sermon in the church, and outside people would be gambling and fighting and shooting at each other." He paused again. "I wasn't going to tell you that part."

"I saw a lot things when I was younger," Joe Daniels said. "I saw a big giant of a man, must've been about seven foot four, beat a little bitty man with a raw cleaned stalk of sugar cane because the little man was a stool pigeon; would go and tell the white people everything the Black folks were doing. And when the sheriff came, that great big ole giant man reached down in his overalls and pulled out two thirty-eights; and the sheriff got back on his horse and rode on.

"I know so many things. I just don't know how to tell it all."

Note

1. Sometimes written McPhaul.

7 · The Side of the Road

Before I was born, when the family still lived in Georgia, there was a bad accident at the side of the road. The road from Macon to Leesburg. Uncle Willie Dan hit a light pole with his Tin Lizzy and his wife, my Aunt Mary, went through the front window face first and got all cut up.

Uncle Willie Dan and Aunt Mary and their five children had been visiting with my family in Macon and were on the way home. My mom and dad and their own five were all in Daddy's Dodge, riding alongside our relatives part of the way back to Leesburg. Just to keep them company. Mom and Dad were going to turn around and come back to Macon and let Uncle Willie Dan and Aunt Mary them go the rest of the way on their own—just riding with them a piece of the road.

All the children were in the backseats of the two cars. That's how it was then, the mother and father sat in the front and all the kids, didn't matter if you had fifty, sat in the back.

Most people, Black or white, didn't even have cars then. Most just rode in a horse and buggy, or they walked. But Daddy Freeney and Uncle Willie Dan were kind of prosperous, you could say. Uncle Willie Dan had a barbershop and was one of the best carpenters in the county; had built the Lee County courthouse and a lot of the fine houses in the county seat. My dad was working for the railroad. So we were all doing pretty good and Daddy Freeney and Uncle Willie Dan had these cars.

Uncle Willie Dan was trying to beat Daddy Freeney driving fast down the road and when he turned a corner, he lost control of the Tin Lizzy and hit a light pole. He was hurt, too, not as bad as Aunt Mary, but they both needed to see a doctor. Daddy Freeney got all of his kids out of the Dodge and told them to get in with their cousins in the Tin Lizzy that was crashed into the light pole. Mom and Dad had some towels and a blanket and Mom wrapped Aunt Mary up and tied her face to try to stop the bleeding. And then all four of the adults got in Daddy Freeney's Dodge and drove to the hospital.

"Now y'all stay right here, you hear me? Do not get out the car. If anybody stop, anybody come over here to ask you any questions, you say we taken them to the hospital. Wait here till we get back."

Not a soul moved. The oldest must have been my cousin Dorothy who was fourteen, then my brother Son, who was twelve, and on down to my sister Sue, who was just two years old then. (Mom was pregnant with Thomas.) Ten children. Two carloads in one car, at the side of a southern road. And they stayed there until the parents got back. Which turned out to be a very long time.

The sun set and people passed along the road, with headlights and horseshoes and just the steady shuffle of shoe leather against the ground. It got late and dark. And spooky. Different people, black and white, peered in through the windows, asking, "What happened? What y'all children doing over there? How many got hurt?" The oldest siblings and cousins answered briefly and respectfully, telling the curious and the concerned that there had been an accident; that the parents had all gone to the hospital. They explained that Daddy Freeney had told them not to go anywhere, to stay together there by the side of the road.

When the adults finally did get back, Aunt Mary's face was sewn up one side and most of the younger children were sleeping, each propped against the others, sitting in laps, leaning on shoulders. They had hardly moved an inch—just lolled their heads over and fell asleep where they sat. The older ones were awake. My sister Mildred was only five, but she stayed awake too. This was segregated Georgia. And even children too young to know the details of the social geography of violence understood a thing or two about dangers. Years later, they all remembered that night. Everybody there remembered it. Even Sue, barely old enough to talk at the time, has a body memory of the apprehension of an uncertain place, surrounded by her brothers and sisters and cousins, waiting in the darkness for their parents to return.

Growing up with the story, I thought of what was unspoken and assumed: the necessity of obedience; the anxiety the children must have felt being left for so long under emergency circumstances; the angst of the adults and the way difficult choices were quickly made; the trust between parents and children; the responsibility siblings assumed for each other—especially older ones for younger ones; the hospital's unknowns—was it a black hospital they went to? If not, would anybody help them? What was Aunt Mary's condition? The image of the children all staying together, hunched at the side of the road, not leaving the spot where they were told to wait, is so moving to me, so haunting, and so very beautiful. It's a kind of metaphor—remembering the will of the elders, now ancestors, and staying together on anxious ground.

Newsprint and Poems

Ella Lee Harris Freeney was a reader. In Georgia, my mother read and wrote letters for people, taught school, and kept accounts for anybody trying to save for something important—tools, some land, a ticket, winter shoes for the children. She read newsprint off the walls by the time she was two. And she was her daddy's favorite child.

Now, all of Mama Liza and Papa Jim's children were intelligent, every one of them. But Ella Lee had charisma too; and a very autonomous way about her that her father admired and encouraged. Ella Lee shared Papa Jim's deep chocolate brown color; she was the darkest of all the children, and she spoke her mind. She read voraciously all her life—five-cent paperbacks and whole Britannica sets she bought from the resale shop; newspapers and magazines. She read almanacs and atlases. She read geography and history. And she loved poetry. When my mom was a little girl, back in Leesburg, before she was even old enough to go to school, the Black teachers would send for her when the white superintendent made periodic visits to the segregated schools. They'd stand her up on the teacher's desk and little Ella Lee would speak flawlessly:

> Great, Wide, Beautiful, Wonderful, World,
> With the wonderful water round you curled,
> And the wonderful grass upon your breast—
> World, you are beautifully dressed.[1]

Mom couldn't have been more than four or five years old at the time. But she was a prodigy. She'd tell you herself. When Mama Liza, my grandmother, was pregnant, the story goes, she fell in a truss between two railroad ties and her water broke. Everybody feared she had lost or hurt the baby. But when Ella Lee was born, a day or two later, she was fine and there was hardly any water or blood—because Mama Liza had lost it all in the accident. "I was born from a clean womb," Mom used to say, to which she attributed many things, in particular her ability to see what was coming before it came.

One day, when Mom was about two years old, they say, she was looking at the old newsprint that lined the inside walls of the small house where the family lived. Little Ella started pointing out words from the faded papers to her mother, "Look at me, Mama. I'm reading."

Mama Liza looked at her toddler daughter and said, "Gal, hush your mouth. You know you not reading."

"Yes, I'm am Mama," Ella said to her mother. "I'm am reading this." Mama Liza couldn't read or write herself so she waited for Papa Jim to come home to find out for sure.

Papa Jim learned to read in slavery time. When he was a boy in South Carolina, one of his jobs was to take the young master Stokes to school in a wagon hitched to a pony. At the schoolhouse, while the white children were doing their lessons in the front, Papa Jim sat in a corner at the back of the room—where he watched, all day. It was against the law to teach Black people to read and write then and most white people were illiterate anyway. But the teacher let Papa Jim stay and my grandfather quietly paid attention and learned. They say he took pride in the way he shaped his letters. They looked prettier than the copied ones in the penmanship book. Papa Jim learned to read and he learned to write, just watching from the back of the room.

So when he came home to his wife and children that afternoon, Mama Liza said, "Jim, this gal say she can read. I don't believe it, she's only a baby."

"Come here sugar," he said, reaching for Ella Lee and lifting her up so she could see a section of the newsprint near the door. "Read this to Papa." And Ella Lee started to read. This was when Mama Freeney was two years old, so the family story goes. She read; she learned algebra; she recited poems and speeches; she was the show child of the county and she became a teacher—of both Black and white children—in Leesburg, Georgia.

"Mama Freeney Liked Smart People"

Mama Freeney invented games, debating contests, speech contests, spelling bees—anything she could think of to keep our minds active and learning. She liked smart people. When the family moved to Chicago, she didn't have the certification to work in the schools, but our home and neighborhood became her classrooms. She made learning a family enterprise and a family entertainment, both. I think it was as much fun for Mom as it was for us—her face lit up when we knew the answers and she'd give a dime or a quarter to the ones who had the highest number of correct responses.

Mama Freeney was always industrious and responsible, but she didn't do anything she didn't really want to do. And she didn't care if you liked it or not. She was an excellent cook with gourmet sensibilities, but once the daughters Mildred and Alma were old enough to make sure the younger children didn't starve, Mom cooked when she wanted and as little or as much as she cared to cook. Whatever she made was delicious. Mildred remembers coming into the house as a young teen and smelling the sautéed liver with onions and peppers simmering in a cast-iron skillet in the kitchen. Anybody else at home would also be irresistibly drawn to the delicious flavors and they'd all stand around the table watching Mama Freeney cook, looking expectantly at her pots and pans, their mouths watering.

"Is it enough for us, Mama?" Because, according to Mildred, Mama Freeney was as likely as not to wake up from a nap with a taste for something—say a polish sausage or some smothered chicken—and cook just enough to satisfy her yen, and not much more.

Mom really didn't like housework. She did it when it needed to be done. And for a while she did day's work for white people on the Northside to supplement the income from the store and Daddy's salary from Brach's candies or Acme Steel mill. But Mom was more studious and sociable than housewifely and she savored an afternoon of stimulating talk about the state of the world over smoked chubs and hard rolls, especially with a conversation partner from whom she could learn as much as she could teach.

All of Mom's children and grandchildren were intelligent. Alma was valedictorian of her high school class, Thomas was an excellent poet who would create lyrical and amusing verses on the spot for any occasion, and Son was an athlete and coach who helped train many of the neighborhood children to win local tournaments in basketball and volleyball. Mom had a special place in her heart for readers and she made sure that all of her children read early and well. For those who showed a particular interest in books, there were special benefits. Charles, my brother Bud's son, Mama and Daddy Freeney's first grandchild, was a playful, sensitive, and exceptionally smart young man. He took after both his mother, Thelma, and his paternal grandmother, Mama Freeney, who were insatiable readers. He eventually became an archivist with a tremendous range of knowledge about everything from North American birds and trains to African American literary history and French Provençal cooking. As a child, Charles would go into the bathroom when the house was full of people and there was no other quiet place, and read encyclopedias and dictionaries from cover to cover until somebody made him come out so that the facility could be returned to its regular, intended use. But Mama Freeney never bothered him. When she got into one of her cyclone cleaning moods, where everybody in the house would be enlisted to help remove the accumulated dust and debris, Charles was allowed to skip the collective task and stay focused on his books.

Mama Freeney seemed to recognize the particular gifts and inclinations of each of her children and grandchildren; and she gave us room and encouragement to lean toward what was naturally in us. My sister Sue was always dynamic and outspoken with a good heart, a sense of justice, and a sharp, sassy wit. "Mama's cussin' child" is how she describes herself. Mama and Daddy Freeney didn't allow any of us to curse in front of them. Daddy Freeney wouldn't even let you say, "Shut up." But from an early age, Sue said whatever she pleased and nobody ever reprimanded her for it. She didn't abuse the privilege, but the hard words were part of the way my sister expressed herself—and it didn't hurt that she did it with aplomb. "Mama always knew I was her kid that would tell my true feelings about anything. She knew that's the way I was," Sue said. "I would cuss even when I was little. And Mama let me. She would say, 'if Sue said it, it needed to be said.'"

Once when they were children, Sue and our sister Alberta were at a summer camp for underprivileged youth run by United Catholic Charities. Somebody asked Sue if she wanted to be in a performance of *Uncle Tom's Cabin*. They offered her the role of Topsy and she said yes, not knowing the story. Once Sue learned the words to the poem that would be recited on stage, she changed her mind:

Don't cry Topsy
Just because you're black as coal.
Underneath it all we know
Your heart is as pure as gold.

And when you die and go to heaven
You'll be so proud to see

The dearest Lord will make you white
So you can be like me.

My sister remembers those words to this day. She told the camp counselors she refused to do the play. "I didn't want to die and get to be white. I was alright like I was, doing my little Black thing."

Sue said, "Mama Freeney always said to us, 'Baby, Black is beautiful.' She always said that. Long before it was popular. My mama believed that and she would always tell me, 'Baby, you are the *prettiest* thing!'" The camp counselors weren't going to make Sue act like Topsy. Not even for pretend. Sue said, "Those white people tried to act like I was a rebellious kid, but I walked off and rolled my eyes at them motherfuckers."

Sue said, "Then here come Alberta talking about, 'I'll do it. I'll do it.' I told her, 'The hell you will. I'll tell Mama Freeney.' So neither one of us did the play."

Mom was thoughtful and good-natured and most of all extremely encouraging to anyone who needed some extra affirmation. She seemed to know exactly when somebody was a little down on themselves and she'd tell you in a minute how good and beautiful and talented you actually were so you'd leave out of her house feeling better than you did when you came in. I remember one time a young woman came to the door wanting to teach us some of the new gospel songs that were getting popular at the time. Norma sat down at the piano to play for the young lady, but the lady couldn't sing. Not a note. It didn't matter. Following Mom's lead we all listened appreciatively and when it was over we complimented our guest. Rather than laughing at her or making fun of her complete inability to hold a tune, Mom praised the words; she praised the woman's enthusiasm. And we agreed with Mom. Some might say my mother lied. But I don't think so. She taught me something I use to this day in my own teaching and workshops. *This is the only moment you have with another person. This moment now.* You start sorting out what is important and what isn't. Most likely, you won't get another moment just like this one. We never saw the woman who visited and sang for us again. But she left our house feeling good. She felt like she was giving us a message of Jesus and we felt like we received it. What does pitch have to do with it? So what if her skirt is hanging?

I saw people come into the house, shoulders bent and tired from all they carried. Mom would welcome them in, give them something to eat, find something to talk about that gave them a hold on hope, and they'd leave out of that house looking different. I saw it so many times.

But Mom was not simplistic or a Pollyanna in her encouragement. And she was an excellent judge of character. She was patient and listened well, and could tell what the "real" problems were, the ones unvoiced. But you couldn't play Mom for a fool. She had impeccable discernment and she'd cuss you out in a minute if you needed it, and when she was finished it was over. She didn't hold a grudge. She spoke her mind. And she took care of herself. Mom lived to be 103 years old. Drinking about a gallon of ice water a day, napping whenever she got tired, fasting when she didn't want to eat, and not letting too many things shock her out of a recognition that the only constants in the world are change and love. "It's a round world," she used to tell us. Meaning that everything is constantly changing. What goes around will come around and there's no need to get unduly upset, because nothing—good or bad—will last forever. Except love.

Mom's Religion

My mother didn't go to church. Not often. Just funerals, weddings, and once in a while for a holiday or special service. She had a simple religiosity. And while she loved good music and dancing and the laughter that was the life-blood of our house, Mom's spirit was in many ways quiet. It was a strong spirit. Watchful, observant, and wise.

When Mom prayed she would go into her bedroom and get on her knees. Sometimes I could hear her hum or speak softly almost under her breath. Sometimes she'd tell God out loud exactly what she needed Him to know. It wasn't that the room was off-limits to us during these times. I remember peering in and seeing her at the bedside with her head bowed or sometimes raised, her hands clasped before her. But Mom liked the privacy of prayer. Mama's supplications were sweet. Fine, like a simple linen. It was something between her and God. And we could see, but she wasn't making a show of it.

Mom's religion was mostly the way she treated people. Or, especially this. She was discerning and she was compassionate and she was full of respect—for herself and for others. She believed in doing what was right, but sometimes she saw that punishment could be worse than the crime.

People took from the grocery store occasionally.[2] I would see them shoplifting—putting a couple of extra cans in their jackets or some fruit in a pocket and walking out without paying. If Mom saw them, she wouldn't say anything to them immediately, but when they got ready to go she would give them a little something extra and tell them, just as nice, "Now, whenever

Mama Freeney in front of 4160 South Wentworth, 1960s. PHOTO COURTESY OF RACHEL
ELIZABETH HARDING.

you want to, you can come back and pay for those things you took." Usually
they looked surprised that Mom had noticed. Sometimes they came back.
Sometimes they didn't. We never did have much money in the cash register
but once in a while we had people try to rob us that way too. A lot of times
people would come and take things because they were hungry.

I remember one night after we had closed, Mom and Dad and I were
upstairs and we could hear somebody moving around down in the store. We
looked down from the window at the grocery entrance and saw a couple of
young men going in and out, carrying things. I asked Mom, "Do you want
me to call anybody?"

"Like who?" she said.

"You want me to call the police?"

"No. Why would we call the police to come and shoot those children?"

After a while we didn't hear them anymore and we went downstairs to
see what was there and what wasn't there. We never did keep money in the
store at night so all they took was food. The boys had broken the lock and
one of the windows and they took a lot of food. We cleaned up the shattered
window and called somebody to replace the lock on the door. The next day,
in the back alley we saw empty tins from our canned goods, brimming from

the garbage pails and scattered on the ground. That told us those dummies lived right down the street from us.

. . .

About three years before Mom passed, she got very sick, stopped eating, and as she weakened dramatically the family took her to the hospital in fear that she was leaving us. But she didn't leave. Or rather, she did . . . and then she came back. She had stopped breathing for a while. Then she started again. Afterward, Mom told us she had "died and gone to New York." It was beautiful, she said, but she had come back. New York's proximity to heaven notwithstanding, when we brought Mom home from the hospital, I was very interested in this "near-death experience" it sounded like my mother had had. And I wanted to know if she had seen things I had read about—like a tunnel of light, or relatives and friends welcoming her on the other side.

"Rose, I came back," she told me.

I said, "Yeah?"

She said, "I came back because you all weren't ready yet. Y'all weren't ready for me to go."

"Oh God, I'm so glad you came back, Mama."

I wasn't sure if there was more she wanted to say about it. But I was curious. We were sitting on the two twin beds in her room in Mildred's house, facing each other. I was helping her change into her nightclothes. I asked her, "Well, when you died, Mom, who did you see?"

She was a little annoyed with the question, as if it missed the most important aspect of the experience for her. She shook her hand in a slight dismissive wave and then she answered me. "Rose," she said, shifting her weight a little to be more comfortable, "you know, yeah, I saw all of those things you're talking about. My mother was there and my father too. And I was glad to see everybody, but that's not really what I want to tell you." She said, "Listen, Rose. When you die, there is nothing, nothing there but love. Everything else is gone."

"Hmm." I listened.

"Nothing but love," she said again. "So while we're in this world, we have to do whatever we can to love people, to love this world, to take care of all that's in this world. Because that's all that matters, the love."

I closed my eyes briefly. The impact of my mother's words made me sway ever so slightly where I sat. "Hmm."

She was ready to get into bed. She was pulling the covers over her shoulders when she said it to me again, "Now don't forget, Rose. There's nothing left but love. That's the most important thing. That's what you need to know."

Notes

1. This poem was written by William Brighty Rands (1823–82) and was a favorite in the early twentieth century. As was "Curfew Will Not Ring Tonight" by Rose Hartwick Thorpe (1850–1939), another poem Mama Freeney memorized as a girl and recited to her grandchildren into her seventies.

2. From the early 1950s, for about twenty-five years, Dock and Ella Freeney maintained a small grocery store and delicatessen at 4160 South Wentworth in Southside Chicago.

II · North

The Mix

We all lived together in those days. Most people in Woodlawn came up from the South, following family members and looking for work. The tones of Mississippi, Alabama, and Georgia were in all the voices, and the tastes of southern hometowns were in the foods everybody cooked. Black people could only live in a few areas of the city so we had a wide mix of professions and economic classes in a single neighborhood. The doctors, domestics, and business owners; the day laborers, teachers, and factory workers. All together. And what a neighborhood it was! Everything you wanted was in walking distance—groceries, clothing, furniture, nightclubs, restaurants, ice cream parlors, drug stores. And all the businesses were run by our neighbors and their families. I must have been about five when we moved to Woodlawn. It's the first community I remember. It was thriving and wonderful.

In the 1920s, starting with my aunts Mamie and Hettie, more than thirty members of my family made their way to Chicago from Macon and Leesburg, Georgia, settling in homes within a mile radius of one another. (Another sister, Bird, was the first of all to leave the South and she went to Detroit. She died within a few years of moving there. But her children then came to Chicago to live with the rest of us.) I could walk a few blocks in any direction and be at the home of somebody in my family. There were always friends to visit too, and along the

Freeney Family c. 1935. Back row, l–r: Dock (Daddy) Freeney, Ella Lee (Mama) Harris Freeney, Alma, Mildred. Front row, l–r: Thomas, Alberta, Sue, Norma, and Rosemarie. The two older boys, James (Son) and Charles Dock (Bud), are missing from the photo. PHOTO COURTESY OF RACHEL ELIZABETH HARDING.

way I stopped to play street games, say hi to a relative or schoolmate, or buy candy. We played tag and root-a-peg with an ice pick, and jacks and jump rope; and in the wintertime we flooded the playground at the school and turned it into an ice-skating rink. For children, Woodlawn was a joy, because we lived inside a wide cross section of African American life and so many people encouraged us to believe in great possibilities for ourselves.

When we first arrived, there were still a few white families in the community, and several of their businesses remained—I remember some Jewish grocery stores—but whites were moving to other parts of the city as African Americans migrated in and Woodlawn quickly became predominantly Black.

Neighbors spent time getting to know each other and helped when there were illnesses and deaths. The doctor lived just blocks away and he would get up at three or four in the morning to see about us in an emergency. Or if one of us got a toothache in the middle of the night, we could walk over to the dentist's house and he would treat the tooth and then have one of his sons to walk us back home. Or, if we needed something urgent from the grocery store after it had closed, we could knock on the door—the storekeepers lived right behind the store, or above it—and they'd get up and see what we wanted.

There was an elderly couple down the street. Every few days Mom would send one of us to check on them and ask if they needed anything. Whenever I'd stop in, the wife would give me a little list and cash to go to the store. Mom taught us not to accept any money for these favors but sometimes the lady would bake cookies and give me a bag of cookies to take home. Our neighbor next door didn't have children either, and Mom sent some of us to evening church services with her so she didn't have to walk by herself.

McCosh Elementary School

When new children from the South enrolled at our school, you could tell they had just arrived, because they looked "country." They were always very neat and clean, but their clothes were kind of formal, as if they were dressing for church on their first day of school—petticoats and things like that. But it didn't take them long to figure everything out. The teachers assigned people to help orient each of the new students. "Take Clara out when you're on the playground. Stay with her and show her where everything is and when the bell rings you bring her with you back to class." It was a special honor to be asked to do this; we were expected to explain things to our new classmates, to make them comfortable, and to be a friend.

McCosh was a two-story building with a basement. The playground was beautiful and large enough to hold several classes during the recess periods each day. There was also a community center with a staff who organized after-school activities for us. I loved to play. We lived so close to the school that I could run home and change, put on my gym shoes, and run back to the play-ground before I had to come in for the evening. There were arts and crafts classes, ceramics, and sewing. Our volleyball and baseball teams competed with other schools in the area, which at the time, were still mostly white.

I had some extraordinary instructors at McCosh. Most of our teachers were Black. They had come up from the South like we had and they en-couraged us to work hard and be studious so that we could benefit from the opportunities that our new environment seemed to offer. Mrs. Turner was the science teacher, and to this day I love the subject because of her. She was excellent; she took no nonsense, and children never misbehaved in her class. We were quiet, earnest; we did the homework and we did not whisper and talk with friends as we might in some other classes. Everyone graduated from McCosh Elementary School already knowing as much about science as we were likely to learn in high school.

Another teacher I adored was Mrs. King who taught seventh grade. She was an immensely creative educator who made learning exciting and memorable for us. She created a courtroom in her class to teach us about the legal system and the responsibilities of judges, attorneys, juries, and other participants in the process of law. Cases sometimes lasted for several weeks and we, her students, took turns acting out the various roles.

One case developed out of an experience we had in class. Mrs. King stepped out of the room one morning, leaving instructions for us to stay in our seats and complete our lessons until she returned. I was left in charge and told to write down the name of anyone who got up or otherwise disobeyed the instructions. Well, one girl did leave her seat, and in doing so knocked over some plants that were resting on a window ledge. They fell to the street below and made quite a commotion. I could tell that the girl really had not meant to knock down the plants, but the teacher had asked me to keep track of the class, and the falling pots made such a disturbance, that I wrote down her name, Edna. When Mrs. King came back, there was some disagreement about exactly how Edna caused the plants to fall. So, Mrs. King decided to use the situation as a real-life case. She assigned roles and gave us time to organize our arguments and then we held the trial. The boy who served as Edna's defense lawyer urged the jury not to convict her because she had knocked over the plants by accident. He made a case that sounded very sympathetic toward Edna, very supportive of her. I was the prosecuting attorney and I knew the only way I was going to win that case was to make her look not so innocent. And I did want to win the case.

I was good at public speaking because I had lots of practice at home. My mother was a fabulous storyteller, a great debater, and she loved oratory and good discussions. She'd set us up in teams and give us a topic and then sit back and be the referee. But we had to debate fairly. You couldn't win if you angered your opponent so much that they lashed out at you, and you couldn't win if you provoked them into a corner so there was no way for them to respond. You always had to leave a little room. Debates had to be fair and fairness meant leaving people with the ability to defend themselves.

So, I said to the class, as they became the jury for Edna's trial, "Let's assume that all the things are true that the defense attorney has told us. Even so, the facts are that the defendant was out of her seat when she was not supposed to be, and the plant that fell could have really hurt someone." I urged my classmates that, for the sake of Edna learning a lesson as well as for the safety of people passing underneath the windows downstairs, she should be convicted. And, she was convicted. Later that day, word got around that Edna was going to beat me up after school.

Well, I knew that my older siblings and cousins would protect me if it came to that—but I didn't want a confrontation with Edna, so I left school early. I love a good argument but I never like to physically fight. On my way home, I was halfway looking around for Edna because she and I usually took the same route from school. I didn't see her. The next day I found out that my friend Tampy had heard the rumors. Tampy was a short, amiable, muscular boy who liked me and was not afraid of anybody. Tampy discreetly talked to Edna and that was the end of that. Although Edna's reaction wasn't the outcome my mother would have desired from the judgment, still I think she was proud of me. I didn't try to hurt Edna's feelings. I was just a bit too convincing in my arguments because I had had lots of coaching and practice.

Baby of the Family

I was my parent's youngest child, the baby of nine, and I had more than a dozen first cousins—most of whom lived in Woodlawn. I was so well loved and well cared for (I guess you could say "spoiled") that I never worried about anything. I just loved to play. And I had plenty of space and time to do that. My oldest brother, James (whom the adults called "Son" and the children called "Brother"), was eighteen years older than me. Bud (Dock Jr.), Alma, and Mildred were the next in line. The middle children were Sue, Thomas, and Alberta. Me and Norma were the little ones. In our family, older siblings helped raise the younger ones and we, the younger sisters and brothers, obeyed them as if they were our parents. Whatever they told us to do, we did. Many times I'd be playing with some friends out in front of the house, running and jumping and having such a good time that my braids would start coming aloose and, as we say, my hair would be "sticking all over my head." I was having such a grand time I didn't notice and didn't care. But walking in from work, Son would look askance at me and send me inside to wash my face and comb my hair "and don't come back out until you're clean." It got so regular that he wouldn't even have to say anything. I'd see him coming up the street and I'd run into the house headed for the bathroom sink and a comb.

I don't want to give the impression that there were no arguments or fights in the family. Like most families, we had our share of disagreements. But there really was a lot of love among us, a lot of respect, and people recognized that some folks were more sensitive than others—some could stand more teasing and others could not. We never joked with someone to make them cry. Sometimes to make them laugh at themselves or at us. But not to hurt their feelings.

When I was a little girl, and while they were still living at home, my older sisters Mildred and Alma did much of the work of running the household. My mother was almost forty-one when I was born, and both she and my father were often working or otherwise taking care of the myriad things that keep a family as large as ours together. Alma cooked for us and Mildred changed diapers and took care of cuts and scrapes. According to Mildred, our mother couldn't stand the sight of blood and didn't particularly like to clean up after people who were ill. Those tasks fell to her older daughters. My sister Mildred would also wash my hair, and braid it or straighten it for me. The older siblings were always buying little gifts for me, clothes and other things that I needed. If I was going to a party or was in a play at school, I could always count on them to really dress me up beautifully. Everyone made me think I was very special.

May Day and the Movies

I was going to be an actress or a dancer. Starting with the "May Day" celebrations in kindergarten, where we danced around a pole with colored streamers, I loved plays, I loved drama, and I loved dance—anything where I could use my imagination and be on stage.

Almost every day, when I was nine or ten years old, I went alone, after school, to the Langley Theatre on 63rd Street. My cousins Perc and Isaac and my brother-in-law, Campbell, worked there, and one of them would open the side entrance for me and escort me to the concession stand, where a very large popcorn machine spilled fresh-popped kernels along the sides of the great glass box. I would get a bag of popcorn and sit in a row near one of my relatives' stations and watch B movies for hours, enraptured. The cool dark spaces of the movie house were incubators of dazzling fantasies that I dared not speak at home or school.

On Sunday afternoons the small theater was filled to capacity. A whole group of us went then, paying our ten cents each to laugh at the cartoons, announce to each other which coming attractions we would see, and settle into our seats, commenting and giggling our way through the feature presentation. Although no one ever asked us to leave, from time to time one of the ushers beamed a flashlight in our faces as a silent instruction to quiet down. We could stay and watch the film as many times as we desired in those days and we would do just that—finally heading home in the evening along a maze of shortcuts through alleyways, small lots, and over backyard fences.

Between school performances and a steady diet of movies, my desire to be an actress was fairly well nurtured as a child. And then there was the "natural drama" of the people in and around my family. There were so many of us kids and we all had friends who liked to hang out at our house. When the house was full I didn't talk much, but I listened to everything, paying attention and taking lessons about what not to miss in life and what to avoid if at all possible.

Another place I loved was the barbershop just down the street from our house where I took my nephew Charles to get his hair cut. The men would lower their voices and tone down their subject matter until they forgot I was sitting there. I found their conversations mesmerizing. They'd talk about all kinds of things—politics, philosophy, sports, relationships. Besides my mother's kitchen table, I didn't know too many places where the conversations ranged that way, and I loved to just sit and listen.

The Tea Party

When I was about seven years old, the little girl next door got angry with me for something and told me she no longer wanted to play with me. We were the same age and often played together after school. I liked her, so I was hurt and sorry when she announced she wasn't going to be my friend anymore. I don't remember now what caused the discord between us, but I went inside, upset and crying, and told my mother. And to this day I am grateful for the way my parents handled the situation. They knew I was sad and they let me feel sad. But they also taught me a lesson in reconciliation that I later found many other uses for—with my students, my children, and in my personal and professional life.

Mom and Dad somehow found time between their jobs to go to a secondhand store where they bought a big dollhouse, miniature furniture, two or three little dolls, and tiny china cups and saucers. My parents fixed up the toys, making new dresses for the dolls and repairing the furniture for the dollhouse. Mom could bake a cake in no time, and once everything else was ready, she did that too. Then she and Daddy put all the new toys on the front porch and brought out a little table with two chairs that I already had, setting the china on the table for real tea and cake.

My next-door neighbor saw all of this, and so did lots of the other children on my block. Everybody wanted to come and play with my new toys and before long there was a group of us on the porch having a tea party. The little girl who had been angry asked, "Can I play too?" I was happy to have her back as a friend and said, "Yes."

Mom and Dad had such a knack for resolving conflict. They didn't say anything negative about my playmate. They simply went out and gathered up the things they knew would heal a discord between two little girls and threw a party for all the children on the block.

Isaac's Death

When I was ten, my cousin Isaac drowned in an accident in Lake Michigan. He was twenty-one years old, Aunt Mary and Uncle Willie Dan's youngest child. He was a big, handsome young man and his death was grievously hard on all the family, especially his parents. There was a trace of foul play in Isaac's dying, but as with my brother Bud, the family never lingered there for long. It was difficult enough to know that our beloved was gone; to focus our anger on a person or persons who may have harmed him was more than our grief could bear. But Uncle Willie Dan went down after that. He just fell to pieces out of sorrow for his boy.

The day Isaac died, Aunt Mary uttered the only curse word we ever heard her say in our lives. She was the calm, reasoning presence in the extended family. The oldest of the aunts; she was the one who nursed us with soft words and gentle hands on our fevered foreheads. Isaac wasn't supposed to have gone to the beach. He was an excellent swimmer, but his father had left instructions for him to wash the windows of the house and he wasn't supposed to have gone out. "Didn't I tell you to tell that boy to wash the windows?" Uncle Willie Dan asked his wife insistently.

Someone had gone to get Uncle Willie Dan at his job, to tell him the awful news. He came back to the full house distraught and looking for a way to understand the disaster that had occurred with his son.

"I did," Aunt Mary responded.

"Didn't I tell you to tell that boy . . . ?" Uncle Willie Dan repeated the question as if he hadn't heard the answer. He must've said it at least three times. He couldn't rationalize.

Aunt Mary said again, "I said, I did."

She wasn't crying or anything. People were talking to her and she was responding, "These things happen, you know. We just have to accept it." Uncle Willie Dan was trying to get her attention. He didn't want anyone else talking to his wife just then. Their son had died. The house was filled with family and friends and more were coming, "Oh Aunt Mary, Aunt Mary. We just heard the news about Isaac. We're so sorry."

And she would say to them, "Yes, thank you, dear. That's . . . things like that happen."

"Didn't I tell you to tell him to wash them windows!?" Uncle Willie Dan bellowed one more time. Aunt Mary turned around and spoke to her husband with the sharpness of her sorrow, "Dammit, Willie. Shut up!" Uncle Willie Dan didn't say anything else.

Snow and Spring

During my childhood, there were other tragedies. We were like any family in that sense. We lost property and all our savings in the Depression and had to begin again from scratch. Relatives died of preventable illnesses. The promises of the North proved hollow and hard for some of us, in spite of tremendous personal and collective efforts. But there was a culture of joy and an insistent hope we shared. It kept us going through very dark places, hinting at the shine whose time was coming.

It was kind of like snow. In the wintertime, toward the end of that cold, quintessentially Chicago season, when the ground has been blanketed for months, it's almost possible to forget what lies under the layers of white and residue. But something in us remembers. And each year when I was growing up, in the slowly lengthening days, before any actual signs of spring showed, I would start to feel a sense of wonder and expectance in my body. The anticipation of a change, something different on the way.

I think the family's general attitude toward the city, toward life, was like this. Seeing snow and feeling spring. Expecting something new. We had come up from Georgia to a place that looked to offer opportunities and changes we could not have achieved where we were before. We were together, we had the vivacity of youth and the wisdom of experience, and we were going to make this new place home.

I don't ever recall anyone in the family being despondent about the move north. In spite of the problems, the disappointments, the sadnesses, my family seemed to live with an expectation of something good, something exciting, something new on the horizon. There was so much joy and laughter around us, it was as if we created a buffer, a measure of strength, against the city's unyielding weight.

When the family would come up against a new challenge—a sick relative, a good job lost, perhaps trouble with the law, or tight times with money—my father would say, in the gentle cadences of the Georgia language he kept all his life, "We passes it." We will deal with it together and it will pass.

Shirley Darden was my best friend. She lived across the street when we were at 6428 Rhodes. There were three girls in the Darden family: Shirley, who was my age; Lucinda, who was my sister Norma's age; and Shirley's oldest sibling, Sarah, who was my idol. Sarah had such grace and charm and looked so grown-up. She wore tight skirts and bobby socks and styled her hair high on her head in a classic bun that I tried to copy exactly. I even mimicked her walk, setting my shoulders in the same uplift and my hips to the roll and sway I admired in her. I thought she was gorgeous. I was so intent on modeling myself after Sarah that my folks surely noticed and probably laughed when I wasn't around—me walking down Rhodes Avenue swaying my hips like Sarah Darden and affecting the elegance I so esteemed. Thankfully they never said anything to me about it.

Shirley, Lucinda, and I played jacks in the hallway or on the landing of their house, sometimes on the sidewalk. On Mother's Day, Shirley and I sold paper flowers on Rhodes Avenue. Red if your mother was living, white if your mother was dead. The lady who made them gave us a little extra change for the work. Sometimes we'd make as much as a dollar each. That was a lot back then. The paper flowers were so pretty, people always wanted them.

Sometimes I went on trips to the country with Shirley and her family. They'd load up a car with fishing rods and a picnic basket and head out to Indiana to a lake or a river where the adults would sit and speak in quiet tones to each other, waiting for the fish to bite. I think they invited me because I could be quiet, all the way there and back. Other children usually asked lots of questions like "When are we going to be there?" and "What time we gon have lunch?" and the grown folks would inevitably send them to play somewhere away from the water. I didn't ask questions and I didn't disturb the fish. I loved the silence and I was just so happy to be able to go, and my mom always let me. Sometimes the adults would even take me by myself without any of the other kids!

The Dardens owned the three-story building where they lived. They rented out the ground floor, and the second floor was the grandmother's home. The parents and the three daughters lived in the third-floor apartment which they shared with the great-grandmother, who had been a slave. Shirley's great-grandmother was old, very old, and she had a lot of stories. Whenever she talked about what she had lived through her face contorted and got hard. I watched her, fascinated and moved. She had long long hair and she looked like a white person. But she didn't love the skin she had. She talked about how mean the white people were. How they beat and abused the slaves. She never used the word "rape" to describe what the Black women had to endure; instead she would talk about how the slave women "had no say" in what was done to them. "We didn't have no say as to who would have us," is how she put it.

I couldn't have articulated it then, but it meant something special to me to be in her presence so I was always glad, even if the stories were terrifying. This was the 1940s, and it was not uncommon for a family to have members still living who had been born in slavery. But my grandparents died before I was born, and I never met Grandma Rye. So, the four generations of the Darden household were a privilege.

My little eyes were following her, watching to see what she would do; if she would get even. Someone had come to the house, "Mrs. Freeney, you not gonna let that man get away with this, are you?"

"Anybody who killed someone is suffering enough," Mom responded. "What more can you suffer when you killed someone?"

Bud was my second-oldest brother. He was our delight. He was as good and smart as he was handsome. He was a bartender at a local jazz club called Joe's Deluxe and was well liked in the Woodlawn community. He hardly ever came home without gifts for his parents and younger siblings, and he was very protective of all of us. Bud had a temper and nobody messed with the Freeney family. He was all of our "favorite" and I was about twelve when he passed.

I remember the events around his death with a clarity as if they happened yesterday. First, there were the roses. It was Mother's Day, 1942, and my oldest brother, Son, was away in the war. Bud brought two cards and two vases of red roses for Mama Freeney, one set from him and one from Son who was fighting in the Pacific Theater and couldn't be home with the family. Almost as soon as the roses and cards were arranged on the table, Son's vaseful began to wilt. Bud saw this and said, "I'll take those, Mama. Let those be from me, the other ones be from Son." Bud moved the wilting roses closer to his own card and put the faultless ones by Son's greeting. Later, Mom said that was the first sign.

A few weeks passed and my brother was killed in a pool hall. He was shot. He had come by the house earlier that day, joyful as always, greeting his parents and the gang of siblings and cousins. I think it was to say good-bye, but maybe not. Anyway, he came by and we were all glad to see him. He said something to me like "I'm gonna go down the street little sweetie; I'll be back." He kissed me and gave me a hug.

It was nighttime when we got the news.

It was a school night and I was sleeping. But the rushing and stunned voices in the living room woke me up. Aunt Mary came first and the rest of the aunts and cousins arrived soon after. The house was full. It stayed that way for several days—through the wake and after the funeral. On one of those days, Bud came back again, like Jesus. I remember him, not saying anything but standing near the end of my bed. The place was filled with people—sisters and brothers and cousins and friends. He came through the oblivious crowd, stood at the end of the bed, and smiled at me. I knew he was dead. He didn't say anything but I "heard" and felt him tell me, "Everything is alright." It made me so happy. I've never forgotten it.

The funeral was held at Lincoln Memorial, the Congregational church in Woodlawn where two of my aunts were Sunday school teachers. The building was packed. As I walked into the sanctuary with the rest of my family I could barely see in front of me for the thickness of the people. There was no room. It was as if the whole neighborhood had come to mourn and honor my brother.

After the funeral, Bud's only child, my nephew Charles, was sitting on the sofa in his little suit, and Mama looked over at him then said to me, "This is your baby now." Of course, he was everybody's baby. Like his father, Charles became everybody's favorite. But I always felt a joyful responsibility for him, like I did with all my nieces and nephews.

Days later I was walking down the street and saw two ladies watching me from the inside of a store window. One of them followed me with her finger. I didn't care. I was so proud of my brother. Nothing anyone could say or do would make me feel otherwise.

Sometimes I think the man who shot my brother did so out of fear. You just didn't mess with Bud, or any of his family. His temper was quick. Another friend said my brother would likely have been a leader in the sixties—he was already highly respected in the community. People were gathering around his words and ideas.

Mom and Dad never pressed charges but they suffered a lot over Bud's death. When they talked with Aunt Mary and other family about it, they never mentioned any retaliation or judgment against the person who shot my brother. When I got older, I asked them why they never went to the police. They told me, "Killing a person is enough punishment. How is that man going to live a human life with that burden on his heart?" My first ideas about nonviolence came from seeing how my parents responded to my brother's death.

When I encountered the Mennonites, a decade or so later, there were resonances of my parents' worldview in the Anabaptist traditions of that church. That is partly why I felt comfortable there. That, and my sister Alma. Alma was already a member of a small Mennonite mission church when I was looking for a religious path. She was so good and so full of integrity, I would have followed her anywhere.

Death and Dying

Death and dying were surrounded by signs in my family. Omens and forewarnings: a whirlwind rising from the floor to carry my grandmother skyward. My brother's gift of red roses falling over new in a vase. Aunt Mary fighting with Death as if he was a man, and her sister, Ella, my mother, helping her to hold off Death's hunger for a little while. The three days of snow when Aunt Mary finally passed on. And the rainbow sign of my father's time coming.

When Aunt Mary was dying she asked her sister, Ella Lee, to spend the night with her. They slept in the same bed and as the night went on, Aunt Mary began to lash out. She was fighting Death with her fists because she wasn't ready to go. "Ella do you see him?" Aunt Mary cried. "Do you see him, Ella?" Mom said she did see Death trying to wrap his arms around her sister. Mom's presence, and maybe other things, too, helped Aunt Mary push Death back for at least that night. When Aunt Mary finally died, there was a three-day snowstorm in Chicago. The heaviest snowfall in decades.

My mother could "see" the impending deaths of family members in dreams and signs. When my grandmother, Mama Liza, passed, Mom saw her stand in the center of the floor and rise toward the ceiling in a whirlwind. Mom also saw a rainbow in her sleep, days before my father died, and knew it was a message that her husband's days on this earth were not long.

I don't know if my mother was conscious that the rainbow is a symbol of the continuity of life and death among the Yoruba and Ewe-Fon peoples of West Africa. Did she know, too, that prodigious precipitation is a sign of the passing of a great soul? Perhaps. But even if she was not aware of these West African signs of transition from material form into spirit, they were somewhere in the collective cultural memory that she carried up from Georgia in her stories, in her wisdom, and in her living.

Mom used to take me with her to visit people who were dying. I grew up with a respect for death, but I wasn't afraid. I watched how my mother and other adults accompanied people in death, through death. How they talked to them about joyful things and shared good stories of earlier days to make the dying person laugh or smile. How they sometimes spoke of the relatives and friends who had already passed over and who would surely welcome the newly arriving loved one on the other side.

In our community, dying people were not left alone and children were included among those who comforted them. It was a very sacred time. And even though I didn't always understand what was going on, I was aware of the special nature of the moment, its mystic quality. There was a reverence for the dead, and we were taught never to speak ill of them.

Most of the people we visited died at home—some were family members, some friends. At that time, in the 1930s and '40s, the practice of dying in the hospital was not common among African Americans. Often we carried food, but sometimes we would just go and visit and sit. The people we visited had come up to Chicago from the South in the same era as my parents, and they would reminisce with my mother about old times, good times in their younger days. Visiting also meant that the families of the afflicted knew they were not alone in their distress.

I enjoyed listening to the adults talk. Their remembrances were always positive, pleasurable ones—they laughed and joked. But I also saw the sadness in my mother's face as she acknowledged to herself that a good friend, a cousin, or a sister, was leaving. It gave me a sense of how to balance one's own grief with the need to help the dying person leave amid as much happiness as possible. The need for joy in the midst of mourning seems to me now a central element in my family's cultural traditions. And mourning is something we all help each other through.

My mother was a consummate teacher. She could use any opportunity to pass on a lesson—and half the time she did it so well you didn't even know you were learning anything until you thought about it later. When I was ten, my Uncle Clarence died of a cancerous tumor in his face. My mother visited him in the weeks before he passed and took me along. Although Mom prepared me, it was a difficult thing to see—Uncle Clarence's entire right jaw was a gaping hole and he was in almost unbearable pain. He turned his head toward us when we walked in, but he couldn't speak.

On the way home from the visit my mother said to me, "Do you know where he got that cancer from? From working with all that bad meat." We could smell the stockyards from where we lived. Sometimes it reeked so overpoweringly we ourselves felt sick. "How many men who work at that stockyard are sick like your uncle?" I didn't know the answer, but the question got me to thinking. "Rose," my mother said, "all races of men work there. And it's dangerous for all of them." Soon my mother and I were having a conversation about the hazardous conditions of the Chicago stockyards where many men labored in a disease-producing environment with little concern from their bosses for protecting their health.

From experiences like this, I learned very early about injustice. My mother was using an African American cultural tradition—that is, not shielding children from the reality of pain and death—as a bridge to help me understand some broader truths about exploitation and social inequity. In the midst of it all were her caring and concern for Uncle Clarence and for others like him. And so, even with her anger, her pain, her sense of the wrong done to so many, Mom talked to Uncle Clarence, tried to make him laugh a little bit and remembered stories that eased the difficult moments.

I think my mother carried me with her to visit our friends and family who were dying because she noticed that, even at an early age, I wasn't anxious in the presence of death. Sickness didn't much bother me either—in fact, after my sister Mildred married and moved away, I was usually the person in the family who looked after those who weren't well. I didn't mind cleaning up accidents and I had patience with people who were weak and disoriented from illness. Also, I always had a kind of affinity for the dead. In Woodlawn, we lived around the corner from a funeral parlor—Banks Funeral Home. I got to know the mortician, Mr. Banks, and he would let me observe the bodies he prepared for viewing and burial. Sometimes I had known the people "laid out" with care and distinction at Mr. Banks's mortuary. At other times, I didn't recognize the faces. Either way I glimpsed a bit of the transition at the end of physical life and that fascinated me. Mr. Banks directed my brother Bud's funeral as well as that of my cousin Isaac, and I went by to see both bodies before the public viewings.

We gather at death. The wake and the dinner after the funeral are unique moments of fellowship and abundance with a plenteousness of everything:

food, people, laughter, liquor, music, and memory. I remember the dinner at my sister Mildred's house, when our brother Thomas died. We call it the "re-past." Every seat in the house had somebody in it and the only space for chairs was in the middle of the living room floor, and that's where a group of older men congregated to reminisce together. They were cousins and old friends of my brother who had all grown up together. They were telling baseball stories, talking about things they had done when they were younger. Leaning back in the chairs, balancing the chicken, macaroni and cheese, ham and greens on their knees, they gestured with their hands for emphasis. They were relaxed and remembering and it was so good to see them that way.

Gatherings around death give us that opportunity to sit and be companions to each other in remembrance. At funerals, family who have not seen each other for years will come back to celebrate and recall the life of the loved one they have lost. Old ties are renewed and new relatives are introduced to each other—the children and grandchildren of cousins, the new spouses, the new babies. It is as if in compensation for the loss, we use the time of death as an occasion to assert the continuity of life, the line going on.

Secrecy and Boundaries

There were certain things in my experience as a child, certain events, that were never discussed. Some stories, some customs, were shared only as knowledge was necessary and then with an attitude of hesitation, reticence. I believe the reasons for concealment centered around two issues. Sometimes, the information revealed was too painful—so tremendously and profoundly painful that the act of recognition risked the release of a haphazard power, an energy whose discharge required a careful, almost ritual attention. This, I believe, was the case in the almost complete lack of conversation about the horrors that sent my family fleeing to the North in the late twenties. It was not until 1960, when I was preparing to go south to work full-time in the freedom movement, and when white vigilante terrorism—and the economic and political system that supported it—was being confronted with a mass movement, that my father and mother began to open up about some of the barbarities they had experienced. Events like the hanging and gutting of a pregnant woman or the lynching of a man and his four sons from the limbs of a single tree were a large part of the reason my family left their farms and fled north. But I didn't hear those stories until decades later. It was as if there had to have been a way out of (or the urgent concern for a daughter who was going into) the madness before it was safe to talk about it.

In other cases, secrecy is a sign of intimate connection to the life force. There are some family practices, taboos around certain kinds of contact at birth and death, that my relatives refuse to talk about on tape. Certain spirit stories that are told only in hushes when told at all. In these instances, the required discretion has to do with a recognition of boundaries. Some things are kept protected—either so their strength will not do harm to the unwary or so their energy and efficacy will not be diluted by misuse and misinterpretation. As with the ghost stories, there is here in the matter of secrecy, a strong element of propriety at work, "a meaning of restraint" as Charles H. Long would call it. A sense of what is appropriate in which time and space; a recognition that a creative and meaningful life is not possible without some constraint.

Dreams and Sight

Closely related to the experience of ghosts and spirits in the African American mystic tradition are dreams, visions, and sight. Anyone familiar with southern folk traditions—Black and white—has probably heard of the "caul." Some people are believed to have the gift of divination or foresight because they were "born with a caul" or a "veil," which means that the amniotic sac was on their head and face when they came through the birth canal. My mother and great-grandmother had this kind of sight. But Mom used to say that she could "see," not because of being born with a caul, but because she came from a "clean womb." In spite of the fact that my grandmother's water broke days before her child emerged into the world, my mother, Ella Lee Harris, was born healthy and lived to be 103 with a number of remarkable abilities, the greatest omen of which she attributed to coming from "a clean womb." Many years later, I discovered that there is a tradition among Tibetans that diviners and seers are born from "clean wombs."

"Sight" or "seeing" is not simply a matter of the ability to foretell future events. It is part of a larger orientation that recognizes the existence of a variety of means of access to information, help, wisdom, and warning. Here, too, as with the ghost and spirit stories, is a vigorous connection between the seen and unseen worlds. Dreams, visions, and signs are other axial elements of this orientation. There is a vast tradition among African Americans of dreaming and paying close attention to dreams. Dreams can be auguries of coming good or ill. Dreams of deceased relatives and friends are often interpreted as forms of communication with them, and the sharing of dreams within a household or among friends is a way to connect with a collective wisdom regarding the meaning of a particular feeling or event.

In the little Black Baptist churches of southwest Georgia (like the one where my grandfather, Papa Jim, was a deacon), there is an old tradition of "seeking"—going out into the woods for days at a time, alone, with only the most simple provisions, to look and listen for the leading of God. Like the forty days Jesus spent wandering in the desert and like the vision quests of our Native American brothers and sisters, these times of solitary communion with the presence of God were an important step in the spiritual journey of many Black folks in towns like the one where Mom and Dad were born. I don't know if my mother ever took that kind of faith journey, out alone in the pine woods, but surely she carried some of its quality, some of its history, in her own approach to spirit, and that mystic seeking has remained with me too.

Some of the oldest Black churches in Lee County, Georgia, started out as "brush harbors," far out in the country where white folks would not easily reach, where first enslaved people and then the descendants went to worship. The earliest of these simply constructed shelters were often open on all sides with just a covering of branches and leaves for a roof. The people who gathered here were folks well attuned to the cycles of agriculture and nature, of planting and harvesting, moon phases and the rising of the creeks and rivers that coursed through the land. Some of this knowledge they had brought with them from ancestral places and some of it they gained from the new land itself. And all of this seeped into their understanding of the new religion, Christianity, and gave it an ancient diasporic scent.

Walking along Rhodes Avenue I was galvanized. By my own breathing and by the rain falling hard. Air moved in and out of my lungs with the same dynamism as the wind around me. 64th and Rhodes to 68th and St. Lawrence is a distance of about six blocks, and my errand was to collect my nephew Charles and bring him home. Rows of cottonwood trees separated the sidewalk from the street, like sentinels, their leaves and branches a lush, dripping canopy. Lightning crackled into thunder and hit something, someplace in the distance. The wind gushed against my back and pushed me forward with a litheness.

Mom knew she could send me. I wasn't foolhardy, but I wasn't afraid either. One of our neighbors had been struck by lightning and died. Not anybody I knew. And I never learned the details. I wondered how the lightning found the person. Was it a woman walking along the street? A child running in the school playground? A man sitting in a doorway or near a window with the lamp on? These were all things Daddy forbade us to do in a storm. When rain came, accompanied by thunder, we were to sit still and not speak until the power had rolled on and it was safe to draw attention to yourself again.

The dynamism was the storm itself, certainly. The charged currents of air and the drama in the ritual cleansing of rain. But it was also the impulse of Mom's and Dad's vitality, their "lifeing" as the theologian Howard Thurman would call it. The way they looked squarely at life's wholeness—its harshness and its joy—with a vision of future good. It was as if they believed whatever the tempest, the path is still promising.

Walking in this storm, I was unhurried but deliberate. I always loved rain showers and never feared thunder or lightning. When I reached the house on St. Lawrence and found my nephew there, my task was half complete. I returned along the same route, holding Charles's hand, the sky now clear. The fresh smell of wet leaves made the air tingle; plants bent from the weight of dripping water, the tree barks sparkling. We passed gardens on corner lots and in the front yards of neighbors and admired the flowers and vegetables there. Then we stopped at the grocery on 65th and Rhodes so that Charles could choose a big handful of the hard candies that brought smiles of anticipation to his eyes.

Both Mama and Daddy Freeney were careful about how they conducted themselves during rainstorms. God was doing His work and we were to be respectfully silent and still. Mom had insisted I bring Charles straight home; she didn't want him unsupervised and away from family in the midst of the deluge. But now that the storm had passed, I figured she wouldn't mind if we detoured a small bit and treated ourselves to a snack.

Howard Thurman writes in his autobiography about the closeness he felt to the natural world, growing up in Florida at the turn of the century. He described trees and woods as companions and felt a special affinity for the moonless, starlit nights of his childhood. "Something in the night," he wrote, "seemed to cover my spirit like a gentle blanket."

Living in the city of Chicago, I didn't have many regular opportunities to be in the woods, but I did go fishing often with friends and their families, and I joined other relatives at church- and government-sponsored family camps for a week or two each summer. In spite of limited chances to get far away from the city in my childhood, I carried an acute sense of nature in my body. This was especially true of the change of seasons, which, beginning in my early teens, I experienced as a kind of exquisiteness, an enchanted sensation that gave me a deep connectedness to the world around me. I was fascinated by correlations I noticed between changes in the atmosphere outside me, and changes in my own mental and physical being. Time, weather, light, and shadow—I could feel the transformations as adjustments in my own material structure.

Winter was like a pause. Summer could be that too—the great heat slowed my energy and gave it a hazy quality like the mist and humidity coming off the lake in August. The snow of Chicago's winters was ubiquitous. It covered everything and turned the industrial city white. It was a gently imposed stasis in the world and I couldn't wait until the snow melted to see what was moving mutely underneath. Surely there was something new and unexpected in the world ...

I think it is good to live in a climate that holds all the seasons. As I think about it now, I am reminded of the way my family lived also with a kind of expectancy that seemed to take its cue from seasonal cycles. Challenges were part of life—deaths, sadnesses, losses. We had been through these things and though we did not anticipate them, we knew that they had their place in the larger pattern of our days. Somehow, nonetheless, my parents and other family members kept a sense of the ultimate good of life, an ultimate balance in the favor of joy.

The apartments on Langley were beautiful then. Dark brick buildings with tall ceilings and wood floors. My cousin Pansy lived there with her family, not far from us, and not far from other aunts and cousins scattered throughout Woodlawn. Everybody in the family pretty much lived in walking distance. As a child, I ran in and out of my relatives' homes whenever I wanted to. I loved going over to Pansy's. I'd go by in the afternoons, or sometimes on a Saturday, and just sit and watch her.

"Hey, Pansy. What you doing?" I would come in and greet my cousin admiring the careful arrangement of her furniture, the doilies on the side tables, the wooden dining table and chairs recently dusted and shined.

"Not too much, darling. Fixing something to eat." Or, "Just straightening up a little. How you doing, Rose?" Pansy would look up and greet me back and invite me to sit and talk with her while she worked. She was always so attentive to her tasks; I was afraid to be a distraction so I was glad if she asked me to run an errand or found some other way to let me help her. If she wanted butter at the grocery store or ribbon from the five-and-dime, I would eagerly run down the street and buy the needed item, happy that I had an excuse to come back and be in her presence a while longer. Once I dropped by when Pansy was making up beds, putting on fresh linens. She smoothed out the sheets, folding the top sheet back over the blanket and then fluffing pillows and setting them on the crisp edge of the fold. "Pull that side straight for me, Rose. That's right. Now help me put these pillows back, sugar."

As she arranged the sheet and blanket over the pillows and swept her hand under the crease to tidy it, I stared.

I was fascinated by my cousin's beauty. Her satin smooth skin was the same deep brownblack as my mother's and her cheekbones had a gentle roundness that lifted and shone when she smiled. But what I remember most were Pansy's hands. Long, dark, and elegant with a gentle rise where the bones bent into joints like something exquisitely carved. As she tucked the white pillows and smoothed the blankets, the contrast of her long black fingers sliding across the fabrics was strikingly lovely to me.

Pansy was my oldest cousin. She had children close to my age and I looked up to her almost as if she were my aunt. She was stately, always so poised and graceful. Even doing household chores. I admired many of my aunts and cousins this way. They were all beautiful women, majestic; most of them dark-skinned and tall. They reminded me—long before the freedom movement and Black Power—of African queens. They looked like sculpture to me and their voices had a lightly amused, singsong quality even in normal conversation. I noticed all of this. They were people who enjoyed life, who met challenges with verve and strength, who held their heads high in spite of disappointments. They carried themselves tall. And they passed these characteristics on to their children.

. . .

Juanita was my Aunt Hettie's only daughter. Hettie lived just down the street from us with Uncle Clarence and their three children—Clarence, Lionel (Billy), and Juanita. Juanita and my sister Alberta were close in age and used to hang out together all the time. They were excellent at every sport they played—from baseball and volleyball to bowling and track. Lean and agile, they moved with fluid grace. When Juanita came to our house to visit, I would watch her and Alberta, their toned arms and legs tossed effortlessly across the sofa or chairs, bright laughing voices, nimble hands gesturing as they talked. I was about five years their junior and they were models for me of what energetic, smart, and beautiful young women should be. Juanita was extremely attractive with short thick hair, what we would call kinky when it wasn't straightened. But straight or in tight natural curls, she was gorgeous and I loved to look at her.

She had a mild, kind manner. A real gentleness of heart. Juanita was also very intelligent, but in an unassuming, even generous way. Mom liked her too. Mom liked smart people; and Juanita often won the thinking games Mom designed for us—spelling bees and geography tests, like contests to name the capital cities of the world. Mom would give prizes of tasty treats or a little money to those who did well. And even though Juanita was quick and clearly enjoyed the games, she was not territorial about her skills. If someone else got an answer before her, she was happy for them. She was just a lovely spirit to be around.

Not only was Juanita brilliant, but she was able to get good jobs downtown because of her charisma and ability to learn anything quickly. It was hard, even for her, because employment agencies in Chicago viewed Black people with so much disdain, so much racism. Even so, Juanita stood out because she was very capable and charming.

My cousin's allure and personality were her own, but they were also inheritances from her mother, Aunt Het. Hettie was the youngest of Mom's sisters and brothers, the baby. In some ways she reminded me of myself as we would talk. Aunt Het told me stories about the South, things she remembered about growing up there. She was the one Mama Liza and Papa Jim would send with my mom and dad when they were courting. A little chaperone, Hettie rode in the back of the buggy and watched her sister and her company get comfortable together. "You should marry him," Hettie blurted out. She liked Dock and thought he was the best of my mother's suitors.

Hettie and I both loved to dance and I remember her showing me rhythmic movements she had learned as a girl in Georgia. That's when I saw the origins of Juanita's gracefulness. Somebody put on a record and Aunt Hettie got up. She moved her torso and shoulders like a flower bending and turning in a passing wind. I could see birds in her movements—the span of wings in her extended arms and gently gyrating back. And then she hunched her neck and slowly lifted her feet and I thought she looked like a gazelle or a deer. Oh, Aunt Hettie loved to dance! In fact, she told me herself she thought some of her dances looked like African movements she had seen in performances or on television. They reminded me of Katherine Dunham's techniques; and Haitian dance. But my aunt learned them growing up in Leesburg.

About ten years after I left Chicago and moved south with my husband, Juanita died. It was a horrible blow for Aunt Hettie. Juanita was her heart. There was an issue of a major national newsmagazine during that time that featured a beautiful, dark-skinned Black woman on the cover. The freedom movement was making real strides and demands on the conscience of the country and the article asked people what they saw when they looked at this face. For me, the woman on the cover looked like Juanita. I saw my cousin's qualities of spirit as well as her physical charm in the model. I bought the magazine and turned to the essay, and as I read the responses of white people who must have been asked what they saw in the face, I was startled. Some said the woman looked angry; others said she looked willful and intransigent. I was amazed. And I said to myself, "They do not know anyone who looks like this, neither are they truly seeing this face." Because if they had met and known someone like my cousin Juanita, their notions of what blackness is and what it has the potential to become would be so different from the answers they gave.

As I think about my family I ask myself, "What helped them survive? What was it that gave them the capacity to navigate their way through so many obstacles?" It had something to do, I'm sure, with knowing they were of great value. No matter what messages we got from the outside world, someone at home was always telling us how beautiful we were, how intelligent, how talented. If you told them you wanted to do something—to be a musician, a teacher, a lawyer, a doctor—whatever good you could imagine for yourself, my family would urge you forward in it. "Girl, you so smart! You go on and do that." Or, "Boy, you great! Can't nobody sing (dance, cook, write, read, recite, do math, spell, etc.) like that child!" My sister, Sue, remembers that Mama Freeney constantly told her how lovely her dark black skin was and how capable and special she would always be. Some of this Mom got from her own father who loved her dearly and encouraged her self-pride, intellect, and independence.

I think this was an important strategy in many Black families from slavery onward: filling our children to the brim with affirmations of their innate merit and praise for their creative and intellectual abilities. Without letting children become arrogant (and, also helping them safely negotiate the limits that racism and prejudice often imposed), the parents nonetheless encouraged them to be hopeful about their possibilities and confident in their worth. I know that not all African American children experienced this, but when I was growing up, it was a staple of my family's child-raising.

Even adults relished in it. Sometimes I felt that friends and neighbors came to talk to my mother to get encouragement so that they could face their hardships with a lightened load. Mom never pushed us to keep jobs that demeaned us, even if it meant having less money or going without until we could get a new job. And then, too, we were able to withstand a lot of mess from the world because we had such a secure place at home.

Around the same time that I saw the *Life* article, I had a conversation with Vincent's uncle, Gordon Broome. We had taken the children to visit him and his wife, back when he was working as caretaker of a private school in Boston, the Windsor School. Uncle Gordon and I hit it off early in my marriage to Vincent. He was easy to talk to and a nice man. When my children were young, he taught them stone-counting games and stories from his Barbados childhood that always ended with the same Bajan rhyme: "I bend on the wire and the wire wouldn't bend and that's the way my story end." This time, as we sat and talked, he told me he had been thinking about the fact that of all the races of humanity, the only people who have tightly curled hair, kinky hair, are those from Africa. "What do you think about that, Rose?" he asked me. "Why do you think that is?"

What came to my mind was images of Juanita and Alberta and Middie Jean and Louise. And all my other elegant cousins. I thought about the joy I felt in their presence and the vitality of their lives, the insistent vitality of their lives. And I had no idea that I was going to say what I did in response to Uncle Gordon, but it just came out: "Well, if it's true," I started. "If it's true that we're the only ones in the world with kinky hair and everybody else has hair that is wavy or straight, then it must be that we, the unusual people, are the first people. And everybody else comes from us." At the time, I didn't know anything about the scientific research confirming the African origins of the human species and the original Black woman who was the mother of all the rest of us. It just made sense to me. I figured that adaptations probably occurred over many generations due to changes in climate and geography as people moved from Africa to other parts of the earth.

But I have to say that my ability to see black people as original people came from my family. There was so much life and strength among us. These were people who had come up from the South just before the Great Depression and suffered tremendous disappointments and injustices in their lives. But what always impressed me most about them were their high countenances. The beauty that comes from the internal work of living through pain and profound frustration without succumbing to despair. It was nothing easy. And Lord knows, they had many falterings. But they understood how important it was to keep one's spirits up. To encourage and take encouragement. And they helped each other through. As I look now at photographs of my aunts and uncles, I see the result of a lifetime of a certain kind of discipline. The effort to live with dignity and compassion, with beauty and integrity (and lots of laughter) regardless of what challenges life sends one's way. That effort, over time, is capable of creating a strong and beautiful character, a brilliant soul.

Whenever I walk from a cold room into a warm one, or, come into a snug heated house from freezing temperatures outside, I think of my father. The house at 6428 Rhodes did not have radiators and Daddy Freeney got up early to bring in coal, stoke the iron stove, and make warmth for us to rise into. All my life I have associated my father with warmth.

There were three rooms upstairs, each with two or three beds, where my brothers shared space on one side of the house and where me and my sisters had the other side. By the time we children woke for school, the flames were blazing and settling into their strength; and the whole house was toasty in spite of the Chicago cold.

Once, years later, sitting in a classroom at Wilson Junior College I was listening to a teacher who came from Europe during the war. She said when she was a child she went to school in a building with no heat and had to sit in the class with gloves on because it was so cold. She said we in the United States didn't know what it was to suffer like that. My heart went out to her and I wished she had had a school with heat and someone to make her cozy in winter. I thought about the blessing of a father who would get up for us in the cold.

Daddy was just that way. He took such good care of his family. One time a man came into our little grocery store on Wentworth with a gun. He wanted to rob us and got mad because there wasn't very much money in the cash register. There never was. My niece Jean was in the store, too, with Mama and Daddy. She was just a little girl then. The man raised his gun and threatened to shoot if he didn't get more cash. Daddy said, "There ain't no more money. But if you got to shoot some-body, shoot me." That's how my father lived. Protecting his children. He was always willing to take the hard knock, to do the difficult things.

Maybe that's where Bud got that impulse to switch the flowers—taking the dead flowers for Son who was away fighting in the war.

. . .

From the girls' perspective, Daddy was the sterling example of a good husband, a devoted father. We knew there were challenges in our parents' marriage—like when Daddy Freeney bought the house and store on Wentworth without telling Mom, or when they lost all their money when the bank crashed during the Depression. But we always saw them work it out. Daddy almost always supported Mama's decisions. He loved and trusted that woman. "Worshipped the ground she walked on," a friend said.

And Daddy was kind to his children. When Alma was little, she was ten-derheaded, and she'd cry if Mom pulled the comb too hard through her hair. If Daddy heard the tears, he'd come and take the comb and break it. He couldn't stand for his children to be unhappy. He very seldom scolded, spanked, or punished us. (That was Mama Freeney's job—and she didn't do it much herself.) But if something serious happened, like the time I acciden-tally set the curtains on fire and almost burned down the house, he could act with much more force and severity than Mom, although on the surface, she appeared to be the one in control. He never hit Mom and neither he nor Mama would stand for any man to hit a woman in their presence.

He was the kind of man we were looking for. Even his sisters adored him. Aunt Bey visited from Brooklyn every other year for the big conference of the National Baptist Church. Around the time the Harris sisters moved to Chicago, the women on the Freeney side of the family—Aunt Bey (who was Catherine), Aunt Rene (Irene), and Aunt Sut (Lilla)—had all moved to New York with their mother, Mama Catherine. The baby, Estelle, had died as a young woman in Georgia. So when Aunt Bey came to visit, she always had lots of updates on the East Coast family and Mom and Dad stayed up long hours with her getting filled in on all the news.

Aunt Bey would stay at our house and sew dresses for Francetta and Jean. She and Mom set up two sewing machines in the dining room and would just sit there with cloth and thread and needles at their sides, telling stories and stopping every now and then to hold up a dress or a skirt to measure against my nieces' quick-growing frames. Aunt Bey loved her brother Dock—I guess he was like a father to his sisters, in a way. Their dad had died when they were all very young and it was the older boys—Buddy Paul and my Daddy—who helped their mother and grandmother raise the little sisters when the father was gone. Alma says Daddy was strict on his sisters, "He watched them like a hawk. But they loved him."

Daddy grew up in a place called Cleages. We never did find it on a map. It's someplace in Lee County, Georgia. Probably a plantation, some land owned by a family with that name. Daddy's family were farmers. Likely sharecroppers in the years after slavery. The story goes that the Freeneys came to Georgia from Louisiana and were not slaves. Free people but poor. Daddy's father was also named Dock. And his mother's people were part Indian—Cherokee or Choctaw.

My Daddy worked all his life—he worked hard and loved work. He grew up in the fields, picking cotton for a few dollars a month. He didn't much care for raising cotton, but he did love the earth. Daddy always had two, sometimes three jobs. When he married Mom he had a job at a sawmill, then he got railroad jobs and was working construction. In Chicago he worked at Brach's candies and Acme Steel and on the side he had a moving and hauling truck and the family store. And he had his gardens, his plot of land where he would go in the evenings and on weekends and put his hands in the earth and know just what it needed to thrive.

"Daddy was smart, very smart," Alma says. He turned a tomcat into a guard dog and trained him to answer questions with meows that sounded like English. Daddy actually worked jobs on two different railroads in Georgia until the foreman on one found out. "Dock," the foreman approached Daddy one day, and asked, "You working here on the railroad?"

Daddy answered him, "Yessir." You had to say "Yessir" and "No, sir" to white men back then, Alma explained. Not just yes or no.

"Well, I hear you working on another railroad line too," the foreman said. "Man, you making more money than I am." So he made Daddy quit one of the jobs.

But Daddy did pretty well anyway. He bought a new Dodge car, a goat and wagon for Son, and a piano for his little girl. Alma wasn't but six months old when Daddy bought that piano, but she was his baby daughter and it was for her.

. . .

Daddy never learned to read or write too well. He missed so much school as a child because he had to be in the fields. But his wife, our mama, was a schoolteacher and she taught him to sign his name. And over the years, he learned enough to get by. His children, and later the grands, read to him when he came home from work or on a Sunday afternoon when he was relaxing. He'd get the newspaper and tell one of the youngsters, "Come and read this to Papa." We called him "Daddy" or "Dad" but he called himself "Papa." That's how they used to say it down south. That's probably what he called his daddy, "Papa."

My father also listened to the radio (and later when television became popular, he watched that too) but always with a critical ear and genuinely interested in what was going on in the world. When the astronauts landed on the moon, he didn't believe it. "That ain't real," he said. While they might have meant something different, a lot of people looking at NASA's budget in the face of so much poverty and need in our country thought the same thing.

I think Daddy's greatest relaxation was his garden. That man grew tomatoes as big as softballs and the best greens and okra you ever had in your mouth. He had peach trees in Chicago. At the last house, the house where he lived until he died, at 41st and Wentworth, there wasn't much land in the backyard, but what was there was absolutely luxuriant in vegetables—corn, string beans, okra, tomatoes, and two or three different kinds of greens. Collards, mustards, turnip greens, bell peppers. He even put flowers and garlic in with the vegetables to keep the insects off. And every day, he would come home from the Acme Steel plant and get in that garden, take care of it. Like he took care of everything else.

When I started working, Daddy would put me on the bus in the early morning dark. "Don't be late, don't be late, baby." Daddy Freeney believed in getting up and getting there early. And to this day, I love the morning, when the air is new and the dawn is coming up. It's so beautiful. Day just breaking and sun striking the buildings with a bright gold leaf. The bricks change their colors then; reds and browns tingle with specks of gold and blue; the rising light giving everything a special clarity. I watch the city mornings and love them; they remind me of my Dad.

The smell of trucks too. Truck smells remind me of riding next to Daddy in the front seat. His moving business was Freeney and Sons Hauling. (Although my sister Alberta said it should have been "Freeney and Daughters" for all the furniture she carried on and off of that pickup.) Daddy could put a three-hundred-pound refrigerator on his back and walk it out to the curb. He showed us how to bend our knees and settle the weight of a heavy thing so that it rested more on the shoulders, which can bear more load than the spine.

The smell of trucks—old leather seats and leftover oils and lubricants, the rubber of the tires. That smell and the coal fires and the early morning suns are my sensory memories of my father. My Daddy and his devotions.

The Public Housing Project

While Woodlawn had an abundance of thriving Black-owned businesses—stores of all kinds, restaurants, clubs, pharmacies and medical professionals, barber shops and beauty shops, all kinds of businesses—in contrast, there was hardly anything in the Gardens. The government did not encourage Black entrepreneurship there and the few stores in the immediate area did not have a neighborhood feel like the stores we knew from Woodlawn. We could get groceries, but for most things—clothes, furniture, other larger purchases—we had to leave Altgeld and go to one of the neighboring white communities, like Roseland, for example, and do our shopping there. So the money from Altgeld's Black community did not stay in that community. I was starting to notice these kinds of things while we lived in the Gardens.

When we first moved out to Altgeld, there was a small farm across the highway. It was just a simple little place run by a man and his family—some produce, a few animals. Kind of rundown really. But by the time we left the projects and returned to the city proper, that man was close to being a millionaire. Why? He sold chickens. And the whole project would be at his farm, if not daily then at least once a week. You know how we love chicken. He raised them there and butchered them there and within a few years he had new buildings and brand-new equipment. All from the Black folks at Altgeld buying his chickens.

The Family in Altgeld Gardens, c. 1948. PHOTO COURTESY OF FRANCETTA HENDRICKS.

Altgeld Gardens was new then, on the outskirts of the city. Out beyond Roseland. Beyond 130th Street. Way far south. It was a housing project that was built very close to a dump, partly on top of it. There were days when the old smells of what lay beneath the earth would come up and pinch the inside of your nose. Some people said the dump held chemical refuse and that the fumes were noxious. I never found out for certain, but the smell could be nauseating.

There was a sort of stigma attached to Altgeld, although we tried not to pay any attention to that. But I did miss Woodlawn and we felt a little isolated in the Gardens as it took a long time to get home if we went into the city for work or to shop or to visit friends or family. At the same time, there were so many good people, creative people, hardworking people there, that we made it serve its purpose and we enjoyed ourselves. The cost of rent in the projects was determined by the income of the head of household, and if you had a number of other people working in the family, you could save up a little money. Many of our friends and neighbors did just that, as did my parents, and within a few years people were beginning to move out again. Altgeld Gardens was the kind of place where people stayed only until they could get enough money together to move and do better.

Actually, a lot of the people we knew in Woodlawn had come to Altgeld. Rents were rising in the old neighborhood and many of the houses were sold. That's what happened to our house at 6428 Rhodes—a jazz musician bought it. He was nice though; he came by and played the piano for us once before we had to move out. The previous owners of the house sold it quickly and we didn't have much notice before we had to find a new place to live. At the time, Mom was working for a white family with connections downtown. The husband knew somebody who got us on the list of families to relocate to Altgeld Gardens and our name came up soon after they put us on the roll.

Miss Radcliff and the Universe

I had just finished my first year at Englewood High School when we moved from Woodlawn. We were among the first families to live in the Gardens and there was a new high school built for us which was named after George Washington Carver. We students had wanted to name the school after W. E. B. DuBois or one of the other more radical Black historians or professionals. We protested the choice of Carver. But the school board had made the decision before we arrived and it remained as they chose.

The education at Carver was not as good as what we had received at Englewood. The reason I know this is that at Englewood I wasn't one of the best students. I mean, I enjoyed school; I had fun and liked my teachers, but I wasn't all that good academically. Once I got to Carver, I was at the head of the class—which probably meant we weren't doing very much there.

I had never really thought about college. Most of the neighborhood kids graduated from high school but not many went on beyond that. The children of professionals—doctors and lawyers—were the ones who knew about the Black schools in the South. Some of their families had been going to those colleges for generations. But working-class Blacks like us usually went looking for jobs right after high school, or they went to a junior college in the city.

Fortunately in Altgeld, I had a teacher, Miss Radcliff, who got me thinking about college. She was the first teacher to tell me I was a good writer. She urged me to write as much as I could—to keep a journal, to write for the school newspaper, and to send stories to literary magazines. Anything to develop my skills. And she told me I needed to take more math. I liked her teaching style and the ideas that lingered in my mind when her classes were over. Her English composition classes were a pretext for discussing wide-ranging philosophical issues that were not much related to sentence structure and outlining paragraphs.

Once Miss Radcliff commented that an essay I wrote was similar to one of the plays we were reading in the class. But instead of suggesting that I might have plagiarized, she explained that ideas are universal. "It's not unusual for two or more scientists, researching many miles apart from each other, to make the same discovery days or weeks apart," she said. "It's just in the nature of things. Two authors writing around the same time might find themselves working on similar ideas, completely unaware of one another. They might set their stories in different historical eras, or use different characters, but the resemblance in their fiction is still appreciable." I was fascinated. "If this happens," Miss Radcliff continued, "it is possibly because they are both working with a concept that is universally experienced. We humans share a lot of collective experiences—feelings, beliefs, physical similarities. More than one person may have access to what we think of as a completely novel idea at the same time." I loved the way she thought and the way she encouraged me to think. Miss Radcliff's class was one of the places where I began to conceive of the universe as a single interconnected space—large, expansive, and all-inclusive.

Vernon and Jerome

There was a community center in the Gardens with after-school sports leagues for the neighborhood children. I always liked team sports and being outdoors, so just as I did in Woodlawn, I spent lots of time playing with friends after school. I was on a baseball team, a volleyball team, and a basketball team. I was pretty good at volleyball and baseball. But even though my brother Son was one of the basketball coaches I was never very good at that sport. It didn't matter though. I loved to watch the games and cheer for my friends and family members who were playing.

One afternoon, I ran into the house from the community center and as I headed upstairs to change clothes Mom called me into the kitchen. "Rose, come here a minute." She was standing behind the table with her full-length apron on, making rolls. The table and the floor were sprinkled with flour and she was kneading dough on a wooden board. Her dark brown hands and arms were dusted white.

"Did you hear what happened to Vernon?" she asked me.

"No, what happened?" I rested my hand on the back of a chair and looked up into my mother's face.

"He had a fight with Jerome and Jerome hurt him pretty bad. They took Vernon to the hospital."

I must have gasped a little. The news surprised me. It wasn't just that someone I knew had been injured. If Vernon was in the hospital, it meant something very peculiar had happened. Something surreal. Vernon had a nasty temper and was known to be brutal when he fought. He usually won. And generally speaking, people avoided him because it didn't take much to set him off. Sometimes, just walking down the street, other children would cross to the far side when they saw Vernon coming. He was just so unpredictable and we were afraid of him. Imagining him hurt now, badly enough that he had to go to the hospital, was difficult, strange. And Jerome? Something awful must have happened.

Both boys were teenagers, about my age. Jerome had a reputation for being very kind and easygoing. He was also sort of physically gentle in his build. Tall and thin. Vernon was the opposite. He was short and stocky, with that reputation for meanness.

Vernon's family had lived in Woodlawn too, and they moved out to the Gardens about the same time as we did. I knew him from the old neighborhood, and although he had never threatened me, I was uncomfortable with him. I had seen him, when we were younger, with a group of his friends, beat another boy mercilessly in an alley near the school. A small crowd had gathered to watch and most of the kids were astonished at how viciously Vernon attacked his opponent. There was so much blood. I couldn't stand to see it and left, walking home, very distressed. I witnessed that before I was a teenager and I never forgot it.

Vernon and Jerome were playing basketball on the playground this day—arguing over whose turn it was to make a shot. Jerome's family had come to the Gardens from another neighborhood, not Woodlawn, so Jerome didn't really know about Vernon's temper. But the crowd knew. And when Vernon rushed toward Jerome and began to pummel him, someone feared for the taller, thinner boy and slipped him a knife. The two boys fought; Vernon with his typical fierce intensity and Jerome, realizing quickly what he had stumbled into, slashing and gouging Vernon with a dreadful determination of his own. Mom said people were talking about how fearful Jerome must have been. Everybody in the community knew he would never start a fight. It was hard to imagine Jerome hurting anyone the way he had injured Vernon unless he feared for his life.

As Mom told me about the fight, I watched her face, her body. Usually it was hard for me to take this kind of news. If it was coming from anyone else, I might leave the room, go back outside if I had been playing, or retreat upstairs. But somehow, when I was hearing it from Mom, I could stand it a little better. I could stay there and listen. I think there was something about the way she carried the news that made me able to hold it too.

We could almost see Mama Freeney go someplace when she received difficult information, or when she had to share hard things with us. Someplace inside herself, I think. And I got the feeling that Vernon, or whomever the bad news was about, was there in that place with her. Those times, she could get very quiet. Not just from not speaking, but as if she was shutting out all the extraneous flutter around her. Often, she would lift her head and steady her breath, her eyes closing slowly or, if open, caught onto a thin, lace haze of strength in the air. She was both firm and supple then. Like she was manufacturing silk from all the contradictions of life and would soon spin it into an uncommon skein of armor and empathy.

I could hear it in her voice. Mom felt the pain of Vernon's injuries and her heart went out to him. And of course, she felt concern for Jerome, too, and could understand his desperation and fear. We were close to Jerome's family. They were our good friends and lived not far from us in the Gardens. But Mom had that kind of concern for all the neighborhood children. And she seemed to have a special sensitivity for what was happening with the young men around us. Maybe it was part of the radar she and Daddy developed from their years in Georgia—being extra conscious of what their sons and nephews and brothers were doing because there was so much implicit danger in the racial landscape. And then, too, a lot of the neighborhood boys would come to talk to Mom. "Miz Freeney, what do you think about such-and-such, or so-and-so . . . ?" They knew she read a lot and was well versed in politics and current affairs. She also listened carefully and gave thoughtful advice. So Mom was conscious of what was going on with the young men.

Whether the threat was external or internal, Mom and Dad had a barometer to gauge it and often did whatever they could to shift the winds.

Months later I saw Vernon on the street. I almost didn't recognize him. He had lost the urgent and brutal look in his face. And even though he was still a teenager, he walked like a much older man. His gait was sore, not fluid. The confrontation with Jerome had taken a lot out of Vernon and I felt some of the same tenderness for him then that I had felt over the years for his victims.

We had our share of fights in the neighborhoods where I grew up. Usually they weren't too serious and usually nobody got badly hurt. But Vernon's fights—the one in the alley and the one with Jerome—made me think about fighting in another way. The violence of it. The damage it did. In my family, and as I grew older, I started to get the reputation as a mediator. I didn't like to see people fight. I was always trying to get my nieces and nephews and friends to negotiate a resolution to whatever the problem was. Like my mother, I loved debates but I did whatever I could to prevent people around me from coming to blows with each other. I think now, this had its roots in those earlier, horrific altercations I witnessed and heard about coming up. Those fights, and Mom and Dad's compassion for all the children involved, no matter who "started it," also gave me the example of a sympathy and concern that could recognize pain that linked perpetrators and victims to the larger circumstances of their lives.

17 · Hot Rolls

(short fiction)

Julia shifted the dough into her hands with slow even turns; she kneaded it three times, counting to herself, then pushed it the length of her arms across the floured counter. Lifting the mixture and turning it again, she started the counting over, the pushing and the gentle raising, hoping her movements would imitate Mama Caroline's easy, expert gestures.

After greasing the long baking sheet with lard and placing the rolls in rows four across and six down, she put the sheet in a hot oven—400 degrees. She sat down in one of the four kitchen chairs, then got up again and adjusted the floral drapes separating the kitchen from the living room, the only two rooms downstairs. Julia glanced quickly through the drapes, as if to make sure the two visitors were still talking to her mother. She lowered the temperature of the oven to 350 degrees.

Two women had come to the front door and knocked several times before ringing the doorbell. They asked to speak to Mama Caroline ("Mrs. Mackinton," they had said, of course), when Julia answered and let them in.

"Please tell your mother that we are friends of her sister, Mrs. Mamie Smith. We work with the YWCA of Chicago," the women explained as they settled into the sofa. Its back rested against the longest wall in the room—the one that shared a common beam with the apartment next door.

Before Julia could go upstairs to her mother's room, Mama Caroline was greeting the visitors from the top of the stairwell. "How are you both? Isn't this a gorgeous spring day?" She must have known these visitors were coming, but she greeted everyone with enthusiasm, making guests feel that they were somehow special, unique, and welcome. The women smiled and cordially reached their hands toward Mama Caroline. She shook their hands, invited the women to make themselves comfortable, and then sat in the armchair across from the couch.

The visiting ladies each carried a small folding notebook-case and a purse. They had one umbrella between the two of them. Both were attractively attired—the taller one wore a teal dress, the other a navy suit with a red blouse. Both women had pillbox hats. To Julia they seemed prim in comparison to her mother who had on a simple floral housedress. Mama Caroline liked her clothing to be comfortable and usually wore dresses one or two sizes too large. Even if she had anticipated the women's visit, she probably would not have dressed differently. Mama Caroline did not "dress up" except for funerals and weddings. She would even go downtown to the Loop to pay bills, shop at the gourmet Stop-and-Shop, or visit a physician in housedresses and shoes too large for her feet.

Julia excused herself and went into the kitchen, just as her mother and the YWCA ladies were agreeing that this was one of those special spring days that only the Onion City, with its breezes and faux-tropic humidity, could create.

"One would have to use a great deal of imagination to explain such wonderfully cool breezes," Mom said. "Especially being as far from Lake Michigan as we are presently." The two ladies glanced at each other as if giving subtle approval to the manner in which Mama Caroline spoke. People were always surprised at how articulate she could be. She didn't talk like that all the time. But she could. One of the women began describing their specific responsibilities at the YWCA.

Upstairs in the house there were four small bedrooms and a bath. All the bedrooms had twin beds except the parents'. The family had moved to Altgeld Gardens from Woodlawn on the Southside of Chicago because the building where they lived at 64th and Rhodes had been sold. To get from Woodlawn to Altgeld one had to pass through several other communities like Pullman Heights, Roseland, and cities further southwest like Morgan Park. These townships had their own bus lines, post offices, and city halls and did not share Chicago city services.

As a matter of fact, passengers who boarded an Altgeld bus in downtown Chicago and paid a fare to go home to the Gardens were not allowed to get off the bus on South Parkway between 67th and 101st. But other riders could get on the Altgeld bus and get off at any intermediate stop. And the only people who rode to those intermediate streets were white.

The YWCA ladies, who had arrived by car from the inner city of Chicago, could have traveled two ways to Altgeld Gardens. One way was to follow part of the bus route. The other was to take Stony Island Avenue, which was pretty far east and would take you past the Chicago city dump. Although there were miles of land and some railroad crossings between the Gardens and the dump, the smells would sometimes fall heavy against the brick buildings in the projects. This afternoon, as the two visitors continued to talk with Mama Caroline, there were no garbage odors in the air.

There was instead the warm, inviting smell of rolls drifting between the two rooms. Julia pulled the pan out of the oven and placed it on a wooden board atop the table. The bread's soft brown shine was like the complexion of her sister Norma's beautiful new baby. Julia turned the rolls over to butter both sides—just as she had seen Mama Caroline do. She took down a china plate, a small bowl, and two matching cups and saucers and scooped some of her mom's homemade preserves into the bowl. This was Mama Caroline's "good china." Julia placed the dishes with a half-dozen rolls on a silver platter with cloth napkins, teaspoons, and knives.

When she walked into the living room, conversation ceased. The visitors watched approvingly, saying "Aahhh, how very nice. Your rolls smell delicious. Thank you." Julia was proud of the way the rolls turned out. She gave a quick glance to see what Mama Caroline's reaction might be. There was a smile, but no comment, no words of praise. *That's typical of Mom,* Julia thought to herself. *She knew I received honor enough coming from the two ladies.* When Mama Caroline did speak, she said, "Mrs. Lewis and Mrs. Davis would like to invite you to an Easter party sponsored by the YWCA. Would you be interested?" Julia eagerly said yes, even before the two women could finish describing how nice and how much fun the party would be.

A few days before the party, mother and daughter went downtown to Carson's department store and bought the first dress they saw. It was perfect—a navy blue and white cotton dress with a floral print and satiny finish. Riding home on the bus, Julia took the dress out of its box and rubbed her hands across the material, imagining the print as tree peonies from her father's backyard garden.

The dress had short loose sleeves that billowed at the ends. The tight bodice flared out into a long skirt that almost touched her ankles. Julia usually had some anxiety about new adventures, but for some reason, this time was different. On the day of the event she stood in the dress, in the long mirror, turning around as if moving to silent music. The fabric followed the sway of Julia's hips and wrapped for a moment about her ankles as she swiveled quickly from left to right. In her mind, she was drifting down from a high plateau where wind and light gave new shapes to the flowers in the dress's pattern. She liked what she saw and how this dress made her feel. It was not yet dinnertime, but Julia was too nervous to eat and left soon to catch the bus. As she walked out of the door a breeze ran across her face and arms. It blew the dress softly around her thighs.

Julia was to meet with a group of young women at a home at 31st and South Parkway. She could see the bus coming as she walked out of the front door, so she ran to the corner. As she got on, the driver smiled. Some of the other passengers looked her way and smiled too. Julia sat down in the middle of the bus, in an aisle seat, next to a middle-aged woman. The woman reminded her a little of the visitors from the YWCA. Except that when this woman began to speak to her, she had a heavier southern accent.

The woman told Julia about the life of pigeons. How they choose mates for life. The woman said that where she used to live in Chicago, before Altgeld, she had raised pigeons on the roof of a three-story apartment building. When she let them out of their cages, the pigeons flew around the neighborhood to houses with lower roofs. The woman said she missed her pigeons when she moved to Altgeld. You couldn't have pets there—no dogs or cats. Maybe you could have fish or small caged animals inside the house. But you weren't supposed to have any pets.

The woman turned her head toward the window and looked out. She said, "It's interesting how they build apartments with just small pieces of land for a garden in the back or grass in the front." And then she turned around and looked at her young seatmate and said, "Well, there is a field over behind the projects where you can have a garden if you like. It's pretty fertile ground too. A lot of people have a little space where they grow things. But you would think that the homes would be built so people could have space for animals, for pets. We need them as much as they need us." The woman turned back toward the window again. "Well, I guess it's just a matter of time. Most of us are out here just until . . . until we can do better."

Julia wondered how long the woman had lived in Altgeld and wanted to ask but was unaccustomed to asking adults personal questions. So she continued to listen.

"That's a pretty dress you have on," the older woman said.

"Thank you. I'm on my way to an Easter party."

"Oh? Where?"

Julia reached into her small black bag and took out the address. "Thirty-one . . . thirty-one fifty-seven South Parkway."

"Oh," the woman said, "You're going into one of those mansions. I didn't live too far from there. But where we were, the houses were smaller. Mmm, is the party there?"

"I don't think so. They told us to arrive early enough to get on a bus that was going to take us to a party sponsored by the YWCA."

"Oh, the YWCA," the woman spoke thoughtfully. "What do you know about the YWCA?"

Julia answered, "Not much. Not much."

"Well, it's an interesting organization," the woman said. "Only recently have they begun to share activities with Black people."

"Do you belong?" the young woman asked hesitantly. "You seem to know a lot about it."

"Oh no. No, I don't belong. But if you read and listen you can learn a lot."

Julia gave the older woman a very close look. So many interesting people live in Altgeld, she said to herself. We have neighbors who play beautiful music; there are singers and dancers and just plain fascinating folks, like this stranger sitting next to me.

Julia got off the bus at 31st Street. She stepped down to the curb and looked at the address, remembering that the woman had told her she would have to cross to the opposite side of the street from where the bus let her off. "Have a good time," she had said.

Walking to the corner, Julia thought about her bus companion and how much the woman knew about so many things. It had been nice to listen to her. Julia often met people in Altgeld like that. So much knowledge, so much experience. She crossed the street and looked at the mansions along the road. They were indeed large and beautiful. Julia found the one she was looking for and rang the doorbell. She was greeted by Mrs. Davis, who had been to the house and remembered Julia by name, inviting her inside to meet the other young ladies.

Everyone was either sitting or standing around drinking something that looked like punch. Julia noticed that most of the women present were young like her: eighteen, nineteen, early twenties. A few of them were holding their cups very properly, their napkins resting on their laps. Whatever they were conversing about didn't interest Julia nearly as much as had the commentaries of the stranger on the bus. Julia stood against the wall, not knowing where to go with her punch. At the door Mrs. Davis had said to go in and talk to some of the other young ladies. But she didn't feel comfortable doing that, so she remained against the wall.

In a little while, the other YWCA lady, Mrs. Lewis, came in and announced that the bus was here now and that everybody would be getting on soon. "If there are any last-minute things any of you have to do . . . ," Mrs. Lewis said.

One of the girls giggled and whispered in Julia's ear, "That means if you have to go to the bathroom or anything."

"Please do it now," the chaperone continued. "We'll board the bus in about fifteen minutes." Fifteen minutes seemed like a long time to Julia. She stayed against the wall for support, to hold herself together. Earlier she had been so excited about the party, so pleased with her new dress that she hadn't had the opportunity to be truly anxious about it all. And just now, coming into town from Altgeld, the conversation and companionship of her seatmate had kept Julia from focusing on the fact that she was alone. She wondered, where did all of these young ladies come from? She didn't recognize any faces from Altgeld nor did she remember them as playmates from Woodlawn.

Soon they were all ushered onto what looked like a school bus. This time Julia took a seat by a window and looked out at the mansions along South Parkway. The buildings were made of stone with windows and doors set in carved wooden frames. And the stones had color that was not painted. Browns and grays and almost-pinks. With wrought-iron designs at the fences and gates. These were some of the most handsome houses on Chicago's South Side, and Julia took pleasure in their elegance.

She watched the young ladies getting on the bus, admiring the array of pretty dresses. But of them all, Julia liked best the one that her mother had helped her select. The pattern of blue and white flowers was just so attractive, she thought, smoothing the material flat across her lap and resting her small black handbag there.

Soon the bus entered a part of the city Julia didn't recognize. That in itself was a little unusual since her relatives lived all over Chicago. Actually, this place didn't seem too far. It was still on the Southside, Julia thought, but farther west. The bus stopped at what looked like a community center. When she got off, she noticed it was a YWCA. The building was very attractive. It must be new, Julia thought.

The young ladies all stood in line as they got off, waiting for more directions. The chaperones led them through an entranceway and down a few steps into a large meeting hall. Inside, standing in small groups around the walls were young men, Black and white, in military uniforms. Some of them were soldiers. Their uniforms looked like those of Julia's older brothers. And some of them were in what looked like sailor's uniforms. The others she couldn't recognize. Although the men stood, chairs were arranged for the women. Some young ladies were already seated, eating refreshments and talking jovially among themselves when Julia and the others arrived. They, too, were Black and white together and Julia thought they must surely have known each other and more than likely came as a group.

At the front of the room were several long narrow tables covered with white tablecloths and beautiful lace runners. At one table, a girl was in charge of the record player. Several other tables held large punch bowls at both ends and in the center a variety of desserts and fruits.

"Help yourselves and have a seat on this side," an older white woman spoke to the newly arrived young ladies encouragingly. "You may dance with whomever you wish. If you do not wish to dance with anyone it is quite alright to say no. The young men have been instructed that they might not get a positive response; but if at all possible, please give each gentleman a chance to dance." The chaperone explained that this was a weekend rest and relaxation for the enlisted men. What she didn't say, but what Julia had guessed from the ladies' visit to her house and their conversation with Mama Caroline, was that this integrated dance, cosponsored by the USO[1] and the YWCA was one of the first events of its kind in Chicago.

In addition to Mrs. Davis and Mrs. Lewis, there were several other chaperoning women, white and Black, milling around among the young people. Some of the men in uniform were older too, and the extra stripes and bars on their clothes led Julia to assume that they were officers. They seemed to be watching carefully over the evening's proceedings.

Julia looked around along the walls where the white young ladies and Black young ladies were seated, and where the men of both races joked with each other across the room, as they got up the nerve to ask the women to dance. Julia had not been to an integrated dance before. Well, not if you didn't count the times she watched her older sisters and brothers dancing to the radio with the O'Day kids in the living room at Woodlawn. The O'Days were neighbors, and they were Irish, which was white, but that wasn't quite the same as this. Everyone here seemed to be—what should she say? Rather stiff, rather . . . well, not so much afraid, but at least nervous.

The first person who asked Julia to dance was a young white man in an army uniform. She wasn't at all sure that she knew the dance steps he knew, or that he knew hers, but anyway she was going to relax. And she did. Even before the music stopped, a Black young man came up and asked if he could cut in. Julia's first partner said yes and backed away politely. But he didn't go far.

"I hope you didn't mind. I couldn't help but notice you." Roland, the Black young man, smiled.

For the third dance the white young man came back and asked her if he might have this one as well. Julia said yes.

The first time she danced with the white man the conversation had been about his time in the army: where he was stationed, places he had seen. His name was David and he said he was from Arkansas and had grown up with both Black and white people. But this was his first time dancing with "a Negro young lady" as he called her.

And she said softly to him, "This is my first time too. Although I've had white friends, all kinds of friends." He asked her, which she thought was sweet, if he might put his cheek next to hers.

"Yes, that'll be alright" she said. His skin was warm and smooth.

While she was thinking this, he said, "Boy, your skin is soft." Then immediately, "Excuse me, did I say something wrong?" as Julia pulled back suddenly, looking at him.

"Not really. Thank you," she responded.

"Oh, you're very welcome. I hope it wasn't too forward."

"No, not at all. Not too forward at all."

When the third dance was over Roland asked to cut in again. As they finished that dance Roland asked Julia if he could have the next one as well. But before she could answer, David was back, wanting another turn. Evidently, the men must have been instructed to consent every time someone asked to cut in. All the music was moderate in tempo, not fast and not too slow. Julia figured the songs were all from records because she didn't see a band.

It went on like this the whole night. Julia danced every dance, alternating between the two men. Toward the end of the evening, Roland asked if he could walk Julia to the door. That was the agreement the military officers and the chaperones had arranged for the young people—no addresses would be exchanged but the boys could walk the girls to the door of the building, although not to the bus.

Julia said yes, it would be alright to walk her to the door. As they were leaving the large hall, her glance fell on her other partner, who gave her a huge smile and a simple, discreet wave with his hand. She smiled back and then turned quickly to step through the door.

Roland said, "I know we're not supposed to give our addresses, but if you want, I have written mine down. You can put it in your purse." Julia said thank you, to be polite, but she was uncertain if she should take the address; she didn't want to embarrass her hostesses. She took it, put it in her pocketbook, and walked toward the street with the other young ladies who were getting on her bus.

She sat in the same seat as she had coming. Her window faced the building and people were still exiting, boarding her bus and other buses nearby. The doors were open and most of the young men were waving and saying good-bye, though not, it seemed, to anyone in particular. David was also standing out there. He didn't wave anymore, but he kept his eyes on her. Julia looked away, a little embarrassed, not knowing the proper thing to do but thinking of him now with a kind of . . . longing . . . for the courtesy, the compliment about her skin and how nice it was that he asked if he could put his cheek against hers.

The bus ride back to the mansion seemed very quick compared to their arrival. One of the chaperones stood up and announced, "The bus driver will make sure that all of you young ladies get home. And we'll stay on until everyone is delivered safely." *Ah, what a relief,* Julia thought. She sat back, put her head against the window, relaxing now and realizing how demanding the day had been. She'd been nervous and hadn't eaten any dinner, but still didn't seem especially hungry. Anyway she knew that Mama Caroline would be waiting up to ask her what the evening was like, and of course there would be something for her to eat.

She was one of the last to get off. The bus had made other stops, even going north before turning back south to Altgeld. Julia closed her eyes as the bus was moving. Not because she was tired, but because she didn't feel like talking. Mrs. Davis and Mrs. Lewis were having an animated conversation with the driver about how nicely things had gone and how well it turned out. This was one of the first formally sponsored military parties with integrated dancing, and the army would use it as an example to encourage more social integration.

Integration was not something Julia had heard much about at all. Now and then there were reports on the radio of Black soldiers demanding more equality or better opportunities. But she hadn't heard the word "integration" used so specifically. Nor had she heard the term spoken with the enthusiasm in the voices of the two women and the bus driver.

Soon the bus was in front of her home and Julia said good night to the chaperones and thanked the bus driver. He smiled. And sure enough, as she walked up the pavement, her mother was waiting with the door open. She must've been watching for Julia, or, as was sometimes the case, sensing that it was about time for her daughter to be coming home.

"Oh yes. I had a good time." Julia told her mom as she was eating dinner. Mama Caroline had stewed a chicken and made turnip greens and a sliced tomato salad. There were soft rolls and butter on a small flowered plate. The house was warm with the smells of food. "I danced with a Black soldier and a white one."

"Ah. How did you like that?" Mama Caroline was sitting across the table from her daughter, watching as she ate.

"It was nice. Very nice."

"Well, that's good." Mama Caroline said.

The rolls were from a batch Julia had made just the day before, her second or third attempt alone. "The rolls came out pretty tasty," Mama Caroline said. "I'm getting it," Julia replied and grinned quietly. She brushed a few crumbs from her lap and noticed again the feel of the fabric and the fine pattern of flowers in the dress. Both women were still thinking about the evening. But neither said more just then.

Julia broke off a piece from a new roll, testing it in the thick, savory broth before her, and chewed it a long time.

Note

1. United Service Organizations.

It was hard for women, too, when I was coming up. But as I think about the young men I knew, my heart breaks. How handsome and brilliant they were, gol-lee! And all Black. All kinds of Black. They were beautiful—from brown-blond to ebony shale, just beautiful men. But I saw so many of them hurt.

I was listening to Noam Chomsky on television the other day and he got it right. He said when poor people make an effort to change things, they suffer. He said there is a lot of meanness done to so-called powerless people in this world. You know, we have to talk about this, and write about it and make some plays so it can be acted out. Because something has got to change this way of thinking that to be powerful means you lord it over others.

I don't remember when I first became aware of the discrepancy in the way Blacks were treated in the city of Chicago, but once I started noticing it, I saw example after example of injustice. One of the first things I saw was that our neighborhoods began to lose what we called the mom-and-pop stores. I used to get very angry at the supermarkets. They would actually put people out of business. They'd lower the prices a little bit, take over the clientele, but then the services were just awful. I mean, we used to could go down the street and get live chickens from the mom-and-pop grocery stores, but once the supermarkets came in, not only did we not get live chickens, we didn't even get *good* chickens. The quality was horrible.

This was just after World War II and I noticed, too, that manufacturers started putting preservatives into everything. My mother was very bright, and she was the one who brought this to my attention. We'd be in the store and she'd call me over to the bread shelf. "Rose, how long has this bread been in our store?" And I would say, "I think the man came last Friday," or something like that. She would look at the bread and pick it up, and then she'd say, "You know, that's too long, and this bread is not spoiling. They must be putting something in this food." Mom showed me that not only were the factories adding something to the food to keep it from spoiling, but they weren't telling us what it was.

Me and Mom used to sit around and talk about things like that. "It's still soft too," she would notice about the bread. The old bread, before they started using all the preservatives, would get hard after a while, kind of tough. But not anymore. And then Mom noticed a difference in the wrapping papers that food came in. She'd say, "Come here, Rose. Look at this." She'd hold the package wrapping over the stove. "Look, it doesn't burn, it melts. What kind of paper is this? What are they putting in it?" From then on she only used the old-fashioned wax paper to wrap things—sliced meats that she sold in the delicatessen, sandwiches, pickles, things like that. She wouldn't use the plastic wrap.

So I learned from Mom to pay attention to what was going on around us: to see the changes that weren't always for the best. This was when we were living at 41st and Wentworth. I thought of my mother's observations as I watched the neighborhood change. When we first arrived, in the late 1940s, there were still white families living in the community. Irish, Polish, and German families. Black and white both lived there. One thing I perceived was that the white young people in our neighborhood—some of whom didn't have as much education as the Blacks—all went downtown and got jobs. The Leonards, the Krantz family, the Zadeks. And there were others. You could tell they had jobs because they'd have new clothes. They'd come in the store and tell us about what they would be doing or how much they were going to make. They were happy and wanted to tell somebody about it. But oh how *often* did we hear from the Black kids how disappointed they were, how prepared they thought they had been, and how they had gone downtown and simply were not hired.

By this time, I had already been out of high school a few years, and all these kids I'm talking about were younger than me. I think that gave me the perspective to observe more. I don't know if the white young people were even aware that their Black friends and neighbors weren't getting jobs.

I think it is rather easy to not be conscious of how others, other races, are treated. Sometimes I think about how easy it is for Black people not to know the horrific experiences that Native Americans have had. Maybe now people are a little more conscious, but when I was growing up, we weren't given much information, and if you didn't go seeking it out . . . I remember Daddy telling me about the Indian ancestry in our family; he said they were treated so bad in Georgia that many didn't want to be identified as Native American. They thought it was better to be Black.

I would watch the Black young men and women coming into the store, and I could actually see the despair in their eyes. Mom would give them a sandwich or a pop, tell them to sit down, and she'd talk to them. And by the time they left they'd feel a little better but they still didn't have a job. And some of them had families to support. Not necessarily children of their own, but they belonged to large families and they needed to earn something to help out. It made them feel proud when they could help.

Along with noticing that Black people were not getting jobs, I saw that the services in our community started disappearing as white people moved out. And I guess the banks weren't giving loans to Black people, because the stores just disappeared. Black-owned stores started closing one after another. And over a decade or so, it got to where a community that had been really thriving and prosperous, like Woodlawn, for example, began to look like a wasteland.

Auntie said that's why she went into the WACS,[1] because outside of the army no one was hiring Black people. She said the only jobs open were for maids, and the older women had those. It was hard on everybody, women and men. But I think it's harder for men. Maybe because they had an expectation of themselves that they should be able to support and protect their families. That's the role this society says men should have. And there was so much—still is—that tries to suffocate that commitment in Black men, tries to kill that determination. But it was hard for everybody. Even after I finished college, I had a very difficult time finding work.

I had applied at the board of education and the state social services offices—and I was waiting for them to call me. While I was waiting, I went looking for work in stores, and factories, and other places. I finally got a job at the Fair department store, but before that I had tried all over the city.

I remember Westinghouse had an advertisement in a window saying, "College Graduates, Come In." So I went in. This was one of many jobs that I attempted to apply for where they were asking for college graduates. There was a man in a little office in the personnel department who looked at me when I walked through the door. He said, "Sit down." He glanced at me for a few seconds, as if deciding how best to handle a situation that for him, I gather now, was odd.

"What's your name?," he asked me.

I told him.

"I'm not going to let you waste your time filling out these applications, Miss Freeney. Because they're not going to hire you. But if you tell anybody I said that, I'll deny it. But I don't want you to waste your time, you see."

I was a little flustered. I didn't really understand yet why people were responding to me like that. So I asked the man, "Is there anything else I could do, or should do, to better prepare myself? I do have a college degree."

"Nope. There's nothing you can do."

I left then. But I had a lot of experiences like that. A lot of them. There would be ads in the newspaper—"College graduate. Looking for college graduates." And they said there were no tests required; they just wanted a college graduate. I walked all over downtown. I went into one office, and I was amazed at how sumptuous it was. I never knew offices could be so lavish. Hmm. You wouldn't believe it. Even the elevator looked as if it were made of gold. The elevator operator man glanced at me as I got on, in the same way the man at Westinghouse had looked at me.

"You look nice."

"Thank you," I told him.

"But they're not going to hire you."

"Well, I'll go on up anyway," I said. It was a high-rise building downtown. Very fancy. I stepped out of the elevator to face a well-appointed reception area with pure leather chairs and a plush carpet. The man in the elevator was right. I answered their description, but they didn't hire me. It happened over and over again. And they always seemed a little surprised to see me. And I was surprised at their surprise. I thought a lot of us would be going downtown to apply for the jobs. But evidently other Black people had better sense than I did. There were so many brilliant young people I went to school with. I was just certain that they had gone on to college and would be applying for these office jobs like me. And I just assumed that many of them would be hired, because they were so intelligent, so sharp, and eager for opportunities.

Note

1. Women's Army Corps.

I studied sociology at Goshen and I became a social worker. But I had wanted to be a nurse. When my older sister Mildred came out of the Women's Army Corps after World War II, she promised to pay for my medical training. She had already paid for my books and other expenses at Wilson Junior College. I was taking pre-nursing classes there and preparing for the entrance examination to nursing school.

I took the exam and I failed it the first time. That upset me terribly because it was my dream to be a nurse. So I studied very hard and took the test again. The second time I passed. They told me I got one of the highest scores possible.

But this was the early 1950s in Chicago and they also told me, to my face, although I think they tried to say it in a nice way, that they were not going to accept me because they thought I had cheated. They said it was not possible for me to have failed that exam once and then passed it so successfully this time. They did not admit me to the nursing school.

I walked down the hall, went into the bathroom, and cried.

(short fiction)

"The call is for your supervisor," Mrs. Rice said. "But I thought you might want to take it. The recipient is in your district . . . you're new, and . . . " Mrs. Rice was the receptionist for the entire second floor of the West Side branch of the Cook County Department of Social Services. She was usually the first person clients saw when they came looking for help and it was her job to direct them to the social workers. She also served as a kind of switchboard operator, putting calls through to where they belonged. The phone on Clarice McKnight's desk was ringing now: two rings then a stop and again two rings. Mrs. Rice prodded a bit, "You can pick it up. She sounds really upset."

"Who is it?" Clarice asked. The receptionist put her hand over the receiver and lowered her voice. Directing her whisper across the row of desks that separated the two women, she answered: the caller was Mrs. Florence Harper. "Harper . . . Harper . . . let me see . . . Harper." Clarice picked through the neatly sorted cases from the previous day's field visits. They had all been transcribed and typed by one of the secretaries in the typing pool.

Yesterday was Clarice's first day of home visits. Her supervisor, Mrs. Patton, had reiterated the instructions drilled in months of training sessions—what to say, how to say it, and what to be cautious of. "Some recipients will surely try to . . . well, you know, try to take advantage of your inexperience. But you just keep to the rules and regulations and everything will be just fine." Then, before the new social workers left to do their rounds that morning, Mrs. Patton gave them each a set of written instructions for conducting the interviews.

The mimeographed sheet was almost identical to ones given to the class of fifteen women and men who were preparing to join the ranks of the caseworkers of Cook County, Illinois, in the fall of 1957. Each day from nine AM to five PM, the trainees sat in a small room on the fifth floor of the State Office Building downtown. They drilled and reviewed sample cases, procedures, regulations, and protocol, and when the training program was over, the new caseworkers were assigned to local branches of the social services department.

The other rooms on the wide corridor of the fifth floor were larger—mostly courtrooms on one side and the offices of state and county agencies on the other. Someone told Clarice that the rooms with darkened glass doors were where the big-time detectives and their prisoners waited until their names were called and they were ushered into one of the courts. Other rooms had high wooden doors whose metal fixtures always gleamed from recent polishing. But the social workers' classroom was tight, with too many desk-chairs and no windows. It was, no doubt, on the Wabash side of the building, because the floor vibrated whenever the El passed, turning over Randolph Street, going west.

The training instructor had been Clarice's art teacher back in high school in Altgeld Gardens. Neither woman ever mentioned the previous association although Clarice was fairly certain they both recognized each other. There was some uneasiness between them these days. The instructor outlined the basic guidelines of departmental protocol—never accept gifts, food, or anything to drink from recipients; they're not supposed to have a telephone; owning a television is not encouraged; if a man is living in the house they probably don't really need the benefits; be careful not to overestimate the needs—all recipients should be urged to economize. It went on like that. Clarice wasn't sure if the teacher actually believed those things or if she was just doing what she had been hired to do—teach the policies. Whatever the case, they sounded ridiculous and mean-spirited to Clarice, and she let the teacher know, more than once.

Now in her newly assigned position at the West Side branch on Roosevelt Road, two days after the classes had ended, and one day after her first home visitations, Clarice tried to address her clients' problems without supervisory assistance. Picking up the phone, she greeted the woman at the other end of the connection. The caller sounded a little surprised, "Oh, it's you Miss McKnight. I wanted to speak to your supervisor, Mrs. Patton."

"Yes, but is there anything I can do to help you?"

"Well . . . yes. Just hang up the phone. I'll call back and ask for your supervisor." Clarice wondered briefly to herself why Mrs. Harper, whom she had just seen the day before, was so intent on speaking to the supervisor. *We had had a pleasant enough visit,* Clarice thought. Mrs. Harper was still talking, ". . . and listen, no matter what happens, stay calm. Just stay calm."

Florence Harper was a keenly observant woman. That was clear to Clarice after a few minutes in her presence, yesterday. Smart. Even so, what she was saying now struck the young caseworker as peculiar. Both women hung up and Clarice looked around the room at the desks of some of her coworkers, where the phones had started to ring. It was almost four thirty and most people were clearing away their papers and folders, making ready to leave for the day. Some had already gathered their coats and jackets and walked down the hall to the stairs.

The main room of the West Side branch of the Department of Social Services occupied a huge space. Twenty-three social workers were assigned to desks—each with a wooden, three-drawer file cabinet. Clarice was impressed with how well some of her colleagues concentrated while so much activity went on around them—the many conversations, the constant ringing of phones, consultations with supervisors, visits from state and county personnel giving briefings on policy changes, and the emergency in-office appointments with clients who needed to see caseworkers.

Yesterday, before Clarice went out on her visitations, she had called the clients to tell them she would be coming for a visit. (The rules did not say to do this.) She asked them if the day she had chosen was convenient and they all said yes. Two were invalids who could not leave their homes; another was a patient of a local psychiatrist. There were four families with dependent children and there was one blind woman. Clarice had been nervous. Not inhibitingly so, but she still wasn't absolutely certain what to expect and she didn't want to make any mistakes. Finally, when the day was over, with all the visits done, she had relaxed as she wrote up the reports and handed them over to the typing pool.

Mrs. Harper lived on the second floor of a three-story wood-frame apartment building on Chicago's West Side. There were six apartments in all, two on each floor—one in the front, one at the back. Most likely the flats had originally been larger, but were now subdivided. The steps up to Mrs. Harper's place were narrower than they should have been given the size of the building. Clarice knocked on the door and when a woman came to answer, she said, "Hello, I'm Miss McKnight from the Social Services Department. May I come in?"

"Yes," Mrs. Harper said, looking at Clarice carefully as she widened the door's opening and gestured to her to come in. "I was expecting you." The small apartment was impressively neat and clean. As Clarice stood in the entranceway she could take in almost the full layout. The living room just in front of her was small and immaculate as was the kitchen she could see through a doorway to the left. Two closed doors on the right were probably bedrooms, or a bedroom and a bathroom. That seemed to be all there was of living space. And then there were the children, sitting quietly on the overstuffed, two-seater couch—two girls and a boy: ages five, seven, and eight respectively, according to the file.

Mrs. Harper introduced her children to the social worker and then, noticing Clarice's roving gaze, she asked, "Do you want to see the rooms?" The question brought Clarice's attention back to the purpose of the visit; it also made her aware that she might have appeared . . . appraising.

"No, I don't need to see the rooms," Clarice responded, taking a seat in the armchair that faced the couch. Mrs. Harper sat down, too, self-consciously upright, in a wooden cane-backed chair, the only other seat in the living room. "So, how are you, Mrs. Harper?" Clarice continued. "I see that the last time a caseworker visited you and the children was about three years ago. Do you all need anything?"

Mrs. Harper seemed surprised by the question. She looked at Clarice as if trying to determine just how she should answer, like there was some trick involved. Clarice seemed not to notice; and faced with Mrs. Harper's initial moments of silence, she proceeded to comment about the children's nice appearance and good manners. She went on, asking about their health, whether they were ready for school, and if they needed school supplies, clothes, or shoes. Mrs. Harper recovered her voice and answered the questions with short, courteous replies. The children were all well, although the older girl had been to the county hospital with asthma about a month ago. She was fine now. Clarice glanced up from her note taking to see that even as Mrs. Harper spoke in a clear tone, she was looking at her visitor with something like puzzlement—as if Clarice was, in some way, a strange quantity to her. When the women's eyes met, Clarice smiled. Mrs. Harper offered coffee.

"I'd love some," Clarice sighed. "It's getting so cold out now. I walked up three blocks from the train." All the while, the children were sitting on the couch like models, their clothes pressed, their hair freshly combed with yellow ribbons in the girls' braids. Mrs. Harper went into the kitchen to get the coffee and returned shortly, still watchful in a ciphering way. Clarice drank her coffee mostly in silence. The boy took a handkerchief out of his back pocket and wiped his baby sister's running nose. Clarice occasionally smiled at the children, who shyly but genuinely smiled in return. She asked the older girl what she liked to do at school.

"I like recess. And stories."

"Her teacher says she reads good for her age," the mother added. After a moment or two Mrs. Harper asked Clarice, "Who's your supervisor?"

"Mrs. Patton," Clarice answered.

"Oh, you got her, hunh?" Mrs. Harper seemed a little more at ease now.

"Un hunh." Clarice was finishing the last sips in her cup. She thanked the other woman and rose to put on her coat. "It was so nice meeting you," she said. "And your beautiful children."

"It was nice meeting you too."

"You sure there isn't anything you need now?" Clarice was moving toward the door.

Mrs. Harper hesitated a moment then said, "Miss McKnight, I do need something. Could you come back in for a minute?" Clarice returned to the armchair and sat down with her coat on and her notepad out ready to write something else. Mrs. Harper went into one of the rooms on the right and came out with a small child. "This is my youngest, Sheila. Sheila, this is your social worker, Miss McKnight." Clarice leaned forward and greeted the little girl. Sheila would be three years old in a few weeks, her mother said, and, as Clarice could see, she was well raised and polite, just like her older siblings. After saying hello, the child went over and squeezed between her oldest sister and brother on the couch. Mrs. Harper was still standing.

"Mrs. Harper, you've had this child for three years and you haven't gotten any money for her?" The social worker seemed genuinely incredulous. The files had only mentioned the older children, and Clarice knew that the money the family was receiving each month was the allotment for three dependents.

Mrs. Harper sat down then. She could see that Clarice's surprise and expression of concern were unfeigned. There was a kind of guilelessness about the younger woman—which her hostess was beginning to appreciate.

"No, I haven't gotten any money for her. I never told the caseworker about her." Mrs. Harper paused, as if waiting for a reply. Or a question. Then she said, measuring her words carefully, as if to assure an exact recall, "They told me that if I had another baby I would be cut off."

Clarice reviewed the major elements of eligibility from memory. "There is no such rule as that, Mrs. Harper." She figured that her instructor and supervisor would not have missed an opportunity to highlight such a restriction if in fact one had existed.

In her report, Clarice carefully noted the youngest child's full name, birth date, and the benefits due her. She promised the girl's mother that additional monies would be secured for Sheila and included in the next month's allowance. Clarice also said that she would see to it that Mrs. Harper received a check for the three years of assistance owed to her in arrears. And she wrote down the reason the woman had not notified the department of the youngest child's birth.

"Is your supervisor going to be in tomorrow?" Mrs. Harper asked.

"Yes, she'll be in. You come by tomorrow and I'll make sure you get whatever you need. I don't know how you've managed all this time as it is."

Mrs. Harper looked at the social worker sympathetically, like a teacher would look at a sincere but overanxious student.

"No, I'll take care of it," she said. "Me and Mrs. Patton know each other."

Clarice put her notepad away a second time and got up to leave. She said good-bye to Mrs. Harper and the children, assuring the older woman that she would not have to wait so long for the next visit from a caseworker.

"Most likely not," Mrs. Harper said and then added, "You take care of yourself."

Now, the following day, Clarice was remembering the visit to Mrs. Harper's house and wondering what the woman was calling about and what kind of prior interaction she'd had with the supervisor, Mrs. Patton. As Clarice was thinking, Mrs. Patton approached her desk. "Miss McKnight, did you make an appointment with Mrs. Harper?"

"No," Clarice answered. "But I visited her house yesterday."

"Did you know that she brought four children in here and just left them in the waiting room? It's almost five o'clock and they have been sitting there without adult supervision all afternoon." Mrs. Patton explained that the client had come into the office just after lunchtime with her four children, requesting to see the supervisor. She didn't have an appointment, refused to see anyone else, and so had been instructed to wait as Mrs. Patton was very busy. Evidently, after a while, she had walked out and left the children. And then called back.

"You know that as her caseworker you are *in loco parentis*, don't you?" Mrs. Patton loved technical terms.

"No, I didn't know. But as I said, I visited her yesterday and she has a new child. A little girl. I told her that we would be sending her the back allowances she's due."

Mrs. Patton's growing exasperation was evident. "Who does she think she is?" she fairly yelled to no one in particular. Except for Mrs. Patton, the four children sitting quietly in the waiting room, Mrs. Rice, and Clarice, the office was nearly empty. Now the supervisor was cursing the children's mother and telling the young social worker, "If you hadn't been new, this wouldn't have happened! You are responsible for those four children in there and you will have to decide the proper action to take. But because this is just your second day and you obviously know nothing of what is expected of a person *in loco parentis* . . . "

Clarice stood up from her chair. She was a little tired, probably from lack of sleep. Since she'd started the social work training, she'd been working during the day and going to the university at night. Her body still wasn't used to the routine. She stood partly to rouse herself, partly in hopes that the gesture would be interpreted as a willingness to take responsibility. Mrs. Patton was right; Clarice had no idea what she should do in the situation. She hoped that standing would give the impression that she was ready to do what was called for, whatever that happened to be. Furthermore, Mrs. Patton's yelling and screaming were less intimidating when Clarice stood. The supervisor's voice had softened a bit by the time she finally instructed Clarice to go sit with the children so that the receptionist could go home.

"Mrs. Patton, line B is ringing," Mrs. Rice said from across the room. Line B was a direct line from downtown. Easing off of her tirade a little more, the supervisor said, "This is a very good lesson in the duplicity of recipients. From here on, you'll know what to expect and how to conduct yourself in future situations." She went to take the call.

Mrs. Rice was getting ready to leave. As she put on her jacket, she explained to Clarice some of what had happened. Mrs. Harper had arrived early in the afternoon with a written accounting of all the back allowances she was owed. She asked to speak to Mrs. Patton, insisting that she couldn't raise four children on what she was getting at the time. When she was not able to see Mrs. Patton after waiting for an hour or so, she left the children in the reception area and went home. Periodically, throughout the day, she called the office and was eventually put through to Mrs. Patton. She demanded all of the money she was entitled to and threatened to leave her children with the agency if she didn't get it. It was after that phone call that the supervisor had appeared at Clarice's desk.

Clarice had been sitting with the children about twenty minutes when Mrs. Patton walked into the waiting room with two large men in black suits and sunglasses. She pointed out the children: "That's them." Clarice and the men were to take the children home. Downstairs, in front of the building, they all piled into a long limousine—the youngsters and Clarice all sitting together in the backseat. The three men sat together in the front.

When they arrived at the apartment building one of the men opened the limousine's trunk and took out a thick manila envelope. They delivered the children and the envelope to the top of the stair where Mrs. Harper stood waiting. When she saw Clarice leaning against the limousine door, Mrs. Harper waved. Then she turned around and went into her building with the children and the money. The limo men were back at the car immediately. "Let's go," one said to Clarice. She got in and closed the door.

. . .

This story happened to me. I don't know why that client had hid the baby from previous caseworkers. As far as I was concerned, it wasn't my business. The child was present and they all had needs that our taxes should provide for—taxes Mrs. Harper and I both paid every time we bought food—until there was no more need.

The children were driven home by limousine. Priorities. Somebody could now afford to send the children home in a limousine. Detectives in fine suits came to the city and county offices to escort them home. But normally the caseworkers were in a pitiable room. One window. Forty cases per social worker. Low pay. This work should be valued. The workers should be valued. When I was teaching social work at the University of Denver, I told my students, "When recipients come into your office, never tell them we don't have enough money. We can find money." We have money for nuclear bombs, for chemical weapons, for missiles. It's all a question of priorities.

When I did social work, I never cut people off at eighteen. I didn't ask who the man was in the kitchen and whether the recipient had a telephone under the bed. It was none of my business. My business was to see to the health, well-being, and education of the children.

My vision of social work didn't come from the books of regulations we were taught by the Illinois Department of Social Services. It came from what I saw my family doing as I was growing up. The values I learned from my parents and my community—that is, that we are all supposed to take care of each other. And everybody is worthy of that care.

Originally I had intended to be a nurse, but the local nursing school would not admit me. Both nursing and social work were related in my mind as ways of caring for people. I wanted to do that.

I saw something on TV a few years ago that made me think again about the way we organize public assistance in this country. It was around 1994 and there was a show on public television called La Plaza that featured stories from Latino communities around the country. Well, this time, the story focused on a young mother with five children who had moved into the Mission Hill projects in Bos-

ton. There were holes in the walls and floor of the apartment she was offered, the paint was peeling, windows were broken, and the whole complex was infested with rats and roaches. The housing authority told this woman the apartment was "all they had available" and she desperately needed a place to stay.

She worked diligently to get off of welfare and for a time held a low wage job but found that she was actually worse off working than she had been on welfare. Because once she had an income, measly though it was, and was no longer receiving welfare payments, she lost health benefits and the new job did not replace them. Also, once she left welfare, the rent in the Mission Hill projects was absurdly inflated and the woman was unable to pay it with her wages alone. The more she tried to pay, she explained, the more the rent rose and the more she was pushed into debt. Eventually she had no choice but to return to welfare.

Many people, especially single mothers, explain that they cannot make ends meet without the help that welfare—grudgingly and paltrily—provides. Of course, this kind of conundrum is created by the lack of national priorities for employment at a livable wage, day care, universal health coverage, and other elements that would strengthen the ability of people to survive with dignity and decency in our society.

And the question is certainly not one of whether or not people want to work. Many people who receive public assistance actually do work. Often the work is "under the table" or in the informal economy. But some form of supplementary benefits is a necessity. Whether babysitting a friend or relative's children in exchange for food or cash or services; doing hair and nails for neighbors; doing odd jobs or other kinds of informal exchange, it is clear that people on welfare work.[1]

As William Julius Wilson, the author of When Work Disappears, reminds us, the problem is one of priorities.[2] Our national government can find the resources in its vast coffers to give billions in what is essentially corporate welfare to businesses who have little or no allegiance to anyone other than their shareholders, at enormous detriment to the working classes of this nation. And yet they refuse to remove the major hindrances to single mothers who do not want to be dependent on (and stigmatized by) welfare—free or affordable, high-quality child care and health care.

We can spend billions of tax dollars exploring the outer reaches of space, moving missiles around on underground train tracks in the Nevada desert, and bailing out the failed ventures of millionaires—but somehow we can't ensure livable wages for the working poor; safe, high-quality child care for women who want to work; or the right of older people to live out their lives without fear of destitution and abandonment.

It is simply a matter of priorities. And of course, anything that is simple is also much much more than that.

Years after my first experience as a caseworker, I decided to study for a master's degree in social work. I remember visiting my Aunt Mamie at the time and telling her what I was planning to do.

"I thought you already were a social worker," she said questioningly.

"This is different," I answered.

"A social worker is a social worker."

"The kind of social work I want to do is putting my hands on people to heal them," I told her.

Aunt Mamie looked at me and said, "Put your hands on me." And so I did. I put my hands on her legs that had bowed beyond the point of standing, and I put my hands on her shoulders, and gently on the soft skin at her hairline. "Thank you, baby," she said. "Go 'head and do that kind of social work." That was a blessing, a sanction for me. I got it from my mother too—but then I had gotten the whole notion of healing as activism from my mother and aunts to begin with.

Notes

1. This story was written in 1997–98, as the Clinton administration enacted wide-ranging changes in welfare policies that drastically reduced eligibility and benefits. The questions raised here about national priorities and the need for compassion and justice in social and economic policy making continue to have relevance today.—REH

2. Wilson, *When Work Disappears: The World of the New Urban Poor* (New York: Vintage, 1997).

Mom loved ghost stories. But she didn't call them "ghosts," they were "haints." Judging from her experience, the woods and little towns around Lee County, Georgia, must have been full to brimming with haints. I remember some of the stories my mother told, but not too many. First of all, I really didn't like being scared. I'd listen a little while, then make my way to another part of the house when Mom got going. I'd find something else to keep me busy while I overheard the squeals from my nieces and nephews as Mom amused and terrified them. She was very good at it.

Even adults would get anxious and unsettled (albeit enthralled and glued to their seats) when Mama Freeney started her haint tales. Her grandchildren had little thrills of terror in their faces as she slid her slippered feet across the floor, hunched over, grumbling in a low voice, coming their way. The children would jump up and run, screaming a laughter-fear mix and Mama Freeney would follow. If she got them cornered in a closet and somebody got too scared or looked like they might cry, she'd ease over and let them all get away. She wasn't trying to traumatize anybody. Not seriously, anyway. But the grandkids say it was usually so eerily delightful that they would try to keep Mom's attention for as long as possible to heighten their own dread and glee.

Sometimes, instead of chasing the children through the house, she would gather all of them around her and start one of her scary stories. Her grandchildren would scramble for a place in the circle, the little ones in the laps of the bigger ones, and all look up into Mama Freeney's face as she started the tale.

"Well now, one time me and your Aunt Itty were walking down the road. This was down in Leesburg, when we were girls. It wasn't dark yet, just getting a little bit toward dusk. You know. We were walking on the side of this old country road, and we could hear a horse coming up behind us. *Clippity cloppity, clippity cloppity,*" Mama Freeney made the sound of the horse, "*Clippity cloppity.* We could hear that horse coming closer and closer, sounded like it was right behind us, and we turned around to get out the road. And it wasn't nothing there . . . "

The lights would be off and the kids would be scared to move. Sitting there mesmerized. She'd actually make you *like* being scared.

Or, she'd tell one about walking home at night from the white people's house where she washed dishes. Mama Freeney had been young then, eight or nine years old. This particular evening, the white people took so long to finish their dinner that it was dark when little Ella was finally able to leave. The older ladies who also worked at the house were worried for the young girl because she had to walk through a thick stand of woods to get home. "Ella Lee, child, you going home in the dark?"

"Yes, I'm going," little Ella told them. "I'm not afraid. I'm not afraid of a thing." And usually she wasn't. Even as a young girl, Mom had lots of self-confidence and she knew the backwoods and trails around Leesburg well enough that she could make it home, even in the dark.

"Oh, Ella Lee, you sure are smart," the ladies said to her. "You are a brave, smart girl." Then they gave her a hug and sent their greetings to the child's parents and waved her good-bye. Well, my mom was indeed courageous and she started out along a little path into the woods, singing to keep herself company. And after a while she saw a lady with a baby buggy up ahead of her, coming her way. The lady had on a big floppy hat with a veil on it and worn-out shoes. Now, my mom wouldn't lie. So if she said this is what happened, it's what happened. As the lady got closer and closer, pushing the buggy in front of her and coming straight toward my mother, she seemed to be blocking Mom's way. There was still some distance between them, so Mom wasn't sure, but when my mother moved to one side of the path, the lady would direct the buggy in front of where Mom was headed, blocking her. Mom moved to the other side and the lady and the buggy moved over there too.

The older women back at the white people's house had bragged on little Ella Lee, calling her brave and smart, and she felt determined; she wanted to prove she could get past this woman, whoever she was, and make it the rest of the way home. The lady and the buggy came closer and closer and every time Mom would move over or try to go around them, the lady pushed that buggy right in front. Well, then, when the lady got directly up on Mom she aimed the buggy for Mom's legs and shoved. That's when Mom saw that underneath that hat with the veil in front, the lady didn't have a head! When the lady jerked the buggy from side to side the hat wiggled because it wasn't connected to anything—no neck, no skull, no scalp, nothing. It was just sitting there where a head should be with the breeze blowing the veil up from time to time so Mom could see the blankness.

That was enough. Mom didn't remember anything after that but coming out of the woods like lightning and jumping onto the back porch at home and into somebody's lap.

. . .

"Don't tell the children those old stories, Ella," Daddy Freeney would come in the room and see us terrified. "You gon have my children scared."

"Did it happen?" Mom would say.

"I know it happened, but don't scare 'em so bad."

Most of the ghosts and haints of my mother's repertoire were essentially harmless even if frightening. But there were other stories that emphasized protective relationships between humans and the spirit world. For example, Mama Freeney and other members of the family have had experiences of being helped by people who show up out of nowhere and disappear the moment danger is no longer present. My sister Alma had this experience years ago in a long pedestrian tunnel in a Chicago subway. It was late one evening and Alma was alone, except for a tall policeman who stayed a few dozen feet ahead of her as she walked. The tunnel was quiet in the resonant way of tunnels and Alma was intensely aware of her surroundings. Once she got to an open gate near an exit, she looked around, and the policeman (who had never turned toward her and never acknowledged her calls out to him, even though he was clearly in hearing range) was suddenly nowhere to be found.

. . .

I met Eddy Van der Hilst in 1992 at an ecumenical gathering in Santa Fe, New Mexico. He is a lovely brother from Suriname who shared in the meeting some insights about the Afro-Surinamese ritual tradition, Winti. In addition to being the name of the religion, Wintis, he told us, are also the spiritual energies who are responsible for each of us and who stay with us throughout our lives. In some ways, these energies remind me of what I know of the orixás of Candomblé—elements of the cosmos associated with earth, waters, fire, plants, forests, wind, and other natural forces. Eddy explained that every one of us is protected and cared for in this life by Wintis. Whether we know this or not, whether we acknowledge it or not, they travel with us through our lives and help us in our struggles. We are their responsibility and when we die, they must tell God how they assisted us, how they accompanied us on our journey.

I don't know if my mother knew about Wintis or orixás. But even if she didn't know them by those names, she was surely conscious of spirits and their ability to help and protect us. Like my sister Alma, my mother had stories of being comforted by an unexplained presence as she walked through frightful and dangerous ground.

One night in Georgia, after a fight with my father, she left him at his mother's house way out in the country and walked with her two young children through a deep woods and back into town. Mama Freeney said the woods were full of sounds she didn't recognize. She started to pray, asking Jesus to help her and her children get safely home.

"Out of the blue," Mom said, "come a man walking up behind us. I saw him coming and when he got close I told him 'Oh mister, I'm so glad that you're going my way. Me and my husband had a terrible argument and I'm going home to my mother, taking my babies.'" Mom just talked and talked as she walked beside the man. Thanking him all the while that now she had somebody to walk through the woods with her. The man never responded. He never said anything at all. He didn't even look at her, but he stayed right there beside her until she got out of the thickets. And then he wasn't there anymore. "That wasn't nothing but God," Mom said.

. . .

Like I said, we believed Mama Freeney's stories. And even if they emerged whole cloth from her imagination, we had seen enough of her mischievous and iconoclastic bent to realize that she didn't have to make anything up to give people a little creep. At Halloween, Mom would dress up as a ghost and frighten the daylights out of the neighborhood children who came for trick or treat. They knew who she was; these were the same children who came by the store for candy and kind words the whole rest of the year, but Mama Freeney was very convincing. She could inhabit another kind of space sometimes, and draw you in there and before you knew it the world was different.

One time, when my niece Jean was a young girl and living with Mama and Daddy Freeney, Mama called her into the front room, speaking just a little louder than a whisper, "Come here, come here girl."

"What is it, Mama Freeney?"

"Come here."

Jean followed Mom into the small bedroom at the front of the upstairs apartment. This was Mama Freeney's room; it was somewhat removed from the rest of the house, off of a den with old French doors, away from the living and dining room, and at the other end of the house from the kitchen. "What you gon do?" Jean wondered, a little anxious at the secret tone of things.

"That sheet gon rise up. Watch."

Jean said Mama Freeney waved her hand over the sheet and don't you know, it started to come up off the bed and hovered for a little while. "How did you do that?" Jean asked, breathless.

"Girl, it's haints all over this house," Mama Freeney said, voice still just above a whisper.

"Mama don't say that!" Jean was terrified now.

"Naw, they ain't gon bother you. But I just want you to know they here." Jean flew out of the room. "I was scared of her sometimes," she said. "I didn't know what she was capable of doing if she could make a sheet come up off the bed. Shoot. You just had to stay out of her way."

I don't know how my mother got the sheet to rise. Maybe it was static electricity, or magnets . . . or maybe not. Who knows? But Mom knew some things about how to transmute energy and change the atmosphere around her, sometimes for prankishness and fun but also, very often, for the benefit and protection of others.

. . .

Carrie Bradley was a childhood friend of my mother's who was as close to her as a sister. They played together as girls, went to school together, got married around the same time, and had their first children within months of each other; both babies were boys. When Carrie's son, Everett, was very young, there was a kind of unwelcome energy, a spirit, that would appear suddenly and drift in the air around him.[1] Carrie would bring the baby to my mother's house anxious and frightened for her child. Each time this happened, Mama Freeney would say something to the spirit, speak its name, and demand that it leave the little boy alone. Although Carrie couldn't see the spirit the way

Mom could, she could sense it, a heavy and threatening energy around her baby, and she would instinctively shield Everett with her body, calling out to my mother, "Ella, tell it to go away." Mom and Carrie would cover the child with their arms, talking to the entity and praying to God to keep the negative spirit away from Everett, and eventually there would be a respite. When Carrie got ready to leave, Mama Freeney bundled up her own baby, my oldest sibling, Brother, and the two women and their children walked down the road to the fork where Carrie and Everett turned off to go home, unharmed.

. . .

There are a lot of these kinds of stories about my mother. But I don't think she was totally unique—neither in the family, nor in the larger community. Stories of haints and spirits are common in the rural South. There are some people who tell the stories extremely well. And there are others who have some expertise in handling the wayward energies that need resettling and admonishment and sometimes forgiveness. Mama Freeney did both.

Note

1. I have changed the names of the friend and her son to protect their family's privacy.

There is something in the upward length. The angels are tall: the policeman Alma saw in the subway, the Pachamamas, and the couple that walked me home.

. . .

Once, when I was a teenager in Chicago, I was coming home from work as the day was turning dark and a couple appeared out of nowhere and walked with me to my house. Just before they appeared, I had gotten off of a bus and I noticed I was being followed by a man. I could see him over my shoulder in the gathering dusk, moving in and out of shadows, slinking around corners and behind the trees. But he never came too close because I wasn't alone.

The couple walked on either side of me and talked amiably as we approached my block and soon I saw Daddy Freeney at the streetlight coming to greet me.

When I turned around to thank the couple and say good-bye, they were not there.

. . .

Daddy Freeney said, "Baby, I saw that man following you back there. That's why I came up this way to get you. But no, Sugar, there wasn't anybody walking you home."

III · South

23 · Hospitality, Haints, and Healing
African American Indigenous Religion and Activism

My family is a southern family. Though we have lived in Chicago for five generations, we are, in many respects, still deeply influenced by the rituals and traditions that traveled with us on the Seminole Limited north from Macon, Georgia. My parents, grandparents, aunts, uncles, and most of my brothers and sisters were born in small Georgia towns—Leesburg, Poulan, Albany, Macon. In the early twentieth century, they began to move north. First my mother's sisters, their husbands, my father, and his brother. Then other relatives—wives, children, parents. They were drawn to jobs in steel mills and railroad yards, escaping nightmares of lynching and the stinging, arbitrary humiliations of daily life in the South between the wars. In some ways they were pulling up roots, moving to Detroit, New York, and Chicago. In other ways, they were simply stretching the roots, changing the contours a bit, but holding fast to the deep nourishment rising there.

The values of Black religion and culture that influenced me in my Chicago youth were grounded in traditions of hospitality; healing practices; ghost and spirit stories; and a welcoming and inclusive community. All of these aspects have deeply impacted the way I live and move in the world. Among them, perhaps, hospitality has been a central model for the meaning of activism in my life. Starting before my children were born, I have been what some people would call an activist—working in political campaigns; organizing alternative schools; training, mobilizing, and reconciling in the Black freedom movement, the women's movement, and the peace and justice movement. I've worked with some magnificent people, deeply committed to spiritually engaged, compassionate social change. People like Bob Moses, Anne Braden, Ella Baker, Septima Clark, Prathia Hall, Gwendolyn Zoharah Simmons, Clarence Jordan, Bernice Johnson Reagon, Marion and Slater King, Jimmy and Grace Lee Boggs, Julia Esquivel, Ndugu T'Ofori Atta, Staughton and Alice Lynd. I've learned a great deal from these marvelous women and men, as well as from many others like them. But as I think about my own movement work and its deepest inspirations, I am continually drawn back to the model of my family—especially my mother, Ella Lee ("Mama Freeney"), and great-grandmother, Mariah ("Grandma Rye"), and the profound mystic spirituality and deep hospitality they cultivated and passed to their descendants.

In my efforts to trace and understand the religious and spiritual values that have come down to my family from Grandma Rye, I have learned from the work of historian of religions Charles Long and dramatist-philosopher George Bass.[1] The meaning of religion for Black folks, they insist, is in the heart of our history, our trauma and our hope. It is what makes us indigenous to this place, to modernity. As Long puts it, Black religion is the way we have oriented ourselves—over the centuries in these Americas and extending back before our arrival on these shores—to "mash out a meaning" of life in the midst of tremendous suffering and pain. Religion, in this sense, is not simply a doctrine of faith or the methods and practices of church; rather, it is all the ways we remind ourselves of who we really are, in spite of who the temporal powers may say we are. Religion is how we situate ourselves, how we understand ourselves, in a particular place and time vis-à-vis Ultimate Reality, vis-à-vis God.

Black religion then, is not only in the music, the drama, the communion, and the interpretation of text within the walls of the physical church; it is also in the orientation of Black people to so-called secular culture. Black religion is Otis Redding and D'Angelo as much as Mahalia Jackson and Mary Mary; it is as much hip-hop as holy dance; and root work as much as the laying on of hands. It is how we make sense and joy out of our human experience. Keeping this understanding in mind, I am looking within the cultural and spiritual traditions of my family for the meanings and manifestations of a distinct southern, African American orientation to being.

This orientation is not unique to my folks. I grew up with many extended families of Black Mississippians, Alabamans, and Georgians—and I lived for many years in Georgia as an adult. I am keenly aware of the pervasiveness of the orientation that I describe. Even now, at the end of the 1990s, there are ways to see it and feel it in African American communities all over the country. It is part of how we have come this far and how we continue on. And it was in the ground where the Movement rose up and offered new fruit to the nation.

Hospitality

My mother and aunts kept a ready pitcher of iced tea or lemonade in the refrigerator and a plate of cookies, a fresh-baked cake, or rolls with homemade preserves on the counter. Anyone who came by to visit was offered something cool to drink (unless it was winter, of course, when they'd be offered coffee or tea) and something tasty to eat. In the years when I was growing up, people visited back and forth at each other's homes more regularly than folks do now and our house seemed to be an especially popular destination for neighbors and relatives. This was partly due to the fact that we had a large family and my older brothers and sisters were all outgoing with lots of friends. And it was partly because my mother and father made the house so welcoming. Sometimes, it seemed almost "too" welcoming—all kinds of people would come through, not just relatives and neighborhood friends, but peddlers and preachers, professional gamblers and union organizers, petty thieves, street walkers, and people we would probably refer to today as homeless. Mom loved "bad" people—that is, people other folks thought were "bad." She didn't judge and she taught us how to respect, how to listen, how to learn from everybody. Mom would set out beautiful china dishes and slices of her homemade pound cake for all of them—especially for the most transient-looking people it seemed sometimes. As if she knew they needed the extra attention and acknowledgment. But then, too, mom genuinely enjoyed their conversation and wisdom.

I remember there was an itinerant bookseller, an immigrant from Europe, who would come to visit mom now and then. The two of them would sit down in the dining room with mom's best dishes and talk for hours about the events of the world and the world of books. The man was not always very clean and sometimes, especially in the winter when the heat was on full blast in our house, we could smell the mustiness of his old and ragged clothes, the heavy acrid sweat of his body. He talked funny too, and as children, we were tempted to laugh—as much from awkwardness as anything else. But if we let loose the tiniest snicker, Mom would cut her eyes at us, and we'd abandon the temptation and keep our faces straight.

As I said, I have a large family. My mother birthed sixteen children, although only nine lived to adulthood. We nine were just one contingent of a large coterie of cousins, uncles, and aunts, some of whom I didn't know were *not* blood kin until I was grown with children of my own. Until 1976 when my father died and my mother sold the house, there was always someone living with my parents at the family home at 4160 South Wentworth—a child, a niece or nephew, then later grandchildren, grandnieces, and grandnephews. Mama and Daddy Freeney always made room and any of us could always come home. Hospitality was a foundation of my family's spirituality, as it had been for so many southern Blacks. The efforts my parents made to be neighborly, welcoming, and to reserve judgment against those the society viewed as outcasts, served as important examples for their children and grandchildren as we grew older.

One of my first tasks as a young organizer in the Southern Freedom Movement was developing an interracial social service project and community center called Mennonite House in Atlanta, Georgia, in the early 1960s. The Mennonite Central Committee (MCC—the service arm of the Mennonite Church) sponsored Vincent and me to be full-time witnesses and participants to the freedom movement. In addition to our work of placing volunteers with various movement organizations, training young activists, and coordinating early efforts at interracial dialogue and reconciliation, Mennonite House became an important place of retreat for many who were struggling and sacrificing so much to transform the South and the nation. Sometimes movement people would call us from the bus station, and Vincent would drive over and pick them up, and they'd stay for a few days or a few weeks, because they needed a place to get some rest. Because of my mother's example, I understood very clearly how important it was to have spaces of refuge in the midst of struggle. Spaces of joy and laughter, good food and kind words. In fact, this kind of compassionate care is a transformative force in itself. As the Cape Breton novelist Alistair MacLeod writes, "We are all better when we're loved."

Healing

Most of the people in the family who remember Mariah Grant are gone now. But the stories that remain of my great-grandmother include recollections of her healing work and her connection to African ways of perceiving and inhering in the world. Grandma Rye was a root doctor, an herbalist. She collected plants and flowers, roots and leaves, in the fields and forests around her Leesburg home and made these into medicines to treat her family members and others who came to her for advice and counsel.

Mama Liza, one of Mariah's daughters, carried on her mother's healing tradition in another way. In Lee County, Georgia, Eliza Harris was known to be an excellent midwife, assisting the deliveries of both black and white women. My cousin Pansy tells me that Mama Liza brought hundreds of babies into the world and that the area's white doctors would often call on her to help them with difficult pregnancies because of her tremendous knowledge. Following Mama Liza, there has been a steady tradition of nursing among women in my family. My Aunt Mary and my sister Mildred were nurses and I, too, studied for a time to practice nursing.

My mother, Mama Freeney, shared many of the healing qualities of her mother and grandmother. When I was a child, she kept herbs in the kitchen pantry to make teas and poultices for us when we were sick. Her pantry was something akin to a local herbal pharmacy, serving friends and neighbors as well as family. She also used home remedies such as placing a sock with thin slices of onion on the foot of a person with fever to bring the temperature down. My mother and her sisters were firm believers in the power of nature and spirit to heal, to transform. When my sister Alma was a little girl, she was struck with tuberculosis of the bone and doctors told the family that Alma's leg would have to be cut off. Instead of yielding to the doctor's orders, Mom and Aunt Mary took Alma home and between prayers and poultices she kept her leg.

In my own life, I am drawn to natural healing modalities, remembering the tea recipes and home remedies of my mother and great-grandmother and learning as much as I can about laying on of hands—massage therapies, acupuncture, therapeutic touch, Feldenkrais and other techniques of alternative care. But even beyond issues of personal health and well-being, I try to follow the examples of my mother and aunts in recognizing the need to create a larger atmosphere of healing and wellness at the level of human relations and societal structures.

Throughout the 1980s and early 1990s, my husband and I co-taught a course at the Iliff School of Theology called, "Healing of Persons and Healing of Society." We introduced our students to the concept that the body politic is, in many ways, analogous to the body human—intensely interdependent in all its parts and very responsive to both negative and positive stimuli. Texts from folks as varied as Joanna Macy, Martin Luther King Jr., Howard Thurman, and Thich Nhat Hanh were central readings, emphasizing that the Spirit, the Universe, does indeed provide abundantly for all living beings on earth. There is truly enough for everyone. The offense is greed and it is just as destructive to societies as it is to the organisms of individual people. As part of the course, we had visitors come to share their perspectives and stories with the class—community activists, philosophers, physicians, scientists, religious leaders, writers. Our students were always deeply encouraged by the connections the guests made between caring for the well-being of individuals and creating more humane and compassionate societies.

In fact, our present work, the Veterans of Hope Project, arises directly from this experience of sharing the "testimonies" and encouragement of older activists with a younger generation of people concerned for justice, healing, and nonviolent social transformation.[2] It is fundamentally to my mother's credit that I am able to recognize and appreciate the links between personal health, generosity and sharing, and social change—for Mama Freeney's hospitality and welcome were as healing as her teas and touch.

Haints

Ghost stories were a tradition of the Georgia woods that my mother brought to Chicago and practiced expertly. She could scare you so bad you'd be afraid to go to the bathroom by yourself to pee. Some of the stories she told were regional favorites that she most likely inherited from older family members like Grandma Rye. But many of my mother's ghost stories were from her own experience. As my sister Mildred says, she wasn't telling "stories"; she was telling "what happened"—meaning, what she said was true. She would talk about the lights that lit themselves in the family home when no one was there, or she'd reminisce with my father about a beloved and well-trained horse that reared up on its hind legs and absolutely refused to cross a haunted bridge one moonless night. The fact that she often had corroborating witnesses only made Mama Freeney's tales more terrifying and delightful.

These stories were a great entertainment for the family. But they were not just entertainment. My mother told the stories as a way to pass on lessons. Lessons about caution, about discernment; but her stories were also a way to acknowledge the reality and presence of spirit. Whether we called them ghosts, haints, angels, spirits, presences, or winds, the beings that inhabited Mom's stories were, on some level, real. The stories gave us a respect for the concealed/the unknown and an appreciation for the transmutability of reality and form.

. . .

Conjure and healing are both forms of transformation, processes of change. As is activism. I recall a story that Bernice Johnson Reagon has told on many occasions about the alchemy of singing in the mass meetings, demonstrations, and marches of the Southern Freedom Movement. Bernice, an extraordinary musician, organizer, and scholar, describes the experience of marching out of a movement church into the streets of Albany, Georgia, and toward the particular store or public facility that was the object of the day's demonstration. Raising their voices with freedom songs, in the cadence and spirit of church, Bernice and her fellow marchers could feel the songs swell into the air around them and *transform* the space. The songs changed the atmosphere, becoming an almost palpable barrier between demonstrators and police, giving the marchers an internal girding that allowed them to move without fear.

The work of transformation, changing the insides and outsides of a situation, is a long and venerable tradition in the southern African American experience. Looking back on our history, one sees a tremendous flexibility among people who had to navigate the vicissitudes of life under an arbitrary and violent Jim Crow segregationist system and yet continually cultivate a sense of their own personal and collective dignity.

Music, and particularly the sacred music of the Black experience, has long been an alchemical resource for struggle; a conjured strength. As Bernice explained in her interview with the Veterans of Hope Project, there is actually something about the experience of traditional Black congregational singing that, over time, "does something to the material you're made of. . . . It really connects you up with a force in the universe that makes you different. It makes you capable of moving with a different kind of access. You're connected to something else, other than what people think you're connected to. And they can't get to you."[3]

Ruby Sales, a member of SNCC who was active in the Movement in Alabama, says that in her moments of deepest terror and anguish she called on the power of Black singing. "[The] thing that got me through is what has always gotten me through, Black songs. Singing those songs and hearing those voices. . . . I sang, 'Will the Circle Be Unbroken?' 'Tell Me How Did You Feel When You Come Out the Wilderness?' . . . 'We've Come This Far by Faith.'" Calling on these old songs, Ruby linked herself to a tradition of sustenance in trauma much older than herself. In fact, she says that as she sang she felt connected to her grandmother and to all that her grandmother's generation had witnessed and survived. "It is in that moment, through song, that I am able to feel something other than myself. I become part of a community. I become part of a struggle."[4]

. . .

Ruby's dynamic connection to her grandmother, through the struggles and the songs, is suggestive of the rich, intergenerational engagement that imbued the lives of many African American communities. In my family, as in most of the southern Black families I knew growing up, children and adults of various ages spent a great deal of time together. Often at least three generations lived in our household, and the young people benefited from the loving presence and guidance of grandparents and other older relatives. Conversely, older members of our family could count on the energetic companionship of younger ones and did not have to worry about being alone or abandoned in the final years of their lives. Children were taught to respect their elders and to recognize that there were spaces and times when they could not enter "grown folks' business."

There was also a certain formality of relations, rooted in southern and African traditions. Respect was shown through courteous forms of address when talking to strangers, persons of authority, and anyone in an age group higher than one's own. Women were always "Miss" or "Mrs." So-and-So and men were called "Mr." (unless the adults were relatives, and then they were called Aunt, Uncle, or Cousin). As children our responses of "ma'am" and "sir" indicated the good "home-training" we had received from the adults who raised us. Even among adults of comparable age and status, who had known each other for many years, there was often a kind of quasi-ceremonial care in the way they interacted with each other. In some respects, this must have been an antidote to the indignities these men and women regularly suffered. But, from all I can tell, this practice of almost exaggerated mutual deference and politeness was an important element of interpersonal relations in many of the West and Central African communities from which the majority of North American Blacks originated, and it was a common feature in Black communities throughout the Americas.

For those of us who lived and worked in the small towns of the rural South during the freedom movement, these relational dynamics became an integral part of the organizing model we developed. Gwendolyn Zoharah Simmons, the SNCC project leader in Laurel, Mississippi, in 1964, describes how she and her teenage and young-adult colleagues in Freedom Summer interacted with older community members with whom they were working to mobilize political and educational reform in the area. Zoharah says: "We were seen as 'leaders,' people who brought a vision, people who brought resources, ideas, materials that they wanted. Books and pamphlets and all of this. At the same time, because of our youth we were also children to them."[5]

Living with local community leaders, Zoharah and other young activists were expected to replicate time-honored African American forms of intergenerational association. Mrs. Euberta Sphinks, a long-standing local activist in the Laurel community, opened her home and her heart to Zoharah. The relationship the two women developed was generally indicative of the way younger organizers and the older local citizens engaged each other: "I had to obey Mrs. Sphinks when it came to what time I could come in and where I was going. I had to tell her where I was going and where I had been. If she said I had to go to church, I had to go. But at the same time, they were willing to follow me into the jaws of the jail. . . . It was a very interesting dynamic."[6]

This "interesting dynamic" with roots in the family and cultural traditions of the Black South was a central element of the organizing strategy of the Movement and a large part of the reason for the Movement's resonance and success all over the region. While there were probably times when the young people of SNCC, CORE, and other movement organizations felt constrained by the behavioral expectations of their elders, those norms of comportment were practical measures ensuring the well-being of the youth who (even if southerners by birth) were often not familiar with the local community where they were assigned. The young activists benefited greatly from being integrated into family and church structures of connection. "Obeying" the elders was a way of showing respect and acknowledging organic leadership and home-ground authority. Furthermore, the closeness and familiarity created by relationships modeled on family interactions were important sources of comfort, stability, and support amid the extreme tensions, uncertainty, and terrorist violence that were constant threats to everyone in the rural southern Black communities.

This indigenous African American organizing model reflects many elements of the religious and cultural orientation I learned as a child. Those who opened their homes, their churches, and their struggles to the young freedom workers exhibited the kind of hospitality and great generosity of spirit that I knew from my own family experience. Relationships between younger activists and older local community members recalled the ways my siblings, my younger cousins, and I interacted with the elders in our family and neighborhood. Finally, it was the pervasiveness of Spirit, the healing and transformative power of Black cultural and religious resources, and a recognition of God's accompaniment in even the greatest of dangers that sustained the Movement—as it yet sustains so many of us still on the journey.

Notes

An earlier version of this essay was published in *Deeper Shades of Purple: Womanism in Religion and Society*, ed. Stacey M. Floyd-Thomas (New York: NYU Press, 2006). It has been substantially revised.

1. See Charles H. Long, "Perspectives for the Study of African American Religion in the United States," in Fulop and Raboteau, *African American Religion: Interpretive Essays in History and Culture* (New York: Routledge, 1997); and Charles H. Long, *Significations: Signs, Symbols and Images in the Interpretation of Religion* (Philadelphia: Fortress, 1986). Also, lectures by George H. Bass in his African American studies courses at Brown University, and the conversations my daughter had with him when he was her professor, 1983–90.

2. The Veterans of Hope Project is an interdisciplinary initiative on grassroots democracy, healing, and religion/spirituality founded by Vincent and Rosemarie Freeney Harding. Housed on the campus of the Iliff School of Theology, the VOHP has been centrally focused on documenting the life stories of elder organizers and activists. Other elements of the project's work include symposia, public conversations, and a program of international exchange centered around the role of religion and healing in social justice activism.—REH

3. "Bernice Johnson Reagon: The Singing Warrior," Veterans of Hope Project Pamphlet Series 1, no. 1 (Denver: VOHP, 2000): 12.

4. "Ruby Sales: Standing against the Wind," Veterans of Hope Project Pamphlet Series 1, no. 3 (Denver: VOHP, 2000): 6–7.

5. "Gwendolyn Zoharah Simmons: Following the Call," Veterans of Hope Project Pamphlet Series 1, no. 4 (Denver: VOHP, 2000): 13.

6. "Gwendolyn Zoharah Simmons: Following the Call," 13.

Black people in Atlanta were intrigued with Mennonite House. This was something new—an interracial social service project tied to the freedom movement, where most of the volunteers were white and the directors were Black, and everybody lived together in the same house. In 1961, this was definitely new. Seeing my husband and me in the leadership roles made Black folks glad and proud. And it impressed them to know that our church (which most had never heard of) had sent us to represent the denomination. I didn't realize the significance of all of this until later. I was just happy to be there.

We moved to Atlanta in the fall of 1961. The student sit-ins had been developing for a little over a year and freedom movement campaigns were spreading to cities and rural communities all across the South. With the Southern Christian Leadership Conference (SCLC) and the Student Nonviolent Coordinating Committee (SNCC) both headquartered in Atlanta, the city was a major administrative center for movement work, and in comparison to some other places in the region, it was a little less regressive in its racial politics. No one knew exactly what all of the social and political changes would mean, especially how white people would react. But we were excited and, in spite of some fear, most Blacks yearned for the transformations the movement was bringing.

Vincent and I came south to be a part of this. We were married the year before in Chicago, my hometown, where Vincent was serving as a lay pastor at Woodlawn Mennonite Church, finishing his Ph.D., and where I was teaching at Brown Elementary School. We were both

Mennonites, but my husband was a member of the General Conference and I was Old Mennonite. I had come to the denomination through my sister Alma and the Westside Chicago Bethel mission church. Vincent learned of the Mennonites from friends at the University of Chicago Divinity School. Both of us were strongly attracted to the Anabaptist emphasis on peace and reconciliation; and we had each been addressing churches and attending conferences on the rising Southern Freedom Movement. So, before we even met, people were telling us about each other, noticing the similarities in our interests, and thinking that we would be a good pair.

After we married, we convinced the Mennonite Central Committee (MCC) that the church should have a presence in the southern movement. They agreed and gave Vincent and me the task of designing and coordinating that presence in line with MCC's long-standing tradition of voluntary service work. Vincent had visited Montgomery in 1958, traveling with a group of Black and white Mennonite pastors, and Martin King had invited him to come back and work in the movement. Increasingly, we met others—like Clarence Jordan, from the Koinonia community—who shared our concern and commitment and who were already deeply engaged in this work. As we talked about it between us, our enthusiasm and earnestness grew. So, with support from the MCC headquarters, we moved to Atlanta to establish a voluntary service unit and join those already organizing for racial justice there.

We followed the general model of Christian service in a context of faith-based community living, but our project was unique in its emphasis on racial justice and reconciliation in the U.S. context. Volunteers were invited to come in a spirit of sharing, a spirit of service, and with an openness to living and working toward justice with many kinds of people. Vincent and I were the first African American directors of an MCC service unit anywhere in the country and our work was closely observed and, I think, largely applauded.

But Mennonite House was more than just a place where Black and white volunteer workers lived. And it was more than an administrative center for their placement with various social service and activist organizations. The house was also a kind of community center—providing a space for people to gather, debate, and reflect on what was happening around us in the movement. It was even an urban retreat space of sorts, a space of welcome for activists who needed safe haven.

With the help of a Black real estate agent, we found and quickly rented the two-story, white frame house at 540 Houston Street that had once belonged to the family of the great concert singer Mattiwilda Dobbs. The first floor had a kitchen, a large living room, a dining room, a sitting room, and a little study that we turned into a bedroom. Upstairs were three or four

Mennonite House, c. 1964. Clockwise from left corner: Vincent, Rachel, Rosemarie, unidentified friend, Charles Freeney, two other unidentified friends. PHOTO COURTESY MENNONITE CENTRAL COMMITTEE FILES, AKRON, PENNSYLVANIA. USED WITH PERMISSION.

more bedrooms with two or three beds in each. At our normal capacity, we easily sheltered twelve people, and when necessary, we put a curtain in the downstairs sitting room and a cot on the landing between the first and second floor to house even more.

Not all of the young people who lived and worked with us were Mennonites, but the majority of the volunteers came from Mennonite communities in the Midwest and Canada. Many had recently finished college and were members of congregations that encouraged church-based service work. They were also attracted to the movement and wanted to be involved in something that was helping our country fulfill its ideals. It wasn't always easy. Some of them were unsure of how they felt about Black people insisting on treatment as full human beings. A few told us the constancy of the marches frightened them. Others had grown up in isolated places and were very naïve about the suffering they were seeing in the neighborhoods around them. In addition, we sometimes had to struggle with a difficult mixture of racism, class privilege, and individual personality differences. For example, some white women at Mennonite House had to ask themselves, "What does it mean for Rose to travel around the South as an MCC representative? She is Black and I am white and yet my role is staying home and doing the dishes and cooking. I've never imagined myself washing dishes while a Black person takes leadership roles."

Sometimes facing those questions was hard. But we had some interesting things happen at Mennonite House. Black men and women would come to our house scarred, with their bodies and spirits battered by the police. They would be in so much pain and they talked about how they hated white people. Now the same white person who had earlier questioned his or her feelings about Blacks would have the opportunity to help nurse this Black person back to health. And both Black and white would have a chance, over the days and weeks of sharing and healing, to feel something different for each other.

Overall, they did well, these young white men and women. We held regular household meetings to talk about the voluntary service assignments and household issues, and every weekend we cleaned. Our volunteers became friends and neighbors to people in the Black community where we lived and they worked at Black organizations and social service agencies. This was all very new and completely different from what most of them had known before. By and large, it worked out well.

When we first got to the city, one of my responsibilities was to make contacts with local groups who might employ our volunteers. I would explain our intentions and talk to them about the Mennonites. I told people we weren't looking for paid income for the volunteers, that the church was taking care of that. (MCC provided stipends of about fifteen dollars per month. There were also allowances for Vincent and me and for the upkeep of the house.) All of the Black groups we approached were very willing to have our volunteers work with them. At that time, Black people were quite open to living and working more equally with whites. They welcomed the opportunity, and a few of the white ones did as well.

I placed volunteers with nursery schools, orphanages, community centers, day camps, Goodwill Industries, and some movement organizations like SCLC. The task of coordinating the service internships was, in a sense, an extension of the social work I had done in Chicago. But this was even more exciting because whites did not normally work in the places where we were sending these young people. At least they did not work under Black people's supervision. This was part of what made everyone so keenly interested in what Mennonite House was doing.

The Koinonia Partners community was one of the inspirations for Mennonite House. After we arrived in Atlanta, we visited Koinonia often and developed a wonderful friendship with Clarence and Florence Jordan and other members of the farming fellowship. We also had friends among the founders of the Reba Place Fellowship in Evanston, Illinois—a group of young Anabaptist activists trying to live a practice of community and service. The tradition of hospitality and welcome from my own family was another strong influence on Mennonite House. The presence of our daughter, Rachel, who was born in 1962, and my nephew, Charles, who was a volunteer in the movement and lived with us at many points over the years, helped emphasize the family atmosphere in the house.

We were also encouraged by our friends John and June Yungblut, who ran Quaker House and hosted discussions and lectures on race relations in their Northside Atlanta location. Quaker House was established a few years before us and perhaps was an inspiration for our name. But our projects differed in that Mennonite House was intentionally interracial, residential, and had Black directors—something very unusual in the early sixties South. We were also more directly tied to movement organizations and participants.

A Houseful of Friendly White Neighbors

When we were first settling in, Edgar Metzler, head of the MCC Peace Section, came down for a few days to help us. Edgar asked me to go with him to greet our neighbors and inquire if they minded an integrated group of volunteers living next door. I told him I'd be happy to go but his question was odd to me. I wouldn't have thought to ask it. Maybe it was a question that needed to be asked of whites, but I knew Black people would be honored, because we want togetherness so much. At least all of the Black people I know love justice and peace and we *really* wanted that then. The people who lived around us sympathized with what we were doing and were very supportive. On one side there was a family and on the other an older lady who lived by herself. She was well-to-do and thought the idea of a houseful of friendly white neighbors was heavenly.

Back then, because of segregation, Black people of different economic statuses lived very near each other. So our neighborhood was home to both wealthy and working-class people. We had heard that the woman in the house across the street wasn't very sociable. She rarely left her home except to get in her large car and drive away, and she hardly ever smiled at anyone. Well, she must have been glad to have us in the neighborhood because she would come out and stand on her porch and watch us from time to time, smiling and nodding our way.

Neighborhood people were stopping by almost daily—just to visit, to talk; sometimes bringing gifts or donating furniture; and always wanting to know more about who we were and what we were doing. They liked the positive environment at Mennonite House; they would tell us this. We were demonstrating integration right in front of them. As people realized what we were trying to do, everybody wanted to help.

Young people were especially curious. There was a high school diagonally across the street and once the students discovered us, some dropped by every day on their way home. They were reading things in the news about changes and challenges in the country, and here was something in their own neighborhood that they could watch and participate in and feel connected to. One young woman began coming over so often that she took to spending the nights in our guest room.

Some of the volunteers who came to Mennonite House stayed for a year or more. Others spent just two or three months, or a summer. Then there were a few people—like Septima Clark and my nephew Charles—who lived and worked with us for much of the period that we directed the project.[1] Septima was running the Citizenship Education Program of SCLC when she stayed with us, and Charles was assisting her. She could have lived anywhere but I think she just loved the idea, the concept, of Mennonite House, and she wanted to be a part of it. There were other movement folks who came for only a day or for a few nights, as they passed through on their way to destinations elsewhere in the region.

Visitors and Conversations: What Sort of Beautiful Nation We Could Create

One of our housemates was a master carpenter who built a large wooden table for the dining room. We had some of the best conversations around that homemade table. People like Staughton and Alice Lynd came by, not only to lecture but just to talk with whoever was there.[2] Howard Zinn did the same—sometimes giving a presentation, but just as often joining the discussion.[3] Andy and Jean Young came also.[4] They had moved to the city around the same time as Vincent and I had and we got to know each other well in the movement days. The house would be so full that all the places at the table were taken and people would stand or bring in chairs to make room for everyone who wanted to be there.

All kinds of people came. I think folks were incredibly intrigued by this group of Black and white people living together. It was a novelty. But it was also something lots of people took as a sign of promise. Even remembering it now, I feel that same elation, that same sense of possibility. It was a moment of immense hope, immense hope in the whole country. People were trying all kinds of experiments to see what sort of beautiful nation we could create.

I remember the Muslims came too—people from the Nation of Islam—and they'd participate in the discussions. I went to some of the meetings at their temple as well. They were always very thoughtful and polite in all of our interactions. I have very good memories of them. One man who visited us several times was Lonnie Cross; he was head of the math department at Atlanta University back in the early sixties. He's now Abdulalim Abdullah Shabazz. I got to know him well and I respected him a great deal. People from the Nation were interested in what it really meant for Blacks and whites to live together, so they came by our house to see. There was a lot of talk among African Americans about *Blackness* and *Black Power,* but underlying all of it was a great concern for fairness, for reconciliation, for justice. Those were the things we discussed around that table and in many other places where Black people got together. We talked about *peace.* The Muslim brothers and sisters were there, so it wasn't as if they were closed to those ideas; otherwise, they would not have visited us and they would not have been interested in what we were doing.

Mennonite House was around the corner from where Martin and Coretta King lived and we became good friends in those years, working together and living nearby. Martin came by the house sometimes, but he was busier and traveling a great deal; so, usually, Coretta would just come on her own. She'd sit and talk with the volunteers or visit with me and the baby, Rachel. Coretta was pregnant herself then, with her youngest daughter, Bunny. I think she found our little community house relaxing, maybe even a bit of a refuge. It must have been a solace to have sympathetic people—Black and white together—with whom to share what was going on her life. I remember once or twice she talked about the insulting telephone calls and threatening letters they received. But Coretta's conversation was more often on the potential of the movement and the encouragement coming from people all around the country and the world. Mostly, she had a real sense of peace about her. An assurance. Like all of us, she must have felt fear at times; but she never let it overwhelm her.

Refuge and Reconnaissance

Mennonite House was also a place where movement people came who needed a retreat, a little rest and distance from the front lines. They were depressed by what they had experienced, or just exhausted and feeling discouraged. Sometimes the people who came to us had been assaulted or terrorized. Fannie Lou Hamer came after she was brutally attacked in Winona, Mississippi.[5] Badly bruised and swollen, she was afraid to go home, worried that her husband might put himself in danger if he saw her condition. So, Andy Young, James Bevel, and Dorothy Cotton brought Mrs. Hamer to Mennonite House for a few days.[6] Sometimes our friends at Koinonia would call us and say, "This young man, or this young woman, needs to just stay with y'all for a little bit." And we would take them in and they would stay with us until they felt stable. The atmosphere at Mennonite House was homey and respectful and full of enthusiasm about the movement. So it was a good place for visitors who needed some extra encouragement.

We had such a strong commitment to the movement and to integration. And we tried to reflect that not only in the voluntary service projects and in our communal life at Mennonite House but also, inasmuch as possible, in our interactions with public institutions and private businesses. Most of the doctors we saw were Black, and we went to a Black hospital for emergencies. The Black doctors easily accepted the white volunteers who needed to be treated for colds or sprains or other illnesses they suffered during their time with us. But we were also trying to find white doctors who were ready to serve a racially mixed clientele. Initially, Vincent and I were the only Blacks in the household and it wasn't so easy to find white professionals who would attend us. Looking back on it now, I don't know if it was even such a good idea for us to try this experiment while I was pregnant.

I was nervous, new to the city, and having my first child away from my family. At first, I was willing to try. My husband and I both genuinely believed in doing whatever we could do to push the barriers back and offer a challenge to segregation . . . but I had my doubts about this project. One of our friends, a white Quaker, had recommended a doctor to us. "He's excellent," the friend said, so we made an appointment.

When Vincent and I arrived at the office no one spoke to us. We sat in the waiting room surrounded by the doctor's white patients but no one greeted us. There were a few hard stares and under-breath comments, but mostly we received a studied inattention, the quiet of indignation. The receptionist was very curt and we sat in the stony chill of the room until we were called to see the physician. He was so distressed he trembled slightly and his hands were damp as he examined me. It was awful. "Listen," I said to him after a short while, "I can see you're uncomfortable. I don't want to upset you and I don't want you to upset me, because all this might be affecting my baby. Maybe we should just cancel the appointment. I'll find someone else." He seemed to catch himself then and tried to summon a confidence that neither he nor I felt. After that visit I decided I wouldn't go back. I didn't need the stress.

But about a week later, the doctor called to apologize. He didn't have his nurse or receptionist call; he called himself and said he was sorry and that I'd be welcome at his office if I cared to return. I said to myself, if he could take that step, I would honor it and reciprocate. But I wondered if the friend who referred us had thought whether this doctor had ever seen

Black patients or whether he would be uncomfortable—or maybe the doctor himself hadn't known what his own reaction would be. After a few visits, he was much less stilted with me and we started having conversations about Mennonite House and some of the work we were doing there. And he delivered my daughter when she was born.

Actually we met many people who were trying to have a positive attitude about integration. But there were also situations where we encountered problems. Once, a Canadian couple was approached by a group of roughneck white youths in a park on the Northside. The couple was babysitting Rachel while Vincent and I were out of town, and the boys surrounded and threatened them as they held my young child in their arms. "This park is for white people," the boys said. They told the couple that the Black baby was not welcome in the park and told them to leave. When the Canadians explained that they were caring for the daughter of friends and that we all lived together, the boys were even more livid. "Why do you want to do that?" they wanted to know. "We don't believe in that and it's an insult to white people."

Later, when our friends reported what had happened it gave me so much to think about. I hadn't realized that many white people saw the freedom movement as a *personal* affront. Of course, I recognized the structural resistance to change that racism created. But it slowly dawned on me that what we in the movement viewed as acts of justice, acts of freedom, acts of Christian community, were perceived by many whites as personal offenses and threats to their entitlements. Their reactions were those of anger, frustration, and the violence of spoiled children. The young men in the park eventually backed down because of the way our friends responded—talking about what they believed and how they were trying to live those beliefs. The Canadian couple had a kindness that I think disarmed the youths somewhat.

In this, Koinonia was an important example for us. The members of that community went through tremendous struggles, great hardships, to live an inclusive vision of their faith, and to make their personal lives consistent with what they were preaching. Whenever we visited the farm, we would leave with more clarity about our own work—the movement work, the voluntary service work. Koinonia reminded us that the emphasis should be in service. Sharing—not only your goods with others, but your whole life.

The importance of Mennonite House was its existence at a time when the student movement was taking off and people were coming to Atlanta from all over the country to join in the effort to transform our nation into its best image of itself. In the early 1960s, Mennonite House was one of the places, perhaps one of the few, where interracial conversation and community was being consciously created in the South. Our work encouraged that impulse in the life of the city of Atlanta and in the life of the freedom movement.

Notes

1. Septima Poinsette Clark was an educator and community organizer who developed important literacy and citizenship education workshops for several movement organizations.

2. Staughton and Alice Lynd are activist lawyers and scholars who have worked together in movements for labor justice, peace, and civil rights for more than six decades. Staughton taught at Spelman College and was director of the SNCC Freedom Schools during Mississippi Summer, 1964.

3. Howard Zinn was a renowned Americanist historian and outspoken social justice activist. From 1956 to 1963 he chaired the Department of History and Social Sciences at Spelman College and became an adviser to SNCC during that time.

4. Andrew and Jean Young were close companions of the Kings and committed community organizers. Andy served in the leadership cadre of SCLC during the movement and later became mayor of Atlanta, a congressman, and U.S. ambassador to the United Nations. Jean was an internationally recognized educator and advocate for child welfare.

5. Fannie Lou Hamer was a sharecropper, a widely respected grassroots activist of the Southern Freedom Movement, and an organizer of the Mississippi Freedom Democratic Party.

6. James Bevel and Dorothy Cotton were staff members of SCLC who worked in the area of citizenship education and nonviolence training. Bevel had been a member of the Nashville Student Movement. Cotton directed many of the voter registration campaigns of SCLC.

Our next-door neighbor at Mennonite House was very wealthy, for a Black woman. She had a large brick house; the largest on the block, with flowers and neatly trimmed grass out front. She kept to herself and didn't have many visitors, although there was a nephew who came occasionally to check on her and several employees took care of her home. There was a woman who came in to do her cleaning, a man who tended the lawn, and someone else who prepared her meals. Because of segregation, people like this neighbor lived side by side with working-class folks in Black communities. That wasn't unusual. But this lady was very proud of her house and seemed to like the fact that her wealth marked her as somehow distinct from those around her.

Like many of the folks in the neighborhood, she was curious about our group. Once we moved in and introduced ourselves, she invited me over for tea. I took one of the young volunteers along and we spent the afternoon discussing integration and the student movement that was opening up stores and businesses in downtown Atlanta to Black people.

Our neighbor was enthusiastic about our project and wanted us to know she approved: "It's quite impressive to see whites and Blacks living and working together so well." Her tone was formal, but with that softness of southern speech. "And with Black people in charge," she said. "That is very impressive indeed. Not something I would have expected to see."

Vincent and I thought of ourselves as giving leadership and direction to the project, going out and making contacts and seeing that our volunteers got to where they needed to be. We didn't use that phrase "in charge," to talk about our role at Mennonite House. But our neighbors, and probably other folks as well, saw it that way. *Black folks in charge of white folks*, and that was new.

"These young people, the students, going downtown to do the sit-ins and all, they really have got the city shaken up, haven't they? And for the better, I would say. I went down to the beauty shop at Rich's last week and got my hair fixed and nobody said a word, except to ask me politely whether I wanted a cut and style or just a wash and set." Our neighbor talked about all the places she could shop now thanks to the sit-ins and the demonstrations. "My, it really is a different time, wouldn't you say?"

Then she said a strange thing. She told us that her family had owned slaves. When she was a child, she was cared for by former slaves who continued to work as servants to her family. I had read about this—Black people who owned slaves—and it wasn't the fact of it that was strange or surprising to me. But I had never met a Black person who admitted this part of their family history with a sense of pride. As she recalled the deference of the older women and men who waited on her, there was in her voice a tone of vanity. Or it seemed that way to me. She must have been at least sixty at the time, maybe even somewhat older, which means that she was remembering events from the turn of the century.

It was just such an interesting juxtaposition. On one hand she was grateful and happy for the current student activism that was transforming race relations in the city and the nation. She was happy that the youth were demonstrating for their rights and insisting on service in stores and at lunch counters. She was benefiting from their campaigns and was now able to go into department stores and be treated with courtesy and respect. At the same time, she was a Black woman proud of her family having owned other Black people as slaves.

I guess some would describe her as "mulatto." She was light and had loosely curled hair that would have been familiar enough to the beauticians at the downtown Rich's department store. But people in my own family had the same complexion and hair and we never called each other by those names. Still, once outside of the Black community, I gather this woman would have fit into the category of "mulatto" or mixed race.

Of course, in our country, especially in the South, if white people knew that you had any Black ancestry in your background, you could be subjected to all manner of rudeness and meanness. It didn't matter what you looked like. If you were light enough and you insisted that you were not

Black (in spite of the fact that there may have been Black people who looked like you), and no one traced your lineage to see if you were lying, then you could get along by "passing." "Passing for white," that's what it was. But this woman wasn't passing. Either because she couldn't or she didn't want to. And now, between the sit-ins and the slaves of the family, hers was a complicated pride.

Essentially, we were representatives of the Mennonite Church to the Southern Freedom Movement. It was a ministry, of sorts, but one that Vincent and I created and defined as we carried it out. The base of our work was at Mennonite House, providing the structure for volunteers who came from around the country to work in social agencies and movement organizations in Atlanta's Black community. In addition to doing the Atlanta-based networking, placement, and community-building work of Mennonite House, we traveled extensively throughout the neighboring southern states observing, learning, and participating with those who were working in the struggle against segregation.

We came to the Movement with an emphasis on reconciliation and Christian brotherhood, as it was called then, and there were many organizations and individuals in the South, particularly among African Americans, who shared a similar commitment to changes in the society. Our focus on nonviolence and religiously based reconciliation resonated with Martin and Coretta King, who were already deeply committed to those values and happy to discover new companions in that way. Of course, there were also people who brought other kinds of political and economic analyses to the problems of racial injustice; and the richness of the time was that these various perspectives often fed each other amidst intense discussions and the day-to-day experience of joint work.

We were a little bit older than the young people at the heart and helm of the student movement that was sweeping the South at the time. So we were colleagues and counselors to them, joining campaigns in various cities and helping to organize workshops and conferences where young activists received training and encouragement for the often dangerous work they were undertaking. As a historian and educator, Vincent was interested in links between the freedom movement and earlier periods of Black radicalism in the nation's history, like during the abolitionist movement, for example. Especially after he started teaching at Spelman and then established the Institute of the Black World, he would often talk about those links as intellectual and spiritual resources for the current struggle.[1]

But a lot of our work involved using the language and witness of Christian faith to help interpret the Movement to influential community members (whites and Blacks) in small cities and towns where the antisegregation campaigns were organized. We met with university administrators, ministers, newspaper editors, business and civic leaders. We would do this discreetly, so as not to arouse unnecessary suspicion or fear. Often, we made a special effort to talk to white religious leaders. And because we were a young couple, representing a nonviolent tradition that was not commonly known in the region (the Mennonites), and sometimes traveling with our infant daughter, there would be, on occasion, an openness to hear and respond to us that might not have been so easily obtained in other circumstances.

One of the people we visited was a wealthy planter in the Mississippi Delta who owned many hundreds of acres near the town of Cleveland. As we approached his place, I immediately thought of slavery days—the stark difference in the status of whites and Blacks; the architecture and layout of the land; the fields of cotton and sorghum. The man was so rich that all the Black people in the area worked for him, and all of them lived on his property. Because of his influence in the area, Vincent and I had been directed to try to talk to this man. And perhaps because we approached him as a couple, who were clearly not from his town, he was willing to converse with us. Out of curiosity if nothing else. He invited us to sit with him in the large gazebo in his yard. And we talked a long time. About integration and the changes it was bringing, about the history of his family in that part of Mississippi, and about his beliefs and what he thought of Black people.

He told us he came from generations of planters; that he had lived around Black people all his life. He said it was interesting to meet folks like Vincent and myself because all the other Negroes he knew were people who worked his fields and tended to his household. "You know, something I've noticed . . . ," he told us, "the colored have a special skill for working the soil. They can make things grow out of this earth like I have never seen anywhere! It's something, how God gives certain people an ability that way."

Earlier in the conversation, when we were telling him about our connection to the Mennonites, the man had recalled a trip to Pennsylvania Dutch country some years before. He had mentioned visiting some of the Amish farms and said that he thought the Amish had a gift for agriculture. I reminded him of what he had said and told him, "If you really look around the world, most people have this gift. God put the land here for the benefit of all of us, and we have all learned to tend and care for it." He looked at me and seemed to acknowledge my deeper point with a wry smile. But I could tell he enjoyed talking with us, was fascinated by us. We stayed out on the gazebo for several hours, and as the afternoon drew on into early evening and it was getting close to dinnertime, I could see the man wrestling with whether to invite us to stay for a meal.

He didn't. And we left after a while.

. . .

But this was the kind of peace work we did, in little towns and cities all over the region. In 1962, Martin asked Vincent and me to go to Birmingham ahead of the major movement campaigns there. He wanted us to talk to white civic and religious leaders before the wave of voting-rights and sit-in campaign workers arrived. The idea was that if we could explain the intent and actions of the Movement to the white power structure ahead of time, it could make the inevitable negotiations and dialogue a little easier later on, and possibly, minimize the violence against the movement activists.

Martin first approached us about the Birmingham trip on a Sunday. Most Sundays when he, or his father, Daddy King, were in town, there was an evening service in the basement of Ebenezer Baptist Church. This particular week, Vincent was traveling, but Martin asked me and another one of the Mennonite House volunteers, Mary Bixler, to come by the church after the service to talk.

Martin said he wanted Vincent and me to go to Birmingham to talk to some of the leaders there and get a feel for the situation before everybody else went in. He told us what he hoped we could do, and as he talked, I noticed a shift in the air around him. Something happened in the light. In his face. Martin looked like himself, but he looked changed as well. For a moment, something surrounding him was lustrous. It reminded me of Florence and Clarence and some dreams I'd had and just a certain sharp quiet clarity in the world. It was a resilience that shone off of him in a shifting moment. A slight thing, but something striking. And I was certain that I saw it.

That evening, after Mary and I returned to Mennonite House, I told her what I thought I had seen, that change in the quality of Martin's countenance, the shift and the light. I asked her if she had noticed anything. She said no.

Note

1. The Institute of the Black World (IBW) was an independent center for engaged scholarship and activism of the African Diaspora, based on the Atlanta University campus in the 1970s. Vincent was a founder and the organization's first director.

Rosemarie, Mildred, and Sue, c. 1950. PHOTO COURTESY OF JEAN FREENEY CAMPBELL.

Rosemarie taught Bible School at Bethel Mennonite Church, c. 1951. She is fifth from the right in the second row. PHOTO COURTESY OF PAUL AND LOIS KING.

Vincent, Rachel, and Rosemarie, c. 1965. PHOTO COURTESY OF RACHEL ELIZABETH
HARDING.

Rosemarie, c. 1966. PHOTO COURTESY OF JULIUS LESTER. USED WITH PERMISSION.

Rachel and Rosemarie, 1981. PHOTO COURTESY OF RACHEL ELIZABETH HARDING.

Jonathan, Vincent, Rosemarie, and Rachel Harding, c. 1998. PHOTO COURTESY OF
RACHEL ELIZABETH HARDING.

Rosemarie, 2000. PHOTO COURTESY OF RACHEL ELIZABETH HARDING.

Rose Singing, c. 1970. PHOTO COURTESY OF RACHEL ELIZABETH HARDING.

27 · Koinonia Farm
Cultivating Conviction

Koinonia was a spiritual retreat for many of us in the Movement. We were so happy to have a place like the farm in the middle of southwest Georgia. Groups from Mennonite House would go down to Americus to volunteer for a few days at a time, to get away from the city and find renewal in the steady physical work of the farm. Florence Jordan had beds made for us when we arrived and the simple cottages, though sparsely furnished, were clean, bright, and comfortable. It was a joyful place; a place of respite for people who were exhausted from the physical and psychic violence of fighting segregation. Even though the farm was in a county thick with Klan members who spent years terrorizing the community, we felt safe on the grounds. How do I explain this? Although we may have been apprehensive on the narrow highway as we approached (conscious of the bullets that had been shot into buildings on the farm and the threats against community members), once we walked onto the land at Koinonia, we felt no fear. We could have been surrounded by rattlesnakes—and we were—but we felt safe, protected, as if angels stayed close to us all the time.

When we visited, I usually worked in the kitchen, helping to get meals ready or cleaning up afterward. Others worked in the factory or helped in the office and still others worked at various outdoors tasks—in the gardens and fields; pruning and planting trees; in the repair shop; whatever needed doing. The air, the earth, the companionship were all healing to us. The Albany Movement was very active then and many folks from that community found their way to Koinonia. SNCC and other organizations held workshops and planning retreats there. We all shared fellowship in this place that had witnessed for twenty years to an alternative vision of relations between southern Blacks and whites.

Clarence Jordan: Bible Stories and My Father's Voice

Clarence was a large part of the reason people came to Koinonia. People liked talking to him. They valued his opinions and experiences. He was plainspoken, thoughtful, and "no respecter of persons." He always said he didn't have any enemies. Although he joked about the times the Klan had come looking for him and he'd had to run, he said he didn't consider them his enemies. That perspective helped the rest of us think about what it meant to love those who fundamentally disagreed with us. To see them as human beings. To see them as children of the Creator.

Whenever he wanted to demonstrate a point to us, Clarence told stories. He was a wonderful storyteller and we'd sit rapt and thinking between our smiles because there was always some moral or political lesson in whatever he told us. Many times, Clarence would take stories from the Bible and relocate them to the red hills and family farms of Georgia. He would make us laugh to recognize the disciples Simon Peter and Andrew as "Rock and Andy, the original Johnson brothers" who might have put their names just that way "on the side of their new fiberglass boat."[1]

Koinonians were often accused of communism in those days, by people who saw racial and economic justice as a threat to "the American way of life." Clarence responded saying: "I don't think a Christian is worth his salt who has not been called a Communist today. Trying to refute that epithet is about like running for your birth certificate when someone calls you an s.o.b."[2]

I loved the way Clarence talked. He sounded like my father. Beautiful—that gravely, southern pitch, where the Black and white cadences slide into each other so that you can't always hear the differences. For me, that voice my father and Clarence shared was a voice full of hope. With humor that made even the hardest lessons something you could stand to hear.

Clarence was born and raised about fifty miles north of Americus in a town called Talbotton, Georgia. Not far from Macon where my parents lived for years before heading north. Clarence *thought* like my parents too. He was very clear about how you have to do right by everyone—and how a society that makes that impossible or illegal will destroy itself with its own meanness by and by. Clarence was convinced that God made us *family* to each other. That we are supposed to treat each other as concerned kin because that is, in fact, what we are.

(Years later, I got to thinking about what there might have been in the land, in the clay, in the underwater currents like veins through the central and southwest Georgia counties, that nurtured that understanding. It sent me back to Grandma Rye. And the Native People who had been there putting strength and blessing into the ground for thousands of years before anybody else showed up. And the enslaved people who sorrowed and sung into that land. . . . I got to thinking about Marion King and the Albany Movement and Bernice and other things . . . but some of that came later.)

Cultivating Conviction

It had been a rough road for Koinonia. At first, in the 1940s, there wasn't much resistance to the new farm community. Clarence generously helped many of the local farmers—Black and white—with mechanical innovations and new farming ideas that eventually had the effect of improving the economic condition of the whole county, and people were appreciative. (Of course, given the structure of things, the white farmers and business owners profited more than did the Blacks.) Clarence showed them how to transform a stationary peanut picker into a mobile harvester and he shared egg-farming innovations that increased the yield from hens. Koinonia held classes in ecologically conscious planting techniques to protect the quality of the soil, such as recycling peanut vines as fertilizer. And, like good farm neighbors everywhere, they helped local friends plant and bring in their crops and gratefully accepted the help of others.

But Koinonia was different from its white neighbors. Blacks and whites worked and socialized together on the property and African American workers were paid good wages. All of this was based in Clarence's deep belief that interracial community was an essential part of what God called His people to do and be in America, especially in the South. The Koinonia folks took the message and example of Jesus and the early church very seriously and looked for ways—like sharing property in common among the members of the community, and embracing nonviolence and pacifism—to manifest what they felt most deeply in their hearts.

As time passed, white people in the outside community grew suspicious and uncomfortable. The practice of Blacks and whites sitting together during meals on the farm was a major irritant to local whites who saw this as a breach of one of the most sacred codes of the southern status quo. Eating together implied a kind of equality, as it was around the table that stories got told, guards let down, and people came to know each other in a more intimate and open fashion. But in the 1940s and early 1950s, largely because Koinonia's practices could be dismissed as eccentricities and not yet manifestations of a greater tide of societal changes, the confrontations were minimal.

Starting in the mid-1950s, however, in the wake of the *Brown v. Board of Education* Supreme Court decision and at the successful end of the Montgomery Bus Boycott, many white people in Sumter County, Georgia, got very anxious about Koinonia. And they started to harass the community in every way they could—with verbal threats, with violence, through the courts, and by means of a years-long boycott that almost put the farm out of business. Even people who might have sympathized with Koinonia's mission were afraid to show any support because of the overwhelming atmosphere of terrorism that reigned against the farm.

Koinonia ran a thriving roadside market along the main highway passing through Americus where they sold eggs, hams, vegetables, fruits, and other produce from the farm. Angry neighbors defaced the market's signs and, after a while, destroyed them. Then, one evening, someone threw a bomb at the front of the building, ripping off the roof and the façade and ruining thousands of dollars of equipment and inventory. The market closed after that. Quickly, Koinonia members found that very few whites in the local community would buy their farm products, and neither would they sell provisions to Koinonia. No gas for their cars and trucks, no feed for their animals or seed for their fields. When one local business did consent to sell some items to Koinonia, it, too, was bombed and a short time later moved to another county.

Lights on the farm's entrance roads were blasted out, buckshot splayed at children in the midst of outdoor games, and bullets aimed into houses under cover of darkness. When I first got to the farm, I could still see where bullets from shotguns and rifles had entered some of the cabins and left a pattern of holes in the walls. Many families who had lived at Koinonia for years left during this time; and among the ones who stayed, children were often sent north to finish their schooling outside of the state of Georgia. Things got so bad that Clarence had to go all the way to Atlanta, to an African American bank, to get loans to keep the farm operating. (He stayed with us at Mennonite House on some of these trips.) White-owned institutions in southwest Georgia—even those owned by people who had previously been friendly—would have nothing to do with him.

It was especially dangerous for Black people to be associated with Koinonia in this time, but some local African Americans so valued Koinonia's spirit and courage that they did what they could to help them through the boycott. Whether bringing a few supplies, offering their labor to assist with work around the farm, or just sharing a word of encouragement, Black folks in the region knew what Koinonia was up against. Perhaps some of them also sensed that Koinonia was contributing to the groundwork for changes that were coming.

When I was visiting Koinonia regularly, in the early 1960s, most, if not all, of the people who lived on the farm were white. There had been a few Black members of the community in earlier times, and that was always the original vision for the farm; but it was hard to maintain as the violence and threats against the community grew. Surrounded by whites who were vehemently opposed to anything that looked like equality between the races, Koinonia was hard-pressed to sustain a residentially integrated community. Still, healthy race relations were very important to them and the farm attempted to nurture the experience in other ways.

I think this was part of the reason Clarence and others from Koinonia felt so comfortable at Mennonite House. We were an interracial group of Christian, community-service volunteers, sharing a house together, participating in freedom movement dialogues and activities and having some success with this model in a southern city. This was encouraging to the Koinonia folks. The fact that as Mennonites we also embraced nonviolence gave them another point of connection to us. And just as Mennonite House represented a kind of respite and affirmation for Koinonia, the farm in Americus offered a space of reflection and renewal for those of us from various parts of the Movement who found our way there.

A Field Visit

In the midst of its own troubles, Koinonia tried to treat all of its neighbors with care and respect, and be unafraid to live the tenets of the Gospel. One night, after dinner, I went out with one of the Koinonia women, Dorothy Swisshelm, to collect some packages from a storehouse. We carried them to a car, put them in the trunk, and drove out to a dirt road. We didn't travel far; maybe a little over a mile along the unpaved way. It was dark. The only lights were our headlights, a sliver of moon and stars. Dorothy pulled over and turned the car lights off. We got out, removed the packages, and started walking across a field. Maybe it was a cornfield. I don't remember now. Or soybeans. As my eyes adjusted to the darkness, I could make out a faint glow, far back into the field. We moved closer and saw the outline of a small cabin.

Dorothy knocked on the door and was greeted by a man and his wife; and around them, their five children. The house was one room, and more shack than house because it was full of holes with newspaper pasted against the walls and rag cloth pushed into the windows to keep out the cold of the evening. They were a beautiful family. The children bright and curious but quiet. The parents welcoming. They knew Dorothy and greeted her with warmth. The packages she handed them were large and might have held clothing and blankets and, surely also, food. They politely asked us if we wanted anything to eat or drink. Dorothy said we really had to be on our way and that she would see them the next time.

As we crossed the field back to where we had left the car, I realized we hadn't called the family to tell them we were coming. I gathered they didn't have a phone anyway. They had not been expecting us. The family were sharecroppers, Dorothy said. The way she saw things, they would never be out of debt to the man who owned the property and for whom they farmed. They were paid so little and charged exorbitantly for everything he advanced them—seed for planting; the ragged house; sometimes flour, sugar, cornmeal and other basic provisions. Sometimes not. They worked from sunup to sundown almost as if slavery had never ended, their children missing school to help with planting and harvesting.

It was never safe for the landowner to know that anyone from Koinonia had visited the people on his property. Families would be evicted, or threatened or physically harmed. And many had no other place to go. The Koinonia people would do as Dorothy and I did that night—wait until it was late and the sky dark so that the night could shield them.

Houses and Pecans

Not long after that visit with the family up the road, I was at Koinonia again. This time I saw models and plans for simple, sturdy houses that could be easily built to address the acute shortage of affordable and habitable housing for poor people in the region. Clarence had been talking with Millard Fuller and others about the need for well-constructed homes that their neighbors could afford, especially as a way to help Black folks get loose from the sharecropping system that exploited their labor and their dignity. The first houses constructed as part of this plan were built right on Koinonia's own land.

I recall that the original intent was that families would live in the homes, presumably paying a very low rent, but not actually holding title to the houses. (This decision was taken in line with the general agreement among Koinonia's permanent members that there would be no private ownership on the farm. All the community's members would own property in common.) But it soon became clear that this policy that Koinonia might choose for itself could not be applied to other people for whom home ownership was an important financial and psychological grounding—one that many couldn't have even dreamed of before. So the houses were financed by Koinonia and its supporters, built by local contractors including African Americans, and sold at very reasonable cost. This project became the seed of Habitat for Humanity, the global affordable housing program that Millard Fuller developed in ensuing years.

Also during this time, because of the boycott and its lingering effects, Koinonia was forced to shift from livestock- and produce-based farming to something less dependent on a local market. Pecans were a common crop in southwest Georgia, but few people were packaging them for shipment to other parts of the country in the early 1960s. Clarence and his colleagues saw this opportunity and the nutmeats became a way to keep the farm going, a way to make a living. Several of us from Mennonite House, including my nephew Charles, went down to Koinonia to help plant new groves. Charles explained to me that the pecan trees had to be planted with so much space between them so that they had room to grow. If you put them too close together, the roots wouldn't get enough water and the leaves wouldn't get enough sun.

Encouraged by friends in other parts of the country, Koinonia developed a mail-order enterprise that featured pecans, peanuts, and fruitcakes (and later homemade candies and granola too) that were shipped all over the nation. Mail order became a way to circumvent the local boycott and, at the same time, develop a national network of people who wanted to help the farm and who supported its interracial vision.

Work and Life at the Farm

Beyond the vision of an interracial community of permanent members, Koinonia also organized itself to provide fair-wage jobs for local Black people. There are pictures from the 1940s and '50s of Blacks and whites (males and females) working together in the fields of the farm; and later, with the growth of Koinonia's pecan business, a shelling and packing factory was built. I remember meeting some of the Black women who worked there on the assembly line. As they sorted and packed the nuts, they laughed and talked together. The atmosphere was relaxed and comfortable and the pace of work accommodated conversation.

Folks at Koinonia laughed a lot. And played games. Even the children were aware of the absurdity of things they experienced and joked with each other about it all. I was sitting out by the lawn one day, watching some of the boys roughhouse with each other—Lenny (Clarence and Florence's youngest son) and a couple of the Wittkamper children who were about Lenny's age. They knew that their parents believed in nonviolence and identified as pacifists. As they tumbled together, one of the children jumped up and hollered, "If you mess with me, I'll *pass a fist!*"

On Sundays I remember we would sit around and take turns reading the comics out loud. You didn't get the sense that people were despondent at the farm, although surely they must have had periods of doubt, especially when they were being attacked. But during the times when I was there, the feeling was just the opposite. I would forget that the surrounding community was so hostile. Inside the grounds of the farm was another reality. Koinonia was a place of joy, palpable joy, where there was support and encouragement for people who believed the world could be much better than it was. Koinonia gave us that kind of hope.

. . .

Clarence died of a heart attack in 1969, the same year that Slater King was killed in a car accident, and the year after Martin was assassinated.[3] Vincent and I drove down to Koinonia with our children when Clarence passed just to reflect a bit; to regroup after the recent deaths and murders. When we got to the farm, I went over to Florence's apartment and she described the funeral to me. How they found a place on a hill Clarence had liked and dug the grave and someone read a selection over the body. And a few people said remembrances. How simple and lovely it was. What he would have liked.

I asked Florence if I could see where they buried her husband. Florence in her wisdom, allowed me the silence to hear what I was asking. Then she began to describe the death scene: Someone shouted that Clarence had had a heart attack. Lenny ran to the small house where Clarence had been working, writing; and he found his father slumped in a chair.

"He was dead when we got to him," Florence said. "We had to get a death certificate and nobody from the county would come out to see us. So we put the body in the front seat of the car and drove him into town to the coroner. Clarence was sitting up there next to Millard." Florence was laughing now. "His eyes were closed and he looked like he was just sleeping. They drove along the highway, passing people and things. You couldn't tell he was dead. If he could've seen himself he would have thought it was funny," Florence said.

Then she went back to my question. "Well, we just got a pine box and put him in it. And he's somewhere over there on the hill." She waved her hand in the general direction of the hills in the distance. "He didn't want a marker. And he didn't want anybody looking for him."

Then she paused again. "Furthermore, Rose, he's not there."

I had to let that sink in.

Florence Jordan: Knowing Her Own Mind

The first time we met her husband, at a church where he preached in Chicago, he was trying to tell us what it meant to live in community. He believed in it, but he didn't romanticize it. He was talking to us about Florence—how independent and outspoken she was and how this was sometimes difficult for the community but ultimately very good for it as well. When Koinonia was first forming, members decided they would own all property in common. Everyone was expected to put everything they owned of any value into a common trust, into the common possession of the community. Clarence said Florence did this with some of the things she owned, but not everything. She insisted that her wedding gifts, for example, were for her alone. And she was very open and clear about it with the community. Some people were initially upset but, Clarence said, it was much healthier for the community, and for their relationship, that Florence spoke her mind and did what she felt was the right thing to do, openly, rather than hold her feelings in and be resentful and secretive. I remember times when a group of us would be talking at Koinonia and Florence would say whatever was on her mind, emphatically. I always loved that. She was not one to demure and she was very honest about what she believed.

There is a story in a book about Koinonia that recounts Florence's decision to rescind the membership of all Koinonia members from a local white Baptist church. One Sunday, the Jordans brought a dark-skinned visitor to the service. The visitor wasn't African American. He was an exchange student from India, but I guess he was dark enough that the specifics of his racial heritage didn't really matter. The ushers got nearly apoplectic when they saw the man entering the sanctuary and asked all of the Koinonia group to leave. Shortly afterward a deacons meeting was called to decide if Koinonia folks should be made to resign their membership in the church. On the day of the decision, Clarence and some of the other men were out of town and Florence attended the meeting on her own with her daughter, Eleanor. When the recommendation was announced to expel the Koinonia members, the chair of the meeting invited a motion from the floor and Florence made it herself, to the surprise of the congregation.[4]

Florence told me that sometime after Clarence died, she received a visit from a group of local white men. Some of them were Klan members and had been among those who attacked and terrorized Koinonia and led the boycott that almost destroyed the farm. She said they came to her and asked her forgiveness for what they had done. Florence listened to the men say what they needed to say, and then she told them she would be honored to forgive them. As I thought about it, I realized it wasn't an easy thing for them to do. Not only did it require a change in their political and spiritual perspective, but also in their manhood. Because to be a member of the Ku Klux Klan, and to ask forgiveness for activity that you were once very proud of, took a great deal of inner strength.

Forgiveness

I have thought about this numerous times over the years. Our friend and mentor, Jimmy Boggs, once said that the most progressive political people he knows are also the most forgiving.[5] He said it is very important to be able to forgive because a lack of forgiveness most likely means we are too entrenched in our own positions and not capable of recognizing that all of us can change. It meant a lot to me to hear that from Jimmy Boggs, one of the greatest thinkers and organizers this country has ever produced. But when I heard him say that, many years ago, I wasn't yet making the connection I'm making now to Florence's story. And the connection is this: not only do people like former or present Klan members need to come and seek forgiveness, but we who have suffered actually *need* to forgive. The act of apology and forgiveness is like a sacrament of human community. It is how we remember who we really are to each other. Furthermore, we need to forgive because forgiveness opens space for maturing and growth and change. It brings a transformative energy into the situation.

As I studied more of the Dalai Lama and began to work with these wonderful Buddhist ideas, I could see that not only do we need to forgive those who come and ask for forgiveness, but we also need to forgive those who are no longer here to ask. People who are no longer in this realm, who are dead, but who still need forgiving. Now again, this is also from my mother and father who helped me understand that there is nothing more lasting than love, nothing more eternally enduring than forgiveness.

So what does it mean to forgive those who are no longer here and cannot ask our forgiveness? There are rituals and traditions among people in various parts of the world where you can do it by proxy. Where one person—perhaps a relative of the one needing forgiveness, but perhaps not—stands in for another and asks on behalf of those who are absent now, expressing their regret and desire for change. Anyone can stand in, because there is no one on this earth who is not connected to everyone else. But if there is a direct genetic inheritance, or a shared experience, the proxy is stronger.

. . .

I'm sure that by the time Clarence died—and Florence a few years later—they were at a much deeper level of spiritual growth than they would have been had they lived a so-called normal Southern Baptist life. I do think the same is true for me and Vincent as well. Lately, almost daily, I think about the ways my own ideas have changed. I'm not saying I'm where I should be yet, but meeting people like Clarence, Florence, and others in the South gave me a great measure of strength and hope. That experience gave me a way to situate all of the teachings I encountered before and since within a broad understanding of human interconnectedness and transformational love.

Since Florence's death, I realize that neither she nor Clarence is "... there." But they continue with me, like all of those I have been close to in this life. They remain with me in my thoughts of them and in my love for them. And in the way I have been molded by my experience of them. And they return in dreams. Wonderful dreams.

Notes

1. Quotes are from Dallas Lee, *The Cotton Patch Evidence: The Story of Clarence Jordan and the Koinonia Farm Experiment* (New York: Harper and Row, 1971), 184.

2. Lee, *Cotton Patch Evidence*, 195–96.

3. Slater Hunter King (1927–69) was a real estate broker, businessman, community activist and a leader of the Albany Movement in the years when Rosemarie and Vincent worked there. The Hardings became close friends of Slater and his wife, Marion.

4. Lee, *Cotton Patch Evidence*, 75–79.

5. James Boggs (1919–93) was a Detroit-based political activist, autoworker, author, and organic intellectual who, with his wife, Grace Lee Boggs, influenced several generations of radical community activism.

28 · A Radical Compassion

*His Holiness the Dalai Lama, Clarence Jordan,
and Marion King-Jackson*

In March 1990 Dharamsala was busy and dusty and full of excitement over the Dalai Lama's extended stay for teaching. On one day,
as I was walking around the town trying to make arrangements for
my return trip to Delhi, I stopped at the side of a road and watched a
group of protesters marching by. They were monks in saffron, young
men mostly, carrying Tibetan flags and banners, chanting prayers and
shouting slogans against the Chinese occupation of their homeland. I
had read about the tortures, the beatings, the deaths. And some of the
young men had shown me their faces, their arms, their scars.

Seeing the monks now, hearing them, I went back in my mind to the
marches in Birmingham, Alabama; in Albany and Atlanta, Georgia; and
all the other places where I had watched and often joined my own body
to the freedom train moving through. I looked at the young men and I
remembered C. T. Vivian leading people to the steps of the courthouse
in Selma.[1] I remembered how Bertha Gober and Cordell and Bernice
Reagon would sing fear out of the room in mass meetings.[2] I looked
at these young monks, some were children really, carrying their colors,
their signs in the street, and I thought to myself: *how many marches I
have witnessed, how many songs rising up from a road's shuffled dust!*

More than once, as I sat listening to the Dalai Lama, I thought of
Clarence Jordan. These two men reminded me of each other: the
wholeness of their visions, the way their commitment, their faith, and

their nonviolence made their embraces wide. The words of His Holiness challenged some of the most militant Tibetan Buddhists present at his teachings. He said that the Chinese people and the Chinese government were not his enemies. He said he didn't have any enemies. That although others may consider him to be their antagonist, he himself did not view any person in that way.

Clarence, too, believed that no person was his enemy. Sometimes in his sermons Clarence would try to help us imagine what was happening in the minds of people whose brutality and racism caused so much suffering. What was it really like to torture another person, he wondered? What happens to your conscience when you are responsible for beatings, lynchings, dismemberment? What kind of psychic contortions must a person undergo in order for the mind to accept these activities? He would think about these things and try to help others of us in the Movement think about them too. I recognized that kind of compassion—at once clear and ample—in the teachings of the Dalai Lama. I had seen it before.

One place I saw it was in 1961–62 in Albany, Georgia. I met Marion King during the Albany Movement—a yearlong campaign to desegregate the city's public accommodations and register the black majority to vote. The King family were among the few black realtors in that region of southwest Georgia—perhaps the only ones. And Marion and her husband, Slater, were respected leaders in the local black community.[3] Clarence and Florence Jordan had introduced us, and almost from the moment I met her, I was impressed with Marion's kindness, her willingness to speak her mind, and her commitment to finding a way to help blacks and whites live together as equals. My husband and I would often stay in the Kings' home when we were in the area and our families became close friends.

Marion and Slater were among the first Black folks Vincent and I had ever met who were interested in Eastern religions. The four of us had many conversations about teachings from India and other parts of Asia on spirituality and peacemaking. And the Kings had an altar in their home where they meditated as a family.

All throughout that summer Vincent and I traveled between Albany and Atlanta, and into the many smaller towns of Dougherty, Terrell, and Baker counties, quietly encouraging conversation between black organizers and sympathetic whites, counseling movement participants, helping to write speeches, and participating in the mass meetings, protests, and marches at the Movement's heart. This was basically the nature of our work—helping to build bridges, behind the scenes, between Black activists and whites who were ready to embrace a new vision. It was such a fascinating and hopeful time.

As Black Mennonites, Vincent and I were somewhat unusual among the legions of Baptists, Methodists, AMES, and other movement participants associated with more traditional Black church denominations. (Mennonites have a long history of war resistance and nonviolence stemming from their Anabaptist beginnings in the fifteenth century. And although the number of African Americans in the Mennonite Church has grown in recent decades, in the early 1960s we were still very few.) Because of our affiliation with this church that espoused nonviolence as a central tenet, and that had done so even before the advent of Gandhi and King, we often found ourselves in conversation with others who were interested in exploring what deeper meanings nonviolence might have for the life of the Movement and for our own lives as individuals.

These were wonderful, searching discussions—not simply about the use of nonviolence as a tactic or strategy, but its most profoundly spiritual and philosophical underpinnings as well. Marion was intensely interested in exploring the widest possibilities of nonviolence and was trying to learn as much as possible about other traditions that embraced peace and compassion as central ethics. She studied Buddhism and eventually became a Baha'i, where she has continued to work for racial justice and reconciliation.

Marion King: A Hard-Won Peace

In the summer of 1962, in the middle of the Albany campaign, Marion and I were both pregnant. She was carrying her fourth child. During the campaign, Marion often visited movement workers who were jailed in local facilities throughout Dougherty and Terrell counties—taking them food, checking on conditions where they were kept, relaying messages. On one occasion as she exited a jail, a policeman who felt she was not moving fast enough kicked her in the back so that she fell to the ground. Marion fell so hard that she lost the baby.

When we, her friends and comrades, first heard the news, we were horrified. Some of us went to see her at her home when she was released from the hospital. As we waited in the living room our shock and pain mixed with anger and we shook our heads and talked in low voices about what a terrible, shameful thing had happened. When Marion finally came in to speak with us, we naturally assumed she would share our sense of indignation and assault. But something else was happening. When Marion came into the room, walking slowly so as not to exacerbate her pain, there was something in her face. A kind of light. Like a victory, a resplendence. It's hard to explain because it wasn't prideful and it wasn't false. It helped to quiet us—our anger, our judgment. And we recognized it.

Many of us in the Movement had the feeling at certain moments that what we were experiencing in our freedom work was something more than just the immediate events. It was in fact something transcendent—capable of transforming us, our adversaries, and our entire society. Marion's countenance and her conversation in that moment reminded us of *that* quality of the Movement. Clearly she had struggled with how to respond to the trauma she had experienced: not only had she been attacked, but the child she was carrying had died. And it's hard for me now to explain her actions in terms that do not sound like romantic idealism or a spiritual naïveté. But what I am trying to emphasize to you in this example is how deeply and how seriously many people were grappling with the meaning of nonviolence during the Movement days and how Marion's reaction had a context and the support of a community of people who understood, or at least were trying to understand, the potential of compassion and nonviolence to transform individuals and societies.

Marion never condemned the man who had beaten her and, in fact, she directed our conversation to other matters and even to laughter. What she showed us in her refusal to disparage or judge the man who had spurned her so violently was a kind of triumph that did not come from a spirit of revenge or even of justifiable anger. Indeed, the words I am using to describe it—"victory," "triumph"—may mislead in the sense that they imply a success *over* an opponent. What we saw and felt in Marion's presence, in her response to the trauma she was living through, had the *excellent* quality of victory, but where otherwise a *dominance* might have been, there was instead *dominion*—a kind of understanding, a place where something very meaningful was shared.

It was this kind of peace we saw in Marion—a resplendent, hard-won peace in which we could see our own failings as well as the failings of others, but where failings were not the issue. The issue was how to live and work for a way to sigh with our adversaries; at some moments to walk with our adversaries, to talk with our adversaries; and how to, at some moments, hold our adversaries close to our hearts. That's what Marion gave us. That lesson. That quality of compassion. Because she was not judging the policeman who kicked her so forcefully that she miscarried, we could see that our own desire to judge was inappropriate. I hope that I'm making myself clear here. I am not condoning the brutality of the police (nor was Marion); neither am I suggesting that nonviolence meant or means uncritical self-sacrifice. Rather, the point I wish to make is about a *quality of spirit* that was present, at certain times and in certain places in the Movement. For those of us participating in freedom work for which we often suffered, that spirit allowed connection to a deep source of balance and renewal that transcended the particular physical or psychic infliction being aimed at us. In fact, it was even capable of including our inflictors in its aura.

Clarence Jordan and the Star of David

The radical compassion I experienced with Marion King and in the presence of the Dalai Lama and other Buddhist teachers such as Lama Zopa Rinpoche had further parallels in my experience with Clarence Jordan. I remember in particular a conversation about the Holocaust.

On Sunday evenings at Koinonia, the community would get together in the common room and talk. It was like church. (And very similar to other Sunday evening meetings I attended at times, led by Martin Luther King Jr. and held in the basement of Ebenezer Baptist in Atlanta.) Somebody would offer a prayer or raise a song and then, too, sometimes we would just carry over the conversations from earlier in the week, looking for meaning in the turbulent times we faced. By the early sixties—when I was a regular visitor to Koinonia—the permanent community had dwindled to about three families, although visitors from all over the country and many parts of the world were frequently present for a day, a week, sometimes a month or longer.

On one particular Sunday when I was there, the evening gathering was small: Clarence, Florence, myself, and two or three of the other women from Mennonite House. This time, Clarence had been talking about the Jewish Holocaust, about its roots in Christian anti-Semitism, about the perils of holding such a contorted view of race and, of course, the parallels with the stigmatization of Blacks in the United States. I was learning so much.

It was in the context of this conversation that I began to realize how widespread anti-Semitism was in Europe. Previously I had thought Germany was the essential offender. I knew nothing about the Spanish Inquisition, for example. "There is not a European language whose speakers have not persecuted the Jews in their midst," Clarence explained. "Spanish, French, German, English . . . " he went on. And yet he warned us of the dangers of judgment. I thought about the Germans, a proud people who had lost wars and blamed their losses on the Jews. It reminded me of my study of my own country between the two world wars. So many of the problems of this nation, too, had been blamed on Black people.

One of the visitors asked Clarence what he would have done had he lived in Germany or an occupied country during Hitler's reign. Clarence didn't say anything for a long time. He just sat quietly. Finally, he said, "We can't always be sure exactly what we'll do in any given situation. It's hard to say, from here. But if we believe that God is no respecter of persons, that He loves us all equally—the victim and those who victimize—then it would've been good if some of us, even just a handful, who believed this way, had worn the star of David." I have told this story at workshops trying to help people understand the possibilities, the resources of compassion, available to nonviolent workers for justice. Often in these settings I am reminded by various individuals of the extraordinary physical and psychic violence of Hitler's Third Reich or that of the Chinese occupying army in Tibet—and I have to be very careful not to romanticize the possibilities of nonviolence.

A Radical Meaning of Accompaniment

And yet it is not simply nonviolence, per se, that I am speaking of here. Really it is a meaning of accompaniment. A kind of radical compassion that understands the essential nature of human relations and the essential nature of human/divine relations to be one of shared experience. There are two traditional gospel songs my daughter likes to sing that help me conceptualize this idea in a more concrete way. One of them is "We Shall Walk through the Valley in Peace" and the other is "You've Got to Stand Your Test in Judgment." On the face of things, these two songs seem to be carrying opposite meanings. The first one states:

> We shall walk through the valley in peace.
> We shall walk through the valley in peace.
> If Jesus himself shall be our leader
> We shall walk through the valley in peace.

It continues with a verse that says, "There will be no dying there . . ." and then repeats the original lines. If "the valley" is understood—as it often is in Christian imagery—as a place of difficulty, of trial, of suffering (as in, *the valley of the shadow of death*), then the message of the song seems very clearly to be one of safety in the presence of Spirit—in this case, Jesus.

The second song, a call-and-response, is sung:

> "You've got to stand"
> > *"You've got to stand"*
> "Your test in judgment"
> > *"Test in judgment"*
> "You've got to stand"
> > *"You've got to stand"*

"It for yourself"
    "For yourself"
"There's nobody here"
    "Nobody here"
"To stand it for you"
    "Stand it for you"
"You've got to stand it for yourself"
    "For yourself"

Further verses sing "You've got to walk that lonesome valley," "My mother had to stand her test in judgment," and "My Jesus had to stand his test in judgment." Here, the immediate impression suggests that the tests of the spirit, the so-called dark nights of the soul that all human beings experience, are experienced at an individual level, alone; and that the correctness of one's choices in these times is ultimately one's own responsibility.

The examples of people like the Tibetan lamas with whom I studied and many of my friends from the movement days (as well as my own experience and the lessons I received from my family) offer a way of understanding both of these songs in terms of a radical meaning of accompaniment. A kind of connection to the divine and to other human beings that allows us to experience the juxtaposition between the reality of the valley—and its terrible loneliness—and the simultaneous reality of accompaniment, compassion.

In the first song, it bears emphasizing that the words are *"We* shall walk . . . " which suggests multiple levels of accompaniment—that of human beings sharing tribulation together and that of the presence of Spirit as an essential companion to humanity. In the second song, the shared experience of the valley, of the judgment test, is not so immediately clear. But if we understand it, indeed especially if we sing it, with an attempt to discern a meaning of accompaniment we can experience it that way. As I mentioned, the song is a call-and-response. At a very basic level, that structure in itself mitigates the idea of a completely individual, unaccompanied experience of trial. "You've got to stand," yes. But immediately following comes an affirmation from outside oneself, *"You've got to stand."* In effect, the second voice or the choir is a corresponding presence, a company for the first.

And while we all have experiences of deep personal, even spiritual crisis in which it seems as if "nobody was there," I believe that at the most fundamental and the most transcendent levels of our experience as human beings, we are never left alone. There is always accompaniment. There are always remnants. What I sensed in the radical acts of compassion of Clarence, Marion, and the lamas was the effort to live, to act from such an understanding of human community. We are all part of one another and none of our judgments is truly separate.

Notes

1. C. T. Vivian was a fearless and eloquent leader in the Southern Freedom Movement who continues, into his eighties, to advocate and organize for racial justice and human rights.

2. Bertha Gober, Cordell Reagon, and Bernice Johnson Reagon were young activists in Albany, Georgia, in the early 1960s and among the founders of the SNCC Freedom Singers.

3. Marion's first husband, Slater, died in the late 1960s. She later married Mr. Bo Jackson, a gentle man who maintained a wonderful and abundant vegetable farm on the outskirts of Albany, Georgia. Marion died in 2007.

29 · A Song in the Time of Dying

A Memory of Bernice Johnson Reagon

When my children were young we lived in a large, wood frame house on the corner of Ashby and Fair streets in southwest Atlanta, Georgia; 201 Ashby Street. My husband, our daughter and son, and I lived on the second floor of the house. Bernice Johnson Reagon and her family lived on the first floor. Most of my daughter Rachel's earliest memories are from that house: running in the backyard under the gargantuan black walnut tree with her little brother, Jonathan, and with Bernice's children, Toshi and Kwan. Watching the Morehouse and Morris Brown marching bands parade down Fair Street at homecoming from the perfect vantage point of Bernice's front porch. Following, instinctively, the allure of the thick, warm, diapasons of the women rehearsing a cappella in Bernice's living room—the Harambee Singers.

There were always friends and relatives visiting the Reagons downstairs. We often visited ourselves—sitting in Bernice's rocking chair or resting in her brother Junior's hammock in the sunroom. The exciting conversations drew us in quickly and the soft-hearty, laughing timbers of Dougherty and Lee county, Georgia, voices mixed memory and present comfortably in my head. My grandparents, my parents, and most of my brothers and sisters were born less than fifty miles away from Bernice's hometown. The family moved to Chicago in the early years of the Great Migration, and although I was born up north, the sounds of southern language, southern music, and southern love were the sounds of my childhood. Bernice is family. And as my nephews and nieces came to stay with us at various times, they, too, formed their own interlaced connections with Bernice, Junior, their sister Mae Frances, and other members of the extended Johnson clan.

Once, in the early 1970s, my mother's sister, Aunt Hettie, came south. Her only daughter, Juanita, had recently died and Aunt Hettie was taking it very hard. Hettie and her son, Billy, came first to Atlanta and then went farther south to Macon, Albany, and Leesburg to see old friends and family there. When they came back to our house from their sojourn in the smaller towns, Hettie was sitting upstairs in the kitchen and my nephew Charles asked Bernice to come up and sing some familiar songs for her.

Hal-le-lu, Hal-le-lu, Hal-le-lu, Bernice began, in the bright-slow, lingering tones of rural Black southern congregational singing. *Hal-le-lu, Hal-lelu, my Lord. I'm gonna see my friends again, Hal-le-lu.* As Bernice continued, Aunt Hettie began to hum a little, raising her hand to shake it gently now and again. "Yes, Lord," she would say softly. "That girl knows all the songs," she looked at Charles, smiling. "All them old songs!"

Bernice would finish one and ease gentle into another, the thick velvet thread of her contralto lining one hymn seamless into the early moments of the next. Soon Charles added his sweet, full tenor voice to the music and after awhile all in the room slipped back into a place half in memory, half in heart. A fellowship of mending. Bernice did that for us, for Aunt Hettie, for Juanita. The power in her voice was (and is) an old power. It is a power of trees and turnrows, of balms and boulders, of aching and making and aching some more. And it is the power of family, of our lacing and unlacing our lives, of our belonging to each other and to those who came before us and to those who left too soon.

30 · The Blood House

(a story outline)

This is the story of a call. A perennial call. It is a mother's hymn, or lullaby, or it's a mother's comfort song. It comes from a place of anguish.

Bob Moses tells a story of a woman he knew in the Movement.[1] Somebody in Mississippi who had been through so much pain, so much loss, she just fell to her knees in despair, one day. She fell on the floor of her kitchen, cradling bad news or pushing away a fresh memory, and from nowhere anybody could see, a sound rose up. It was within her someplace between her waist and her lungs, a vast place more guttural than the throat, a sacred place. And it was a deep haunting sound. Not shrill. But it rose and was full. The tone rose up out of this woman's body on the floor, on her knees, and when she was done, everything was alright. She was alright. She had made a road.

I'm imagining the desperation of slavery—Grandma Rye and the other mothers and fathers. The iron taste in their mouths.

There is a way of believing, among some Africans—and among some Native folks on this side too—that all people belong to us. The Africans thought this even before Western science found the bones of the mother of the world in Tanzania. We always knew. Can you imagine going through slavery, going through the Middle Passage, and feeling these are your children doing this to you?

When I was researching Ida I found a reference to a house, a woman who owned a house that had blood coming out of the cracks. The house was in the upper south, but I'll put it in Georgia for my story.

It was a horrible house where captured runaways and the steadfast re-calcitrant were beaten until resistance left their spirits or until they died. The blood runs out of the sides of the house, the floors bleed. The walls bleed and the soil soaks what it can. People tell stories about the house. They talk about the woman there. She was abandoned by her mother and abused by her father. This woman, who is white, catches fugitive people, breaks them and collects a reward or sells them for a profit. This is her legitimate work. Torturing slaves. And she enjoys it. Once in a while she takes free folk with no papers and no white people to vouch for them and resells them to slave gangers passing through to Alabama and Mississippi. She doesn't crack the whips or turn the stretcher herself. She makes other Blacks do it. And she watches. Most know they don't have long to live. She kills everybody she doesn't sell.

She has some very unsavory white people working for her as well, people who are able to tolerate the work. In the story, they are in shadows. After a while, the depth of the pain they have inflicted comes back to them. In dreams and nightmares, but also in a growing mistrust among the shadows who work in the house. The white woman, we discover later in the story, is not, really. Not really white. She isn't the only one trying to exorcise unclaimed Blackness in that house. All the shadow people look white, but toward the end of the story, it's not clear *what* they are—white, Black . . . maybe haints?

The woman has a brother, a man as light as she is but who identifies with their mulatto mother, with the slaves, and he is captured with a Black man who is their half brother and the two men are brought to the house as runaways. The woman recognizes her brother.

Mariah comes to Georgia in the war. She leaves the ship captain in Cedar Keys and walks from Florida with her husband Robert, and her children, Ella, Willoughby, Liza, and the baby, Hester. They moved along the roads when they could and through the swamps when they couldn't, passing other people going their same way, everybody looking for some new place to start. When they get to Leesburg, they stop. Cedar Keys to Leesburg is already a long way to travel with little ones.

People whisper about the house out in the country. Everybody knows, although the white folks don't talk about it as torture, per se. During the war, the house is "mysteriously" set afire. And it is left, cindered, in a little clearing out back in the woods. Nobody goes there.

Well, we'll have to figure out how she gets the notion, but about twenty years after the war, Mariah starts going out to that clearing to sit. She sits and listens to the spirits out there. A little baby whose mama was in that dungeon. Baby spirit come looking for its mama. The baby had been cut out of the mama's womb, they was both dead down in there. And there is shouting in the ruins covered up with so much death it sounds like whispers.

And there are white people too—she doesn't know their story exactly, but they are haints now. And crying all the time. Carrying severed limbs in their hands. (Now, you know this is some morbid shit. I don't know if this scene is really going to be like this. We'll see.)

Some of the chaos Mariah hears are strange languages. Old languages. Some from Europe. Some from Africa. Some Native. Some even Asian. A hard dissonance that rises until all the voices merge into that wailing, anguished sound Bob Moses was talking about.

Grandma Rye asks the forest spirits if she can dig some roots from the woods around the clearing. She does that. And she brings water from a creek out back of where the house used to be. She makes a water salve that she pours all over the remains of that house. And she prays. She does this for weeks. Then she gets her son-in-law and some other men to come and take the cinders and burnt bricks away. They tote it all out somewhere. They don't tell nobody where, just she and they know. And she sends a bucket of her herb water with them and they sprinkle the ashes some more in the new place and then they leave it all there for the wind to disperse and the earth to swallow slowly.

And over the days that Grandma Rye works, the sound becomes less and less tormented, until finally it's only a murmur—and you can't tell if it's coming from the ground or from the trees.

Note

1. Bob Moses was the legendary organizer-leader of the Mississippi Freedom Movement of the 1960s and is founder of the nationally recognized Algebra Project. He is a devoted practitioner of yoga whose example was an inspiration to Rosemarie's own spiritual practice.

31 · Spirit and Struggle
The Mysticism of the Movement

One of the most exciting things for me about being in the freedom movement was discovering other people who were compelled by the Spirit at the heart of our organizing work, and who were also interested in the mysticism that can be nurtured in social justice activism. We experienced something extraordinary in the freedom movement, something that hinted at a tremendous potential for love and community and transformation that exists here in this scarred, spectacular country. For many of us, that "something" touched us in the deepest part of our selves and challenged us in ways both personal and political.

There was an energy moving in those times. Something other than just sit-ins and voter registration and Freedom Schools. Something represented by these signal efforts but broader. As I traveled around the country in the sixties, it seemed to me that the nation—from the largest community to the smallest—was permeated with hope; the idea that people can bring about transformation; that what we do matters. C. T. Vivian talked about it as a time when the Movement made so many cracks in the foundation of the status quo that "creativity broke out all over" like a celestial sun, and the power structure was rushing around trying to stuff it back below the horizon but it was too late.[1]

Nonviolence and Change

For Martin, nonviolence was a central tool for building an inclusive justice movement. He believed very profoundly in nonviolence. Martin felt that you couldn't build trust, you couldn't build organizations, you couldn't build the capacity to work effectively with people if a violent response was ever an alternative. Without nonviolence, there would always be the possibility that you could just get rid of someone, literally or figuratively. The option of violence provided a way to deny your connection to your so-called enemy. Martin was very drawn to nonviolence and was always interested in people who did activist work from that perspective. I think that's why he was open to meeting with Vincent and the interracial group of Mennonite men who came down to see him in Alabama in 1958. Howard and Sue Thurman believed that way too.

Nonviolence in the Movement meant that there was room for everyone—every ethnic group, every race, males and females. You constantly made room for the oppressor. The very way in which you were protesting was a form of reconciliation. That was the significant thing about the Movement. Its mode, its approach, contained the seeds of inclusiveness, openness, and forgiveness. This made for a very different kind of revolution. But if you didn't experience it yourself, I guess you could get tired of watching your world turned upside down every day.

I remember being in an airport in the sixties and passing a white woman on the concourse as she was looking at a newspaper where the lead article was about the sit-ins and marches that were constantly in the news in those days.

"When is all of this going to be over?" she said in a loud, exasperated voice, to no one in particular. (There were plenty of Black people, too, who wondered when the marching would stop, when the protests would finally settle down.) It was interesting. By then the ongoing movement activity was *normal* to me, and a lot of us inside of it realized this was a process that would demand our full attention for a long time. And, too, I think the idea of confrontation—even nonviolent confrontation—was uncomfortable to some folks.

It didn't dawn on me until much later that for those who grew up receiving the privileges of segregation, it must have been emotionally wrenching to see the people you never acknowledged, never addressed, remain in the news with their vindications day after day after day. Vincent once heard a southern white man say that the changes the Movement brought to his world were like being surrounded by a forest of trees whose shade, fruit, and wood had been taken for granted for generations—and all of a sudden, one day, the trees started talking.

But that wasn't the way I was looking at it. I was ready—and maybe this was a little prideful—but I felt ready to take this movement around the world. I thought, *we can do this. Why can't we? If we've learned anything about the transformative power of nonviolence, why don't we tell others about it?* It may have been beyond my individual capacity, but those were exactly the thoughts in my mind.

A Transforming Presence

Martin and Coretta and Anne Braden and Ella Baker and others like them had a beautiful effect on people who spent time with them. Living and working in their presence hastened changes in your own thoughts, your reactions, your priorities; even if you weren't always cognizant of the shift. It's like Bernice Reagon talks about in her Veterans of Hope Project interview. She recalls how she and the other children in her small southwest Georgia church congregation would "sit up in the singing," not joining in at first, but surrounded by the energy and power of those songs, the molding fellowship of that worshipping community. Bernice said the music, the simple but mighty a cappella music of the church, "did something to the material you're made of," and transmitted a kind of cognizance, an understanding, a strength that was, fundamentally, a connection to the life force. "We were just connected to the higher things in the universe," is how Bernice put it.[2]

What I'm talking about is similar. Being constantly in the presence of people who lived so fervently in the power of nonviolence, who believed and acted from the understanding that love and forgiveness were essential tools for social justice; being surrounded by people like that fed those commitments in me, in many of us. And it infused the nation.

These people didn't necessarily call themselves "nonviolent" or even "religious" but they lived with such integrity and fairness. And after you spent time with them, even if you didn't remember particular teachings or incidents, you kept a "feeling" for doing what was just and what was fair. Those feelings moved a lot of us, Black and white, to have great *hope* for the possibility that men and women of different races, religions, economic backgrounds, can have respect and love for each other as fellow citizens of the nation. I saw this again and again in that time. And I've seen it since.

In a way, Martin's assassination marked the nation's rejection of his ideas and so much love was lost. Of course some people never stopped—Clarence and Florence Jordan, Grace and Jimmy Boggs, C. T. Vivian . . . But we have to find another direction now. Our challenge is to create new ways to keep

Vincent and Rosemarie at Morehouse, c. 1969. PHOTO COURTESY OF RACHEL ELIZABETH HARDING.

building on what we've gone through, building on all the things we've learned. There is so much good work to be done to bring us together. We have to find another way to keep walking this road. Raise up a new rhythm from the old. Maybe this is why I'm still searching so much. We have to let these young people know that they are not abandoned, that their elders love and trust them. That we are going to keep working with them to bring more humanity, more integrity, more compassion into our nation. There was so much coming together during the movement time—different ages, different professions, different races. *That part* was beautiful.

Spiritual Appetite

For a lot of people in the Movement, our participation gave us a craving for spiritual depth. I think about how Zoharah Simmons was led to Bawa Muhaiyaddeen, and Bob Moses to Paramahansa Yogananda and the Self-Realization Fellowship; how Slater and Marion King had an altar room in their house in Albany, Georgia, in 1963 and eventually found their way to the Baha'i tradition. How Anne Braden did yoga for many years and Wazir (Willie) Peacock embraced Islam and became a master bodywork therapist. Diane Nash, Sonia Sanchez, Bernice Reagon, Julius Lester, Victoria Gray

Adams—all of these people have gone into deep spiritual pilgrimage since their years in the Movement.

So many of them, like Prathia Hall and Bernice and Zoharah and Ruby Sales and Charles Sherrod and Nelson and Joyce Johnson, so many of them had those deep mystic traditions in them to begin with. A lot of the young people in the Movement came out of the tradition of rural southern religion. They came out of those country churches; places where the droning, lined-out hymns put you in the mind of Tibetan monks' double-voiced chantings. Places where the ancestral memory comes up out of swamplands and riverbanks and hills of clay and flat delta black earth, carried along in the old songs and the sung prayers and the days of seeking, deep and alone in the piney backwoods.

I think about how Bernice and the Harambee Singers were doing those old-style songs. Stretching tones and words so you move yourself into another consciousness, a way to access some discernment and build up your strength.

So many of the young movement activists were filled with spirit. Sometimes not knowing what was right or wrong in a situation, they had to be quiet about it. Had to go somewhere and just meditate about it. Pray on it. And then sometimes they just had to take risks. Not knowing who would go to jail and who would not. Who would be beaten and who would not. They were taking great risks.

Dharamsala: The Lamas and the Movement

In Dharamsala, His Holiness the Dalai Lama told us stories that reminded me of these folks. I was there for a month in 1990, studying with people from all over the world, climbing up and down the hillsides of McLeod Ganj, day after day, to get the teachings. I sat among hundreds, with earphones to catch the translation of his words. The Dalai Lama talked from the Buddhist scriptures about monks and geshes who were constantly meditating—some who stayed secluded in cave hills and simple mountain shelters praying unceasingly for the well-being of the world. Others who kept up their devotions even as they went about taxing daily routines.

His Holiness was talking about people who were examples of the kind of life that most rewards us, a life that fulfills our role in the world, the life of broad compassion and concern for others that is the life we were meant to live in this body. I had my notebook out and when he would start talking like that I'd jot in the margins of the pages "Anne Braden" or "Mom and Dad." I thought of so many people I had known in the Movement, so many people who lived with the kind of active prayerfulness His Holiness described.

It was kind of funny, because he warned us, he said, "Now don't feel like you need to apply these scriptures to people that you know." But I thought to myself, *I can't speak for any of the other folks here, but I definitely know some people like those lamas and geshes*; people who catch the sufferings of others and have given their lives over to meditating and praying and working on behalf of healing, on behalf of peace, on behalf of the world. If they are not the same, they certainly have a lot in common.

Global Influence of the Movement

The teachings in Dharamsala helped me more clearly see the connectedness between a world spiritual tradition, like Buddhism, and the experiences of people I knew from my childhood community and from the movement days. But long before I got to India, I was beginning to understand the global impact of the freedom movement.

The first time I left the country was in 1964 when Vincent and I made a lecture tour to Europe on behalf of the Mennonite Central Committee. We traveled as representatives of the Mennonite Church and as spokespersons for the Movement. The American civil rights struggles were gaining tremendous international attention, as, almost daily, nonviolent challenges to segregation (and the often severely violent responses) were documented and broadcast around the world. We shared our stories and perspectives with communities in France, Switzerland, the Netherlands, Poland, and Czechoslovakia, speaking before church and civic groups, and sometimes at prisons and schools as well.

Beginning with that visit, wherever I have traveled outside this country, on every continent, I meet people who tell me how inspired they have been by the African American freedom struggle. Our movement affected people all over the world. We met Sandinistas in Nicaragua who told us they took Martin Luther King's book *Strength to Love* into the mountains with them as they organized to fight Somoza's U.S.-backed army. Vietnamese and Southern African friends who came to the United States in the seventies and eighties described how they took encouragement from the African American freedom struggle and told us how proud they were of what we had done to transform our country.

But just as some in our government feared the fundamental moral challenge the movement urged upon the nation, there were similar reactions in other parts of the world. Many Central and South American elites were desperate to keep progressive economic, political, and social transformations from happening within their borders. Throughout the sixties and seventies, violence and repression grew in Mexico, Brazil, Argentina, and elsewhere in the hemisphere—in attempts to keep those marginalized people (students, workers, women, Indigenous people, and people of African descent) from claiming democratic rights and insisting on more inclusive societies. I witnessed the effects of some of this on a visit to Brazil in 1980 with the American Friends Service Committee—five years before the end of the military dictatorship there. The universities had been closed, campuses deserted, and prisons were filled with political resisters. And among people working for change there—in both open and clandestine ways—many took inspiration from Martin, Malcolm, and our freedom movement in the United States.

Strength for the Journey: The Spirit and Struggle Retreats

In the early 1990s, Vincent and I organized a series of summer retreats for faith-based activists from African American communities around the country. Called "Spirit and Struggle" these weeklong intergenerational gatherings brought together older folks from the movement days and younger organizers working on a variety of racial- and gender-justice issues, prison reform, international solidarity movements, environmental justice, grassroots politics, and movement scholarship. It was such a rich combination with all kind of folks, including Michael Eric Dyson, Sister Souljah, Zoharah Simmons and her daughter Aishah, Prathia Hall, Mwalimu Imara, Art Jones, the Moses family, and about two dozen others.

We started each day with meditation and yoga. Massages and healthy food were available and we spent most of our sessions sharing the struggles, our turmoils and joys, and the deep internal places we go for strength in storm. Of course we sang a lot, and laughed a lot, and in the intimacy of the time and place there were plenty of angers and tears too. But those were extraordinary gatherings. Full of spirit—they gave us a chance to reflect on the twenty to twenty-five years we'd come through since the movement days; time to gather with the rising generation of organizers to get some sense, some wisdom, for the journeys ahead. And the biggest resource, I believe, was the rejuvenation we shared with one another, the acknowledgment of our individual and collective struggles and the inspiration to keep moving on.

We need to do that more often. People have been asking for it. The replenishment. The re-collection of who we are to each other and what our responsibility is in the world.

So many movement folk went searching. Looking for the healing spaces. We had to. To keep from being destroyed. To keep from going insane. There was so much stress—we were harassed, terrorized really. Not just by police and people like the Klan, but there were provocateurs inside our organizations. We saw and experienced so much violence—people beaten in the streets, in jail. The subtle torture of death threats and jobs lost; and nasty, startling phone calls in the middle of night. People we knew were murdered. Ralph Featherstone and Che Payne blown up by a car bomb meant for H. Rap Brown. Sammy Younge Jr., Jonathan Daniels, the Mississippi Summer workers. Ruby Doris Smith's death wasn't an accident either. There was so much grief in our anger. So much trauma. All of these things affected us.[3]

We had experienced something so precious, so extraordinary in our struggle. But we were tired too. Those were hard times. So many of us got weary. Anybody speaking out was under a lot of pressure. But we went on. People have gone on—those who are not dead. And the gatherings like "Spirit and Struggle" help us recall what we sometimes forget we know, about how to strengthen each other and how to rest and how to ask the ancestors and the Spirits for help.

Surveillance and Angels: An Occasion in El Salvador

At the last "Spirit and Struggle" retreat, in 1992, I told the story of an experience I had in El Salvador; it was something I didn't normally talk about; an experience that troubled me for many years. In 1984, Vincent and I organized a delegation to Nicaragua for Witness for Peace (WFP). Witness for Peace is a global, ecumenical Christian organization of nonviolent resistance to U.S. imperialist intervention. For several years in the 1980s, while our government was illegally supplying arms to the contras, WFP staff and volunteers maintained a presence in the capital, Managua, and in other cities of that beautiful Central American country. We were trying to both document and minimize the violence against Nicaraguan people through exerting the political pressure of our presence as North Americans. The delegation that Vincent and I led was primarily people of color and included students, activists, and religious leaders from around the United States.

Because ours was an unusually inclusive group, and because several in our delegation had been participants in the freedom movement, there was some added interest in our visit inside Nicaragua. We met with president Daniel Ortega and the minister of culture, Ernesto Cardenal; we visited hospitals caring for people wounded by U.S. artillery; and we traveled to towns that had been bombed. We talked with mothers in Jalapa whose children had been kidnapped and killed, and read a statement in front of the U.S. consulate condemning our government's support for the contras. We were the first WFP group to travel to the Atlantic coast of the country, to Bluefields, an area with a strong Afro-indigenous presence, and we spent time with religious and civic leaders there.

Shortly after we returned, Vincent was asked to go again as part of a special, smaller delegation. He had a schedule conflict, but suggested that I travel in his place. While he was on the phone talking to the delegation organizers, he attributed some provocative political statements to me. At the time, we both knew our phone was tapped, and we were generally careful about what we said by telephone. As Vincent spoke these things, I got a sick feeling in my stomach and something told me it would be a mistake to make that trip in his place.

The night before I left, I dreamed I was looking in a store window at a white lace wedding dress on a mannequin with no head. I wasn't sure what it meant, but the image was striking and I remembered it when I saw it again, in waking life, a day or two later.

There was a little girl on our plane who must have been about four or five years old; she was just the sweetest child you'd ever seen. Something about her smile was joyful and calming at once and she laughed and played in the aisle of the plane, walking up and down and looking at everybody with a sparkle in her eyes. For some reason, when she came to my row, she wouldn't move away from me. There was something absolutely beatific about this child's brown face, her smile. I was in the aisle seat and I played with her and talked to her until she had to go back to her row when the plane was about to land. Later, after everything else happened, I thought the little girl had been an angel. A sign of divine company.

We had a layover in El Salvador for what we were told would be a brief stop. But as we got off of the plane, heavily armed soldiers were patrolling the airport. All of the passengers found seats in the waiting area. I sat with the others in my group and looked around for the little girl and her parents, but didn't see them. Then, some of the soldiers approached me, saying that I should come with them, that they needed to ask me some questions. I was the only person in my group singled out in this way and while I didn't know how to respond, I knew that I didn't want to go anywhere with these men carrying automatic weapons, and wearing helmets and heavy boots in the airport. At the time, the country was run by a vicious military dictatorship. Our plane wasn't supposed to have stopped long, and we had been warned to be circumspect about our conversations and comportment in San Salvador.

But now it wasn't at all clear what was happening and how long we would have to wait to continue on to Nicaragua. The whole thing felt eerie. I understood a little Spanish, enough to know the soldiers were telling me to get up and follow them. They were insistent. My two traveling companions tried to intervene, but neither of them spoke the language well enough to be of much help. Fortunately, as the situation began to attract the notice of others in the waiting room, a young white woman came over and sat next to me. She was from the United States but she spoke Spanish well. She spoke firmly to the soldiers, demanding that they not remove me from the group and saying that if they did, she, too, would go wherever they took me.

I didn't know her. I had seen her on the airplane and maybe I smiled at her or spoke a word of greeting, but I didn't know her. Later, she introduced herself to me and I found out that her father, William McLoughlin, was a professor at Brown University, where my daughter was in school. The young lady stayed with me until the military men eventually left me alone. The next leg of our flight was canceled until the following day. Our small group was put in a van and taken to a hotel in the city. We were nervous and didn't talk much on the ride. The military presence was obvious as we drove through town and the feeling was tense and uncomfortable. At the entrance to the hotel were a few shops. Fancy little stores with picture windows.

It was growing late when we checked in and we hadn't eaten much all day. So after getting our room assignments we went into the hotel restaurant and sat down to order. We were the only guests there. We ordered our meals and after about fifteen minutes the plates of my traveling companions arrived. They waited a little while, politely, but my dinner was late, so they started eating. My dinner was very late. And when it finally arrived, more than a half hour later, it looked to me as if there was a shiny film on my food. I noticed it, but hunger dampened my suspicion and I took a bite. Immediately, I had the feeling that I shouldn't eat anymore from that plate. I set my utensils down and within a few minutes I was feeling ill, very nauseous and sweaty. I excused myself to go up to my room and as I passed the stores again, in one of the windows, I noticed the wedding dress from my dream. I wasn't sure what it meant, but I took it as both a warning and a sign of protection.

I was very sick. In the room, I vomited over and over again and was sweating so profusely my clothes were soaked. I was frightened and anxious and sicker than I had ever been in my life. I thought I might die. But I didn't tell anyone for fear they would come and take me to a hospital and I was even more worried about what might happen there with no one around to protect me. I was almost delirious with pain and retching. Somehow I knew not to eat anything at all and to drink only the smallest amount of water. And to pray. All night long, I was in such horrible discomfort I couldn't have slept anyway, I prayed. When the morning came I had just enough energy to get down to the van before it left for the airport again.

I was weak for several days, and after that first night, I took only bottled water until I felt better. In years since, I've wondered if the strangeness of my present illness—the rare complications of diabetes, these odd, inexplicable pains throughout my body—might be somehow related to what happened in that hotel in El Salvador.

. . .

There was another experience, a year or two later, in an airport here in the states (Rachel was with me and she remembers), when a man with a briefcase came up beside me as I stood in a boarding line and for a brief second I felt as if I had been stuck with a pin or a needle in my hip. I turned around to see what was going on, but the man was walking away, and at the time, I didn't think it was anything except maybe a stray sharp point from his case.

These were difficult times. We had been under surveillance since the sixties. The Institute of the Black World was ransacked by the FBI and our phones were tapped. Like a lot of other movement people, Vincent sometimes got letters and calls from white supremacists threatening to harm him, or me and the children. I preferred to throw those letters away immediately, but he saved them. I was accustomed to speaking my mind equally about both the potentials and the problems we faced as a nation. And in my public life—when Vincent and I spoke and wrote and lectured together, I still said what I felt moved to say. But after the experience in El Salvador I was more cautious.

Sometimes now, on a plane, or in other places, someone will ask me, out of the clear blue sky, what teas do I drink? What kind of herbs am I taking? As if to say, *how is it that you have survived all of this? What are you doing?* As if I should be dead by now.

Notes

1. C. T Vivian interview with the Gandhi Hamer King Center (Veterans of Hope Project), 1998, unpublished.

2. "Bernice Johnson Reagon: The Singing Warrior," Veterans of Hope Pamphlet Series 1, no. 1 (Denver: VOHP, 2000): 11–12.

3. Ralph Featherstone, William "Che" Payne, Sammy Younge Jr., Jonathan Daniels, and Ruby Doris Smith were all organizers in the Movement whose deaths were related (directly or indirectly) to their activism.

IV · The Dharamsala Notebook

32 · Sunrise after Delhi
(poem)

through mist
like so much snow haze
sloping over growing things
over fields
over telephone poles
and wires of early morning announcements

long rays hiding among white
gas tanks
running train tracks
covering colored land
like a mother
blanketing her growing children
close
chasing the chill
out of a multitude of voices

I Returned to Delhi by Bus

I returned to Delhi by bus, a trip I had been warned against taking. Sometimes, in the absence of railings and strong brakes, buses fall off the hillsides as they descend through the steep and stunning Himalayas. And even when they stay firmly on the road, the views can make the ride harrowing. But I didn't want to go back by train. I had come to Dharamsala that way a month earlier. Traveling with an Asian American friend and her family who had invited me to join them for meditation and study with the Tibetan Buddhist lamas based in this northern Indian town, the capital-in-exile of the Tibetan nation. Dharamsala is the headquarters of the Dalai Lama and the base from which he offers periodic teachings to local people and pilgrims from all over the world.

I had been in the city for over a month and was now making my way back home. I would go to Delhi for a short stay and then return to the United States, via London. On the trip up to Dharamsala from Delhi, the train passed through a region where there were palpable religious tensions. As we waited at a depot to collect and discharge passengers, even as we sat in our seats, we could feel the strain of conflict in the searching glances that reached us through the windows, and in the faces of those newly boarded. Also, I felt there was a greater risk of robbery on the trains—as people who traveled that way were generally more well-to-do than those who traveled by bus.

Mostly, I wanted to feel safe. I am a Black woman from the United States, but in India, I look Indian. I was traveling unaccompanied now because my friends had left some days earlier, and I was concerned that there could be a misunderstanding about my identity in a place where such a mistake might be costly.

Already in Dharamsala I had many experiences of people assuming I was Indian. I was flattered and happy that I could walk around without a stark sense of my physical distinctness from others around me. On some occasions, however, the assumption had more complicated consequences. Once, I stopped in a restaurant to order some pastries to take out. (Dharamsala, with its mixture of Tibetan and Indian gastronomies and the influence of many international visitors, has some of the best food I've ever tasted.) This particular eatery was a place I had visited once or twice before, always with white, English-speaking friends who were, like me, studying with the lamas during the special session. I recognized the owner of the shop from my earlier visits, and I am pretty certain he also remembered me. This time, however, I had come alone and when I asked him for the sweet rolls I wanted, he began speaking to me in Hindi, in a disdainful and increasingly agitated manner. I wasn't sure what he was saying, but I could tell he was upset with me for some reason. As I was gathering up my purchases to leave, someone who had been watching the exchange approached me and explained that the restaurant owner was accusing me of putting on airs, trying to pretend I wasn't Indian. He didn't know. I would have considered it an honor.

. . .

On the bus ride back from Dharamsala, I sat in the first seat by the door, across from the driver. I chose that seat because it was in plain view of everything. I could see the driver as well as all the people as they entered and left the bus in a beautiful array of colors throughout the fourteen-hour ride. Also, I had a clear view of the elaborate altar in the front window, and I watched the driver make simple gestures of genuflection each time we stopped and each time we started again. He was burning incense so that an earthy piquant smoke drifted around the entrance and down into the first rows of the bus. As the passengers boarded in Dharamsala, a young white man took the seat next to mine, and that was fine with me. I didn't want to sit by myself; and later, as we traveled and the young man fell asleep on my shoulder, I didn't mind people presuming that we were together.

The altar was just above the driver's head, in the upper part of the large glass pane. He had decorated it with all kinds of ribbons and gorgeous beads. There were pictures of deities and banners of different colors. I asked two nuns sitting behind me if they knew the meaning of the altar and one of them said she thought it was for protection. *That's a good thing,* I said to myself, thinking about all I had been told of the treacherous turns of the mountain roads.

I was fascinated to watch people as they arrived, selected and settled into seats on the bus. One woman who got on—if she didn't remind me of some of my relatives . . . She was one of the earliest to board. She was traveling with younger family members, maybe a daughter and granddaughter. The older woman got on first, and loudly; quickly scouting out seats for her people and having animated conversations about where to place luggage and other things they carried. I *liked* her. She was claiming her space with a boisterous voice and a pushy presence and making sure that everybody in her little group was comfortable. She had an aisle seat across from her relatives so she could more easily maneuver to scan the surroundings and stretch her legs and feet when she wanted. At one point, the seat immediately next to her was empty and a young Indian man indicated that he wanted to take it. He spoke to the older woman and I don't know what he said, but she responded in such a quiet and sweet voice. She didn't even look at him directly, but lowered her head and eased to the side to let the young man take the seat. Just a second ago she had been raucously dominating the spot where she and her family sat. But the moment the young man appeared, she became a different person. Demure, quiet. He hadn't spoken roughly at all, and he was young enough to be her son. But it seemed to me that the change in her composure was about the place of women. And the older woman knew that place. And played the part.

The young man, of course, wasn't noticing anything in particular about the scene he was an integral part of. Not the way I was noticing. He was just being a courteous person, announcing his desire to take an available seat. The important thing to me was that I observed it, this sudden and complete change in the woman.

The bus stopped many times along the way, picking up passengers, and letting people off to buy food and use the bathroom. There were some steel-nerve moments on that ride. Especially when another bus or truck was speeding toward us from the opposite direction. The road wasn't wide. Our bus was on the inside lane around the mountain, so there wasn't so much danger of falling off the steep side, but sometimes I just wouldn't look. We rode through the night. The seats were hard, and the ride was dusty, but I was glad to be going back safely and I didn't care about the small discomforts.

It was dark as we rode, so we couldn't see much of the terrain, but the women were beautiful in their saris. Flowing colors, wispy silks and cottons, and the jangle of their jewelry. Their traveling clothes were lovely. Everyone was courteous and nice to each other. People smiled at me and said things in kind voices in Hindi that I didn't understand. But I smiled back and nodded politely. Halfway through the trip two families got on and the women sat just behind me. After overhearing me speak to my white seat companion, they asked, in English, if he was my husband and what part of India I was from.

Dharamsala

In Dharamsala, I see very dark-skinned people living among the Tibetans. Some are well dressed. Others are begging. Most of the beggars I see are dark-skinned. Some, I think, are Dalits, descendants of India's oldest indigenous inhabitants. I see, too, perhaps an illusion of darkness—a light-skinned woman rubbing dirt on her child's legs and arms, on her own face. I'm not sure why. It reminds me of a dream I had of nine Indians walking down into the depths of the earth, covered with gray/ash/earth/dirt. They were envoys for all the world's people.

I arrive in Dharamsala on a train, from Delhi, in early March 1990. With the Champan family—friends who are Asian American Buddhists.[1] Delia is an engineer; we are traveling with her mother and oldest son. I had met Delia a few years before through other friends. When she discovered my interest in Buddhism, she invited me to join her family on this trip. I needed to come and was happy for the invitation.

People are kind. When I am settled I will wash my clothes. I thank God for everything. For Delia and her family, for a safe trip, and for the care we receive as travelers. At the hotel in McLeod Ganj, the old colonial outpost town adjacent to Dharamsala, I am given a nice room on the first night and later told I will have to move to a less desirable one. I am grateful for a hot shower and a clean bathroom for this evening. But I wonder about the move. Something similar happens in Delhi at the end of the trip where I stay for a few days before flying back home. You don't always know if the inconvenience is legitimate. Sometimes it is. But I have lived my whole life as a woman with dark brown skin and I know people sometimes make choices based on the assumption that we who are dark can be treated with less regard, less care.

Coming into town from the train station, our group shared taxis with a German young lady who plans to take me shopping in a few days. She is adventurous and seems to know a great deal about the area, has been to India many times, and knows what to do and not. She feels my color makes things easier for me here. In some ways she may be right. Now, however, I work to refuse a sense of despair and suspicion. At this moment, a young man is cleaning the second room very well for me. He is kind and helpful. I am grateful to him.

. . .

Bob Marley is everywhere. A restaurant run by two Tibetan monks serves delicious vegetarian meals that don't cost much. And they play reggae all the time. I listen to "One Love," "Africa Unite," and "So Much Trouble in the World" over the loudspeakers up in these Himalayan hills, paired with delightful savory dumplings; and I think of the ways different places and cultures vibrate their wisdoms. How they share what they know about strength and survival.

Dharamsala is at the meeting of breathtaking mountains and fertile valleys with Tibetan and Indian flavors and languages crisscrossing like the streams and hills of the landscape. The town sits in the foothills of the Dhauladhar, or "White Ridge," range of the Himalayas. It's one of those places in the world that pulses a strong spiritual energy of compassion and healing. You can feel it in the air, an energy cultivated for so many generations that it is now part of the soil. The city attracts people who need what is here. And it resonates with people who can help replenish and revitalize that spirit as well. I came to Dharamsala looking for help and I am receiving it. Space, study, clarity, thinking about my own faults, my family's patience and generosity. The goodness of God. The chants, the city, my friends, the teachings are all doing me good.

I have my list of prayers. My children, Vincent, other relatives, friends. The Italian woman, the German girl. Delia and her family. Some here who are sick—maybe from the altitude or something they ate. Colds. Coughs. Fever. Or it may be the adjustment inside their bodies, their spirits.

There are so many fascinating people in this place. The monks and nuns who have traveled from all over the world to study. Maria from Malaysia born on the Chinese mainland. Paul, an engineer from Rochester, taking a year off work to travel. He lends me a book he is raving about, *The City of Joy*. Charlotte from Denmark who remarks about my braids, "This must have taken ages." Ann, a wonderful acupuncturist from Vancouver who arrives the day after the teachings begin. My new nun friends Nai Jin and Tan Den. So many people coming for the teachings. Finding space. Making connections. The nuns belong to a Taiwanese and Chinese order. They say they will show me the library and the Tibetan medical center the next time we are out. They are staying at the guesthouse with me and I have questions for them: *Where can I learn the Tibetan language? I know some things about traditional healing from my parents, and from books—how would one go about studying elementary Tibetan healing traditions, in English, here? Where can I cash traveler's checks?* I want to buy soap and a bucket to wash the door of my room, the mirror, clothes. I need a cloth to hang up to the window.

I speak to the owners of the guesthouse about putting a cloth to the window of my room. They say *yes*, but maybe mean *no*. I put up a blanket.

Rain came today. On wind like a chinook, knocking away anything unsecured in its path—everyone runs for cover. The city is filling up for the teachings. Rooms are more and more scarce. There is an elderly man willing to sleep outside my bedroom, in the open, no enclosure. They are offering him a bed and a blanket for protection from the rain; it won't help much with the cold. There is a charge for hot showers and toilets. A roll of toilet paper costs the equivalent of a dollar and doesn't last long.

The Tibetan Teachings

Oh, the monks are beautiful! Nothing is pretentious at all. You don't have to sit with your back straight. The monks don't even sit that way. They sit in whatever way makes them comfortable. The whole atmosphere is relaxed. They have their rituals, but they laugh at themselves too. That's what I really like about it all. No, there isn't any special aura about the place. It is beautiful and ordinary and dusty too. And the monks are just so kind! They serve tea and little snacks during the breaks in the lectures. They make sure everybody is taken care of.

The teachings always begin with chanting—beautiful sonorous prayers. We arrive early at the Gompa, the temple, and sit on cushions on the floor of the main gathering room. There will be more than five hundred people here. The monks give us a sheet of paper with the words so we can follow along. If you lose yours or leave it back at your room, you can just listen. The Dalai Lama gives his lectures in Tibetan. I have a notebook and a pen and headphones through which I listen to the translation. I am writing quickly. Abbreviating and condensing as I try to get down as much as I can. I want to read and reread and think about these things later on. The wisdom gives me a sense of joy—I see Mama and Bawa and Bob and Grace—so many of my teachers are in these words. I am trying to take it all in.

It takes time to discipline our minds—so be patient and don't become depressed. If not in this lifetime, then in the next and next. Do not expect a lot to happen in a short time. Keep making the effort. We have mental tension when we expect too much.

Start slow and moderately in your practice because our minds are not yet disciplined.[2]

The temple where the Dalai Lama gives his annual spring lectures is up the side of a mountain. We have to walk a ways from where we are staying in little hotels and guesthouses farther down. His Holiness speaks in the mornings, and in the afternoons we go back down the mountain to classrooms and to the library and archives. Some people prefer, after hearing the lectures, to just sit quietly in the library and read. But I really want the discussions; I want to make sure I understand.

It is through other sentient beings, through help, that we are able to survive. All we have, all we use, all we are, is because of the sacrifices of other sentient beings. All sentient beings have become our mothers, fathers, friends. Only practice generosity in relationship to other sentient beings. Good personality comes from practicing patience and tolerance and can only be developed in relationship to other sentient beings.

Do not rely on expectations and hope, but on practice, practice, practice. Pray for all sentient beings. Give, share, help—and supplement your giving with ardent prayer.

In the margins of my notes, I write "Clarence and Florence [Jordan]." They believed and lived this with so much integrity. Faith and works. The teachings remind me, too, of Bob Moses and his decades of study and practice with Paramahansa Yogananda's Self-Realization Fellowship. Bob says it's possible to live a life, a full life, in struggle for what is right and humane. Meditation and spiritual study give that life of struggle direction and meaning.

One chooses what practice and what method is appropriate to serve other sentient beings. Choose a practice that will help train and discipline the mind, stop non-meritorious actions, start reciting prayers. Find time to meditate on the teaching, start with a small scope and increase one's practice.

Vincent was teaching at Swarthmore College from 1985 to 1987 and I was working in the Dean's Office as a special counselor. I had only recently begun to do Vipassana meditation, to study it, although I had a long-standing interest in Buddhism and other contemplative traditions. At Swarthmore, I met Don Swearer, a professor of Buddhism who gave me books and told me about the Vipassana Retreat Center in Shelburne, Massachusetts. I went twice. The first time, Rachel and I went together for a ten-day silent retreat. It helped me so much that I turned around and went right back to do another one. It was a difficult time at home—my husband had new confessions. The meditation helped me pass the traumas through my body, not hold on to them. There was something very healing in the stillness. In the guru Goenka's instruction. Vipassana was not my first experience with Buddhism, but it was my most intensive. Years before, Vincent and I had met the venerable monk and teacher Thich Nhat Hanh when he came to Atlanta to talk with Martin and others during the Movement. He spoke at Canterbury House, the Episcopal student center on the Atlanta University campus, about the affinity between the nonviolent spirit of the Southern Freedom Movement and Buddhism in the resistance movement in his native Vietnam.

> *Everyone is under the spell of delusion. Tibetans are concentrating on the inner development—these experiences that are beyond understanding. The good nature, the heart of the Tibetan people is in keeping with Buddhist teaching.*
>
> *We are trying to stand up from the place where we have fallen. All religious traditions teach to take care of people. Buddhism also teaches to care for all sentient beings, for clean water, air, and all of the environment. Buddhist teachings are for the rights for all human beings—education, human rights. Even if we do not have schools, we have elders as teachers, we have their examples.*
>
> *Others may think they are above the Tibetan people, may call them names to mean lesser people, but Tibetans are educated by their elders, by the example of their compassion, by their lives.*

We who are visiting from other countries exchange addresses and information outside of the classes. Recommending things to read, music to listen to. I am learning to say greetings in Tibetan. A woman from Hertfordshire, England, discovers that I am from Colorado and asks me if I would contact a family in Grand Junction with whom she lived as an exchange student twenty years earlier. "They took me on holiday. They even bought me a graduation gift. I never properly thanked them," she said. I told her I would take their names and try to pass along her message.

There are books I want to purchase, *The Essence of Nectar* and *The Yoga of Tibet*. A cloth for the table in my room. Gifts for the family, for friends. Some earrings, silk scarves. Also memory pills, a mandala, and more chants.

There are people in the street selling wares, offering services. I take a pair of my shoes to a shoe repairman who has set up shop along one of the streets I pass daily between the guesthouse and the teachings. The man fixes the shoes for me while I stand aside and wait. Then he tells me what it costs.

A young monk is nearby watching. He hears the shoe repairman announcing the charge for the work, and he objects. "That's too much," the monk tells the man "You are charging her a very high rate." I don't know what they are saying at first. They speak to each other in Tibetan. After they exchange a few words, the shoe repairman gives me a new, lower price.

Thupten is a young monk from the Sermey Monastery in Mysore, in southern India. We met on the street in Dharamsala, just like that. He was visiting the city and participating in the lessons as part of his studies to become a geshe, a scholar trained in the Tibetan Buddhist monastic tradition. He was born in Tibet but his mother died when he was a boy and he has been living in India as a refugee. I paid for my shoes and we had tea together at a restaurant nearby. I would see Thupten often as I walked to the temple; his room in the monastery was near the road. Slowly, we adopted each other—having tea and conversations about the Buddhist teachings. Thupten looked out for me while I was in Dharamsala, like a son. Before I left, I told him I would be honored to be another mother to him.

> Understand the qualities of a spiritual master. It is important to distinguish between a spiritual friend and a spiritual master. Masters should have more qualities than faults. Disciples also need qualities—impartiality, intelligence and strong effort. They must have a sense of discrimination and not simply be a good person. Be able to listen. Be able to understand the teacher's faults. The relationship between a disciple and a teacher must include faith in the teacher—it must be an emotional relationship as well as intellectual. It is very important that the disciple wait until she or he feels comfortable with the teacher. Before accepting someone as a spiritual master, accept him or her as a spiritual friend. Take your time.

In the small group sessions, nuns and geshes respond to our questions. An American young lady asks why there aren't more women in leadership. The geshe answers her, saying that the leadership of men has been a tradition among Tibetans, but that people are becoming more open to women serving as religious and political leaders now. Especially since the revolution, since the Chinese took over their land and destroyed many of the temples, women are naturally taking leadership roles because there is such a need and many of the men have been imprisoned or worse.

Sometimes in the afternoon sessions a teacher will give additional lectures. Lama Zopa Rinpoche is one of those gurus and his talks span many days, even after the Dalai Lama's lectures are formally over. Someone tells me, "You never know how long Lama Zopa's lectures will last—how many days or weeks. With Lama Zopa you can never say, *Okay, you're going to get a lecture for a week.* No, you get a lecture for as long as he feels that there is something he needs to say." This time, his talks last two weeks.

> *We can examine our own conduct. We can know what will become of us in the next life. We do not need clairvoyance. The joy we have, depends on the amount of compassion we have for others.*

We took refuge one evening, until after midnight, in the Gompa room at the Tushita temple. Lama Zopa offered the ceremony for any of the students who wanted to participate. There were about thirty of us from around the world. A nun responded to our questions first: why the prostrations, why the mantras? Some she could answer, some she couldn't. Lama Zopa Rinpoche gave blessings to everyone who desired them. Staying late and long, as long as he felt the need was there. He seemed tired by the end. But was still pleasant, still sensitive.

> *Meditation sterilizes the imprint of delusion. If I don't get angry today there is less imprint. My mind is easier to control in the future.*
> *The mind is like a child, a baby. It needs discipline, encouragement, guidance and subduing. Buddhism has a great effect.*

I remember Lama Zopa telling us a story about a man who made up his own chants. Well, the man tried to do the regular chants, but he didn't understand them, and he didn't know which chants were meant to be said on which days, so he ended up creating something, really of his own. I mean, it seemed arbitrary and foolish what this man was doing. But the beautiful thing about it was that what the man made up, what looked to us like he created on his own, was acceptable to the Buddha. And the man did good work, good spiritual work because he was sincere about it. That was something. Being in the presence of the lamas and studying with them makes this very clear: the *holy* is not something that one or two people can claim as their own. It takes many forms.

> *There is one Source and many Buddhas. One Source and many Gurus.*

When the lectures are over, the monks have a farewell ceremony for all who came to study and meditate with them. They bring out treats and goodies they have prepared and pass around trays, offering something to everyone. Lama Zopa gives everybody ten dollars. In case you need food, in case you need something—it is symbolic, but it is lovely to see. I don't know how many hundreds of us are here. But he gives something to everyone. And then we are invited to stay and have a final meal together. A few of us even come back for an evening meditation and lecture after the meal. I have befriended seven women. We walk together to and from most of the teachings. So I am never alone.

Meeting the Dalai Lama

The Dalai Lama makes time to see anyone who wants to see him; anyone can receive his blessing, his counsel. I actually see him twice. Once I meet him privately with a small group of American Buddhists and another time I get in the line for a public audience and just go up there on my own. When I see His Holiness with the Americans, he has such a kind and unassuming spirit. An older Asian American couple asks what he thinks about the future of relations between China and Tibet. And the Dalai Lama answers mindfully, trying to get at the heart of things. He says—and these are my words now—he says that as human beings, we have a need for spirituality. We have an inner urging—it's the way the world is constructed—to interact with God and to find a peace in our interactions with God. He says unless communism is going to allow for something that connects people to spirit, there will always be a need. He thinks the Chinese people themselves are going to turn things around in China. What I think he means is that the change won't necessarily come from outside of China.

Then there is a third time I try to see the Dalai Lama. I am escorting a friend, a woman staying at my hotel who has recently arrived and who has not seen him yet. I take her down to his office to get tickets to see him, because the monks say that anybody who has not seen him should come for these special tickets. So I take her, and I ask for another ticket for myself, so that I can join her. But the man in the office knows me, because I am the only one there who looks like me.

"Haven't you seen him enough?" He speaks with a tone between query and reprimand. "You don't need to see him again. Let somebody else who hasn't seen him go." It is true, because the Dalai Lama has so many people to see. And he sees EV-ERY-BOD-Y who wants to be seen. And there isn't anything you can't ask him. Not only will he have a sense of who you are and what you need, but he'll do his best to help. I don't have anything specific I want to ask. It is just a blessing to be in his presence.

I saw him again when he came to Boulder, to the Naropa Institute, some years later. Vincent was speaking to the audience as the Dalai Lama came into the hall. Vincent had everybody singing a freedom song and they were just finishing when the Dalai Lama was ushered in. His Holiness said he was moved by what he heard. He said he couldn't understand what they were saying, but he was moved. And I *think* he nodded at me and recognized me.

Well, I'm not going to be so presumptuous as to say that. But there weren't a lot of other Black people in Dharamsala when I was there. In fact, if there were *two* that was a lot. I saw one other lady, but she was not at the lectures and meditation places like I was. Maybe she was just visiting as a tourist. And there was a beautiful Black man who looked like an African prince; he was all in white, very regal and handsome. I wondered how he kept his long clothes so spotless in the rain and dust of the city. But I think I was the only Black person from the United States at that time. I had also met the Dalai Lama at a conference in Costa Rica so perhaps he did recognize me in Boulder. Then again, he's a very polite man and maybe he greets everyone that way. He smiled and bowed a little when he passed me as he came into the hall at Naropa. But I was so shy, I hardly looked up. But I felt the good. I have to say that. For weeks after I saw him I felt better. My pain eased. The man just has a beautiful spirit. He just has it. And it touches us. He didn't get it by accident. You just have to work at it. Work and discipline—I think that's what he was trying to tell us. That you work very hard at living and very hard at being humane. That is the gift of our lives.

> We learn from our discomforts, from pain. Never quit.
> Never give up; persist like water flowing into the ocean.

Note

1. Delia Champan is a pseudonym. I have changed her name to protect her privacy. —REH.

2. This extract, and all extracts that follow in this chapter, are taken from notes on the lectures of His Holiness the Dalai Lama and Lama Zopa Rinpoche, Dharamsala, India, March–April 1990.

Wherever We Stand in the Mandala Is East

These are the notes that came with prayers and wanderings in the hill town, and what I remembered of Mama Freeney as the lamas spoke:

    I. A clean meditation room clears distraction.

       Bowls of water
       Scented for the guru's heart
       Saffroned for joy

       Dedicate merit to all sentient beings. Devils as well as Angels.
       Whatever merit I have may sentient beings have.
       Whatever sufferings, may I experience alone.

    II. The Devils and the Hell-Cats liked Mama. They came in the store. Some of them lived in the house. She fed them, protected them, kept the fighting down, made pallets on the floor, served fine china tea and pound cake. Listened to their sorrows. Cussed them straight out. She blessed their children. Made their fires rage less wild.

    III. *Remember people's kindnesses so that you will not see them as bad. See the good, the greatness, the kindness in others. The Buddha's instruction is to have compassion for all sentient beings—feed the hungry, give water to those who thirst, heal the sick. Take care of each other. This is the Dharma. Discipline your mind and show the right path to all sentient beings.*[1]

IV. Buddha has a response to every question. Mama can say one thing that will answer even the questions you have not yet asked.

Buddha mind is omniscient—has equal compassion for all human beings. Mama, birthed sixteen, raised nine. Made milk in her seventy-year-old breasts for twin great grandsons. Said, "I love all my children."

She would send us out into the city, downtown to do business, pay bills, buy better food, visit family across town. If we hesitated, fearing that we would not find the way, she'd say, "Girl, you mean to tell me that this Chicago is bigger than your mind?"

His Holiness said we are always fearful at the time of death. It's a natural thing. A sign we have died before. Aunt Mary fought death with her fists, the square-toed messenger, wrestled him down in a corner so he sat and waited. Came back another day.

Mom must have been a great teacher in a past life.

V. *Medicine benefits you and destroys disease. Similarly, what a person does to harm your ego is really a benefit to you. So this person who hurts your feelings, your greed, your desire, is not really harming you. In fact she or he is benefiting you in destroying your desire and self-importance. Buddhist teaching is to remedy and cease desire and attachment, the source of all the problems.*

Do not see anyone as an enemy. See every person as a friend. A kind friend, a best friend, someone who makes clear your shortcomings—like X-rays—so that you can see what needs to be done.

A person who is always praising, giving you smiles, increases your desire. This does not help to develop our mind.

VI. Red stones are blood strengtheners.

Apache Tears strengthen the chakras.

Trace a figure eight with crystals over the body;
this is good for the energy.

Any pendulum will work,
but Apache Tears works best.

Clean the pendulum when you finish,
dip into water and throw the water away.

VII. *The greatest enemy is the inner enemy. The enemy of disturbing thoughts. The enemy of an angry mind, an angry heart. Anger gives many reasons to do harm. We become violent from pain in the heart.*

Try to live without anger. It becomes easier all the time. One year becomes three years becomes six years. See anger as the mind creating delusion. Think of clear light. Try. Try to live without anger. The mind can be trained this way.

VIII. Mama would go sit with the ones who were leaving here. Keep them company. Take food and stories and family and silence, so they could remember something beautiful in their final hours.

Death is not the end of everything. What comes after death is just as important as what comes before. Practice Dharma to leave a strong imprint of positiveness at death.

Knowing too how to make the separation: The last conversation. The last morsel of food. One has to separate completely.

When Daddy died, Mama sat at the side of his bed and he asked her if she would go with him. She whispered to him, "No, fool! Are you crazy?" She was kissing him and crying and holding his hand. She told him no. Everybody tried to make him as comfortable as possible when he passed. But he had to go alone. They were waiting on the other side—Mama Catherine and them—Daddy's people. My mama knew that.

(In my father's house are many rooms. I go to prepare a place, that where I am there you may be.) Buddha went ahead to discover what is real. Mama brought reality into our home, gave us an example and sent us into the world to practice.

IX. *Our mothers have been especially kind to us in this life—they gave us space in their wombs and love us despite the pain we cause them. See all human beings as one's own mother—because we have all been each other's mothers. When we serve others, see them as our mothers. Serve them as we would serve our mothers. See their suffering and take it to heart. Recall all the qualities of kindness our mothers have shown us—the sacrifices of pain, of thirst, of hunger, of labor, of going-without.*

Then project this love and compassion to others. There is no love more precious than that of a mother.

What we are now we owe to our parents, to those who have loved and cared for us. Without love and affection we would not be who we are now. How kind sentient beings have been to us! We have to do something to repay the kindness. This is the attitude with which to seek enlightenment. Enlightenment is for the sake of all sentient beings.

x. White light, a light like pearled water, cleanses all impurities, the lamas say. It is clarity with no duality. A brightness that does not blind. Whenever any of my family travels, or if friends are passing through pains and struggles, I imagine them covered in a soft and shining white light. The energy of shelter. It is what I remember from the room. What entered and stayed with me all those years.

XI. *In human beings, positive qualities are stronger than negative qualities. More dominant. Love is more dominant than anger in all of us. We have an instinct toward the positive. Our survival depends on love and compassion in humans. This is because our natural tendency is to want happiness rather than suffering. We survive only through our dependence on each other.*

XII. *Show your heart completely to sentient beings.*

Note

1. This passage and all italicized passages in this chapter are quoted in Rosemarie's journals from the lectures of His Holiness the Dalai Lama and Lama Zopa Rinpoche, Dharamsala, India, March–April 1990.

v · Bunting

: a seed-eating songbird
: flag cloth; streamers for decoration
: a warm, protective wrapping

(Rose's Memory)

I was sitting in the waiting room of the diabetes and metabolism section of Brigham and Women's Hospital, in a wheelchair. My daughter was sitting next to me. I don't remember anyone else in the waiting room. Maybe there was a couple, or was it a woman by herself, along the window side of the room? I don't remember.

I was not in a good mood.

I didn't see him come from around the corner of the tall desk. I didn't see him stop for a moment and pass a word with the attendant there and then pick up a folder. My daughter told me later: for a second, it looked like he was going to go straight to one of the consultation rooms in the other direction. Only for a second. Then, he must have seen me. Slumped over in that wheelchair in so much pain that I was furious. But with no energy to express it. He came over and put his arm around my shoulder.

(Rachel's Memory)

We were sitting in the waiting room of the diabetes and metabolism section of Brigham and Women's hospital. It was a cool September day, and bright. My mother was in a wheelchair, slumped over, her mouth and eyes cast down, shut up close and tight. She was tired of the pain. Angry-tired. I sat next to her, watching the people I had just spoken to behind the high reception desk. The room was nothing special, seawater green paint on the walls and the square columns that supported the ceiling. It all looked regulation. And, if not depressing, at least not very inspiring. We were a little late.

My mother was still slumped when the doctor came from around the corner of the desk. He came directly over to us and put his arm around her shoulder. He looked at me briefly, nodded, and said something gently to my mother—some word of encouragement that I can't recall now. He stayed for a while, noticing her distress and speaking kindly to her. Then he went down the hall.

I wasn't sure it was genuine. "A doctor?" We had been through a lot of doctors. Probably thirty by that time (when we left Boston, the count of physicians, health practitioners, and therapists my mom had seen in a year topped fifty). And although some did their best to help us, most were just overworked and desensitized by the assembly line atmospherics in the hospitals and clinics where they worked. So, to have a doctor—one who had not even met us yet, clearly had not even opened the folder with the basic patient information forms—respond so immediately and emotionally to our misery, seemed just a bit . . . staged.

Later, when we were down the hall in the little exam room, the same man came in to see us and introduced himself.

(Rose's Memory)

In the little room he took my hand while he talked to me. All of my bones ached and my blood felt like the sharp tips of pins inside my veins. He moved carefully as he listened to my heart and felt my pulse and looked into my eyes with his pinpoint light. Not too much else. But I remember he rubbed my back when he talked and he never stopped holding my hand the whole time.

(Rachel's Memory)

I don't know how you do that. How do you give an examination and never let go of the patient's hand? Dr. Arky's voice was calm, assuring, and respectful. He called my mom, "Mrs. Harding" when he was talking to her, and "Mother" when he was talking about her to me. He asked us a few questions about her medicines and how much insulin she was taking. But mostly he seemed to want to comfort us, taking account of Mom's troubles, wanting to do nothing that might increase her worry or her pain.

"Let's just see if we can take care of the pain and get some more weight on you for now," Arky told Mom. "We won't bother about the diabetes control so much right now. You have to eat and gain weight to get better. Eat whatever you want. Just eat." Later, on the telephone, he told me: "This condition that Mother has . . . it's very rare. I've been practicing a long time and I have only seen it once or twice. Usually it lasts a few months and then goes away. The patient loses a lot of weight, the pain is severe and we don't know exactly where it comes from. The most you can do is try to control the pain. Either the patient gets well, or . . . sometimes they die."

(Rose's Memory)

The way out is a long way around. I am still hurting. My face, my arms, my legs. I can barely speak from pain. My baby is pushing me in the wheelchair along the narrow hallways of this building. Every time we move from one part to another, there is a small incline, with, it must be, ridges. We go either up or down. Pushing. I offer to get out and walk. But my daughter knows I am still hurting. She moves slow, tries to ease down the ramp, holding the handles of the chair tight to make the ride a little smoother. But I feel the bumps anyway. I'm not saying anything though. It hurts to think.

(Rachel's Memory)

I help Mama into the car. It's a little Hyundai, from before Hyundais got a makeover. We bought it at a car repair shop, and the front tires go flat every couple of days. I got them fixed and they still go flat. Almost every time we go out I have to stop at the gas station down the street and pump some air. We drive back over the bridge. I need to get a pillow or something for Mom to sit on. This car doesn't have good shocks.

We are living in Cambridge, Massachusetts, for a school year, 1997–98, on Broadway in a large one-bedroom apartment that a friend found for us.

Mom is here to do a fellowship at the Bunting Institute. We told them I was coming, too, because she needed help. They said, *come*.

(Rose's Memory)

I was in horrible pain for months. Maybe a year by the time I got to Cambridge. I didn't know what was causing the stinging sensations in my hands and along my spine, the fire shooting through the veins of my arms, the feeling that I was being pummeled with somebody's fists.

When I first heard I had diabetes, I wondered for a while if that was really the case. It's not common in our family. But I felt better when I discovered that, like many illnesses, diabetes can be controlled with diet, by drastically reducing the consumption of sugar, and getting good exercise.

Even before the diabetes was diagnosed, I was reading things. My eyes were working well then and I had lots of books around the house about health and healing. I knew something was wrong and I was trying to figure it out. I was losing weight; I was tired easily. And I didn't care about whether the house was clean. I just didn't seem to have the energy and I didn't even want to be in the kitchen around disorder. So I knew something was going on.

When I would take my trips to Berkeley for classes, I discussed all of this with some of my classmates and teachers—medical doctors who happened to be in the class, sometimes psychologists and so on. And I got good counsel. They were saying what I was reading—*watch what you eat; remove yourself from stressful situations, if possible.*

I was studying Feldenkrais. The gentle manipulation of the body and the connections between neurological, physical, and emotional health were fascinating to me. I always loved any kind of physical movement anyway. And putting my hands on people. This was a good fit for me. We were almost finished with the four-year program, and in spite of the pains and everything, I looked forward to developing my practice back home when I got the certification. During the final week of my training, the week before our graduation, I was having some trouble walking and feeling very tired. One of my classmates, a doctor, suggested I take a blood test at the hospital where she worked. Turns out my sugar level was extremely high. The doctor got the results and said she'd take me in for treatment the next morning. I had mixed feelings. I didn't know if I really wanted to go through all of that. And honestly, I wish that I had not. Because I think I could have lowered it myself. But I had a good rest, especially in the first days—they gave me lots of liquids because I was dehydrated and didn't know it.

The hospital sent all kinds of people to talk to me—endocrinologists, neurologists, social workers, nutritionists. Somebody suggested I talk to a psychologist: "You know, stress can be a cause of diabetes. There's a mental and emotional side to this disease too." I wasn't ready to hear any of that.

While I was laying there in the hospital I got to thinking about this pain. Where it came from. How long I had had it. It started long before the diabetes was diagnosed. I wasn't so worried about it back then because I could alleviate it with massages and acupuncture. Once in a while, if it got too bad, I'd take some Tylenol. So, I guess I just weathered the storm. And there were times when it really did get better. And other times when it was flaring up like nobody's business.

(Rachel's Memory)

I came back from a year of research in Brazil in 1995. I worked two years after that to write my dissertation and Mom was sick the whole time. She had seemed fine when I'd left the country. When I came back, she and Daddy met me at the airport. Mom was standing in the Jetway door wearing some beige jeans she got from one of her resale shops, cinched tight with a belt. They must have been a size four, but the pants hung off of her hips like a croaker sack. She couldn't have weighed more than eighty-five pounds. Skin and bones. Daddy was standing there next to Mom. I was astounded. Speechless. I'm looking at him like, *wtf? What's going on here?* Looks to me like he should know something, but he acts as if this is not the strange homecoming it most certainly is. They both hug me. Mama doesn't want to answer questions in the middle of the concourse and I can't let go of her hand.

We took her to doctors in Denver and Boulder, trying to figure out what was wrong. One diagnosed the diabetes, but that's as far as we got. Nothing to explain the pains, the lethargy, the constant diarrhea. The one thing that seemed to keep Mom going was her Feldenkrais certification classes in Berkeley, California. She'd go three or four times a year for a few weeks at a time. Even though she was getting weaker and in almost constant pain, there was something about the training (and perhaps the location and time away from home too) that seemed to revive her. She always looked forward to the trips.

Two weeks before my dissertation defense, she was out in Berkeley and I got a call from someone whose name Mom had mentioned to me once or twice.

"*Where are you? Do you know your mother is in the hospital? Don't you know your mother is sick?*" Maurilio Gonzalez was a caretaker at the bed and breakfast where Mom stayed. (Later I found out he was a *santero*,[1] too, his one-room apartment at the side of the guesthouse consumed completely with a spectacular floor-to-ceiling altar of *soperas*[2] surrounded by candles and cigars, beads and statues, and abundant fruit offerings to his orishas. I doubted many people on the staff had been in that room.) I was defensive. Mom had mentioned to me she was going to the hospital for some tests, but I was so focused on finishing my work, I figured I'd wait to see if she *really* needed me to come.

"You *need to come out here*," Maurilio told me.

I dislike hospitals now. But I remember that one, the one in Oakland, one of the first of our sojourn through sick bays in four cities, and it reminds me of the good parts. When I first got there, Mama was in the far corner of a room with three beds, all occupied, separated by curtains. She was by the window and I excused myself as I passed the people in the first two beds, looking around the final screen for my mother's face. It was a narrow space—the space where her bed sat between the curtain and the wall. She smiled a warm smile at me, although it was obvious something was wrong. I pulled up a chair and eventually got her a private room with a recliner for me to sleep in, and I stayed with her.

That became our routine. Anytime Mom had to go to the hospital, I went, too, and stayed in the room with her. Three days. Ten days. Whatever it was, we did it together. People complimented me on how well I took care of my mother. That was nice to hear, but we were taking care of each other. And it was this illness that showed me the power of Mama's spirit and how much strength I drew from her. Something passed between us in the years that she struggled to regain her health: it was in our conversations trying to figure out our next steps, in gestures and prayers, in bits of songs we sang together. I was very conscious of us as a team. I also saw the mix of her vulnerability and her amazing vitality. Maybe my own too. We kept encouraging each other: sometimes at the same time, sometimes each of us alternately holding up the banner when the other was worn out.

She didn't really want to go back to Denver; she was close to finishing the Feldenkrais program, but the doctors encouraged it and I was afraid to leave her in Berkeley on her own with new diabetes paraphernalia and no experience giving herself shots. It didn't take us too long to discover that the insulin itself gave Mom severe edema; and for seven years, until just days before she died, we struggled with doctors to get them to recognize that something was really wrong with her reaction to the very thing that was being used to control the diabetes.

(Rose's Memory)

My daughter came the day after I got to the hospital and she stayed with me there. She talked to the doctors and helped me formulate my questions, making notes about all the treatment options and the medications I was given. I was glad for the company.

But I didn't want to go back to Denver. On the way to the airport, we stopped to say good-bye to my classmates. When I saw everybody getting ready for graduation, I got very depressed. I have to confess that. Not only would I probably not see those friends again, people I had been in the program with for several years, but I wanted to be part of the celebration. I had come so close to finishing. Rachel was giving me the medication under doctor's instructions and I had such mixed feelings. I didn't know what to do. My sadness didn't help my condition because when I got home the pain just got worse. That's the way I remember it. But that's the way pain usually is for me. I really don't remember how it was before the present moment. The present seems to be all I can handle. I just thought it was horrific and I didn't understand where it was coming from and I didn't know how to stop it.

And the swelling too. By the time I got home it was really pronounced. And I was disappointed that the weight I thought I had gained in the hospital was just fluid accumulating in my body. Rachel and I adjusted the level of insulin down, and that seemed to help the swelling, but I still had the pain. And oh! I don't know how to describe the pain.

I think people didn't believe me. Most people with diabetes don't go through this kind of physical distress. Every time I would begin to explain it to somebody, even doctors, they would listen, but soon I would see something like disbelief, or at least amazement, in their faces. And I am telling you, this thing was from the top of my head to my toes. It was so unpredictable, so arbitrary, I couldn't tell where it would start, or when or how long it would last. It chased me and there was no where I could hide. I just cried because I didn't know what else to do. I think I went into a deep deep depression, so deep I wasn't even conscious of it. I could hardly get out of bed. But the family was so supportive. Jonathan massaged me. Rachel kept account of my medicine and made sure I had anything else I needed. Vincent massaged me, too, and helped as best he could. I'm so grateful to them, I really have to say that. But nothing any of the doctors could do was making any difference to the pain. Sometimes, I'd see a bodywork therapist, or an acupuncturist, and I'd feel some relief on the table. But as soon as I got home, the pain returned. I was screaming. I would cry out and fall down on the floor, rolling until I felt some kind of relief. And it would come; relief would come. I'd be able to sleep a little. The screams helped.

When I first started to lose my sight, I wondered what it was I didn't want to see. I used to "shush" myself, and then wonder what I no longer wanted to hear. I had lost so much weight. I looked so gaunt, you know, I was in a terrible state. After a couple dozen different health care practitioners, and hospital stays in Denver and California, we still had no idea what was going on with me. The doctors tested for everything—cancer, AIDS, tuberculosis. All of the tests came back negative. The practitioners were giving me things to build up my immune system, to help my diet; herbs and things to improve my digestion. But no one seemed to know what to do about the pain.

(Rachel's Memory)

Dr. Arky wasn't the only doctor who helped us. Others tried. A general-practice physician and family friend in Denver was the first person to diagnose the diabetes. He put mom in the hospital several times when the pain and diarrhea became excessive, but none of his colleagues were able to figure out what was going on. Two wonderful practitioners of Traditional Chinese Medicine were also a great help, and their acupuncture, moxibustion, and magnet therapies gave Mom temporary relief. But always the pain would come back and her general condition was deteriorating.

Keith Block is an internist who runs a nationally recognized cancer clinic with his wife, Penny, and a staff of both allopathic and holistic practitioners, in Evanston, Illinois. My folks met the Blocks in the early 1980s when they were all studying macrobiotics. Keith had cured himself of his own illness through a combination of the Japanese-inspired diet, exercise, supplements, and both Asian and Western medicine—and he has since developed a well-respected and successful practice that uses a similar blend of therapies with patients from around the country. The Blocks came to Denver a few times as guest speakers for my parents' "Healing of Persons and Healing of Society" courses at Iliff and they kept in touch over the years.

Finally, one night, Mama was wailing and rocking so bad it was like she had left us and was hovering in some acicular air, pleading with God and all the angels. We didn't know where else to take her. None of the doctors in Denver seemed to have a clue.

"Bring her right away," Keith said when Daddy called him.

(Rose's Memory)

In the middle of all of this, somehow, I got an application for a fellowship year at the Bunting Institute at Radcliffe College. I remember I was hurting so bad, sitting in the living room on the couch, rocking myself back and forth and trying to stay focussed as Rachel, Vincent, and I were filling out the paperwork a day or two before it was due. We called Bob Moses, Grace Boggs, and my social work professor, Enid Cox, and asked them to write letters of recommendation for me. They all agreed.

After we sent it off, I didn't think about that application too much. But it turns out Bunting was a house of refuge. They offered me a Peace Fellowship to write about spirituality and social activism and I wanted very much to do that. I wasn't sure if I could, physically. But the opportunity meant a great deal to me, and if it was in any way possible, I was going to try.

Keith Block arranged for me to come to his clinic from Denver on very short notice. Vincent and Rachel went with me. I was in such hard pain. When we arrived, while we waited in the consultation room, my husband and daughter rubbed my hands and consoled me with their voices singing, *The storm is passing over, hallelu . . .*

Dr. Block made appointments with two of his colleagues—a neurologist and an endocrinologist—who saw me immediately at the end of their workdays. I was in a wheelchair. I don't remember the details well. The neurologist said I had the appearance and symptoms of a concentration camp survivor: bent over with trauma and pain, but with a quiet buried rage.

(Rachel's Memory)

The neurologist wouldn't let Daddy or me answer any of the questions. Mama's voice was small and cracked, like every other inch of her. The doctor was a stocky man, with dark hair, and his office was a nondescript single-story building with no particular amenities. We parked on the side in a lot, eased mom out of the car, and got the wheelchair out of the trunk. We didn't have to wait long. We were the last clients of the day. The neurologist looked at Mom intently. Asked what was going on. She couldn't talk much, or loud. Or wouldn't. He said she looked like she'd been under extreme stress; what he said was "She looks like the women I've seen who've been in concentration camps," and dictated his thoughts into a small tape recorder for his secretary to transcribe and forward to Dr. Block. He said she should go to Cambridge and accept the fellowship. It would help.

The next day, we went to see the endocrinologist. He had fit us in after his last scheduled patient too, and when he saw us, he was soft-spoken, efficient, perhaps a little overburdened, and apologetic about the wait. In less than twenty minutes he took a brief history, examined Mom, and gave us a diagnosis. *Diabetic neuropathic cachexia*, a debilitating complication of diabetes that causes severe weight loss and almost unbearable neuropathic pain. Nobody knows where it comes from. And it's not common. We asked him what he thought about going to Cambridge. He said to see his teacher, Dr. Ronald Arky at Harvard.

(Rachel's Memory)

We stayed in Evanston for two weeks in the late summer of 1997. We went over to the Block clinic daily for bodywork and blood tests or consultations with different members of the staff. They were doing everything they could to help—pain patches, pills. Mom couldn't eat too much and the nutritionists were supplementing her food with Ensure and vitamins. What seemed to help most were massages. The therapy room was a dim, quiet space with no windows and just enough area for a massage table and two or three chairs flush against the walls. The therapist, Michael Huff, sat at one end of the table, his hands gently and firmly on Mom's head and shoulders; and Daddy and I sat on the sides, talking softly to Michael—asking him about his life, his work. We laughed some and Mom slept. This was one of the few times she could relax and drift off. She wasn't sleeping much at night. There was still so much pain. Some of the medications were too strong; others had no effect at all.

At night in the hotel, pacing the length of the large room, Mom seemed to be going through almost an exorcism. Everything hurt. Everything. Hurt to stand, hurt to lay down. Hurt to eat. Hurt to sleep. Nothing could touch her. Nobody. Not even clothes. Sometimes she took off every stitch she had on and marched and stumbled around the room cursing the pain and crying. Naked and insistent. Window shades up or down. It didn't matter. *Jesus, Jesus! Help me!* and *All you motherfuckers can go to hell. I got to get well.*

(Rose's Memory)

When we left Evanston, we went to my sister Mildred's house. The day we got there, she cooked smothered chicken, greens and okra, cornbread and sweet potatoes, and something good every day we stayed. I ate more than I had eaten in a long time. The food was a home feeling for me. It was six years since I had been to see my sisters, my family. Mama died in 1991 and I had not been home in six years. Rachel and I slept in Mama's room. I slept in her bed and they brought me food and tea and medicine. Mildred and Rachel rubbed my feet and we laughed and talked in the memories. Norma was there for a few days, smoking on the back porch and checking in on me. *How's Rose?* Everybody came by to give a kiss and a hug. My nieces and nephews. My sisters Alma and Sue. Nobody knew if I would make it.

All the doctors said I should go to the Bunting. No matter the pain, I should go. And thank God, Rachel finished her degree just as I was going through all of this. She finished everything and she was there to help me. Because my eyesight was going quickly. I had cataracts. First the right eye, then the left too. Blurry to where I couldn't see anything at all. I thought all the women at the Bunting were Black because I couldn't see color!

The acceptance we found at the Bunting Institute was just unbelievable. Being there made all the difference in the world. Those women helped me get well. They helped me get well. I was honored to be in the presence of scholars, writers, artists, all knowing what it is to be a woman in our society; and all creating such magnificent work out of their experiences, their perspectives, their scholarship. So many of them went out of their way to assist me and Rachel. They were so kind.

I had dreams at the Bunting. New kinds of dreams. Dreams where I would see times long past and a future beyond the twenty-first century. I saw the people, the homes, the clothing from all stages of human history, and the dreams were telling me to *be* a part of the newness; embrace the experiences coming to me and *live* inside them unafraid.

The year before I went to the Bunting, Mrs. Sue Thurman was getting weaker and I dreamed that her husband, Howard, appeared to me, upset and concerned for his wife. There was an urgency in his presence, as if he was telling me I needed to see about her. To go and be with her. Howard and Sue Thurman were very dear friends and mentors to Vincent and me. They were people with a powerful sense of the connectedness of life and faiths and deeply committed to social and racial justice in the world. They were models for us. Vincent really saw Howard as a kind of father and they loved each other that way. Sue, too, was this marvelous, wise, and gentle woman. I watched her embrace and embody the great diversity of her heritage—African, Native, European—just as she embraced the unity of Spirit.

After the dream, I began to put pictures of Sue around my altars at home, but I didn't get to see her, physically, before she passed. I felt bad about it. For weeks after her death, Vincent and I both felt Mrs. Thurman's presence with us. It was very strong. I let go of some of the guilt for not seeing her when I remembered what Mama Freeney told me about death—*all that remains is love*. That's what I felt from Sue Thurman's spirit. I felt it after she passed, and I have felt it here.

So many people have prayed for me. I feel the prayers. Friends, family, people unknown to me. I feel those blessings helping me accept new dimensions and develop myself on a higher level. That is what I have asked for. This illness, I think, is to help me go deeper, help me to grow more. When it struck me the way it did, I was calling out to God to help me rise. To open me and give me understanding. I feel a presence—maybe it is an individual, or the composite of many who have kept me on their hearts. It is something—through the grace of God—coming to assist me at this particular time.

(Rachel's Memory)

> *Oh Death, have mercy*
> *Oh Death, be easy*
> *Death, have mercy*
> *Spare me over another year . . .*

Me and Mama were whisper-singing the stanzas, just loud enough for us and Jesus and the square-toed messenger who tracked us to hear. It was 1997, ten days before Christmas. We were on our way to Chicago. Mama was still weak then. We were still waiting for the miracle. Praying hard.

A few weeks before, I had dreamed of Iemanjá in a fury unlike anything I'd ever seen or imagined, coming to get my mother. A few times in my life I have had dreams so stark and full of power that they wake me up with the force of an explosion, my pulse racing, my body on full and immediate alert. One was a vision of Mom's face contorted to the grotesque in pain. That came just as she started to experience the worst of the illness. I was still in school, writing my dissertation, and the dream's message was to finish quickly because Mama's need was beyond urgent.

This time, the meaning wasn't immediately apparent to me. But the urgency was there again. In the dream, I saw a Black woman hanging upside down in a yard, her pregnant belly slit open where her near full-term unborn child had been ripped out and both left to die. From that same yard, Iemanjá, the Great Mother orixá, stormed onto the porch of a house where my mother was inside and reached wrathfully for the door. The Goddess was pure fury and determination. And she had come to get my mother, as if she were angry that some essential task had been left undone. Some precious time wasted. Some vital gift underestimated and abandoned.

I don't play with the orixás. They don't come often, unmistakably, in my dreams. And when they do I pay attention. They are my most steady and dependable sources of support and counsel. This dream terrified me. The image of the lynched and disemboweled pregnant woman was horrifying enough. But to then see Iemanjá at the height of her ire with designs on my mother sent me into panic. What was this about? What was Iemanjá saying to me, to my mother? I don't think I had ever been more astonished in my life. Ever. Normally, I do not fear the orixás. Not because I am unaware of their potency but because, in my life, they have been enormously merciful and patient spirits. Old souls who have watched me with the solicitousness and care of grandparents. Intellectually, I know that in their representations of the natural forces of the universe—Xangô as thunder and lightening; Oyá as tempest and wind; Iemanjá as the ocean's mighty body and all its mothering muscle—their axé is a poetic balance of destructive and constructive energies. But in my day-to-day life and beseechings, I had been shown so much benevolence. For me, Iemanjá was a compassionate, if sometimes stern, maternal figure with an unconstrained capacity for care.

I sat utterly straight up in the bed. Mom was still asleep. I looked at her carefully, watching her breathe and trying to judge that nothing was amiss in an obvious way. My mother was *already* sick. I couldn't quite get a clear narrative out of the dream, but I could see that Iemanjá was furious. I felt it was a warning. Something hadn't been done. Something needed to be done. It was kind of like, *if Mom didn't get up and do what she was supposed to do . . .*

. . .

I know this is very hard to explain in a "logical" way. Even if you believe in God. Even if you believe in the Orixás. And then again, it's all poetry. It is all poetry, y'all. It is all story. But let me tell you that the poetry is real. The story is truth.

I was so afraid, I would not talk about this dream out loud for years. The only person I told was my friend Vincent Woodard. I called him and asked him if I could send him a ticket to come from Texas, as soon as he could, to help us. And he came. Vincent was an initiate in Vodou and an amazingly beautiful and perceptive man. He and I met at Cave Canem, the Black poets retreat. The first one. Vincent came to Cambridge with his bones, crystals, and incense. We bought rum and candles and he spit the liquor behind the door of the apartment with prayers to cleanse and bless the house. And he called on the *lwa* and the orixá to bring healing and comfort to Mom. He stayed with us for a few days and when he left to go back to Austin, Mom and I took a plane to Chicago for Christmas. That was when she really started to get well.

> *What is this that I can't see?*
> *(Spare me over another year.)*
> *Cold icy hands all over me.*
> *(Spare me over another year.)*

Mom did in fact get a good deal better. She did start to do the work she was meant to do—the writing, the sharing of her wisdom, her experience, her healing axé. That part of the dream I felt I understood, eventually. And it was affirmed by our priestess friends in Bahia. They told Mama, "Do what healing work you can. If you had been born here, you would be one of us now. But do what you can where you are." That part I understood.

> *Oh oh oh death, have mercy*
> *Ooh oh death, be easy*
> *Death, have mercy*
> *Won't you spare me over another year.*

I leaned in close to Mama on the plane, so our music wouldn't disturb the other passengers. Even quiet, she was singing with a determination in her voice that was, I am sure now, lined up with that fury of the Goddess, that innate resolve, that *way out of no way* she possessed to make death sit in the corner longer than he expected.

(Rose's Memory)

When I first got to the Boston area and was so sick, my friend, Makota Valdina Pinto, suggested that I see Dr. Fu-Kiau Bunseki, a great Congolese philosopher and healer who lives in the city. Valdina, who is herself a brilliant priestess in the Afro-Brazilian Candomblé tradition, had met Dr. Fu-Kiau some years earlier when he visited Bahia, and she considered him a mentor. "Call Fu-Kiau," she told us. We invited him to dinner in our apartment one mid-fall evening, and he came. After we had eaten together, Dr. Fu-Kiau began to talk to us about healing.

"Nothing is ever lost," he said. That interested me. He said that what we inherit from our ancestors remains with us, whether we are conscious of that inheritance or not. And we do remember, perhaps more in the body than in our intellectual awareness; perhaps more in the heart. It sounded like what I had heard from Bawa, about the essence that remains "in the indestructible place in the heart." That remnant of peace, of grace, that all of us carry. What we inherit from those who came before us, among other things, is a link to the ancestors and ancestral traditions of everybody living in this world. We help each other find our way home. That's why I see so much of my own tradition—that southern African American spirit—in Buddhism, in Islam, in Native wisdom. I see it in Judaism in people like Rabbi Abraham Joshua Heschel, and in Sufi tradition in my teacher Bawa Muhaiyaddeen. Those connections, those ancient connections, are never lost. They are the love that remains.

(Rachel's Memory)

This was the year of Mom's work and the miracles. When she came to Bunting she was barely able to walk and stand on her own. Legally blind with cataracts. Winced and sleepless with irresolvable pains. And thin as a rail. But her pain-wracked body housed a spirit of bottom earth and iron. By the time she left, with forty hours of audiotaped recollections and insights, the initial chapters of her memoir, and two book proposals with interested editors, she was so much better.

At the time, the Bunting Institute was a program of Radcliffe College (before its final merger with Harvard), and the fellowships were specifically intended to support women, of promise and accomplishment, who may not have had sufficient opportunities to develop their work due to family responsibilities or other constraints. It was a setting tailor-made for my mother and she found so much encouragement, so much understanding. From the associate director, Renny Harrigan, who made sure that I had access to the libraries and other facilities to help Mom with her work, to members of her cohort of awardees—including Ruchama Marton, Carol Ockman, Esther Parada, Marion Bethel, Deborah Levenson-Estrada, Odile Cazenave, and Indira Ganesan—all were tremendously accepting and encouraging of her.

We worked hard that year: to get the illness to subside, to get the diabetes under control, and between visits to doctors, therapists, and pain clinics, we wrote Mama's story. She made dozens of tapes: recollections, stories, pieces of plays and poems, and rituals for a healed and healing America. I was so proud of my mother.

For her public lecture at Bunting, Mom had a packed house. She read her chapter on hospitality, haints, and healing and afterward two visiting scholars from Hawaii came up to tell Mom that the southern African American traditions she described were strikingly similar to what they knew from their home. Linda Mizell, a graduate student and family friend, thanked Mom for articulating the grounding she always knew and intuited, but had not previously heard in that way—of an indigenous southern African American philosophy.

Mama was diligent in her healing. As if every day, she pushed herself to do a little more, to get a little stronger, by force of her will and God's grace. I'd be reading or writing somewhere in a corner, late at night, and peek into the living room, and Mom would be trying to walk, slowly, balancing every step with her arms extended and head held high. *Come on Rose, you gonna do this thing.* She worked so hard to get well. That determination. And this with pain so massive it could make her cry. Every day.

Mom really did not want to return to Denver. She asked me to talk to Dr. Arky about helping me find a job in the area so that we could stay. She said she could be a nanny, anything not to have to go back. We weren't arguing. She was just telling me she thought it was dangerous for her to go back to Denver. Dangerous for her spirit and for her health. She was not happy there. I was nervous. I had a couple of job offers in other cities but Veterans of Hope was just starting and Daddy asked me to come back to Denver to help with the project. I really didn't know what to do. I decided to go back home and I promised Mom we would finish the book.

Notes

1. A practicioner of the Afro-Cuban religious tradition Santeria, also known as Regla Ochá or Lucumí.

2. Porcelain vessels in which sacred elements of the orishas are consecrated and kept.

Vincent and Rosemarie, c. 1986. PHOTO COURTESY ESTATE OF WALTER LEE DOZIER.

Over many years, my husband and I have created and led workshops and retreats for teachers, community organizers, social workers, and others in helping professions. These are often developed around themes of racial reconciliation, peace-making, and the relationship between spirituality and social justice. The gatherings are, in a sense, a ritual space in which whoever comes is able to release some of the burdens of their heart and in which the group as a whole finds and shares encouragement for the ongoing work of compassionate, spirit-based activism.

Our model is very organic and very flexible—always including rich storytelling and music—but changing with each group and incorporating many other elements and insights as we discover them and sense their usefulness. We usually begin with sound and silence. We set a tone with spirituals or jazz and then with a more formal welcome where one of us outlines the intention for the time together, and always, we do introductions around the circle. I think it was in Denver, after we came to Iliff, that we began to ask participants to identify their "mother's mother" as part of the introductions. We know that grandmothers have traditionally played a pivotal role in the formation of cultural and moral identity among many peoples, and so we began asking people in the workshops to talk a bit about their grandmothers (or, if they didn't know their grandmothers, to talk about an older relative who was important to them). This was a way to begin to acknowledge the importance of ancestors. Also, as I learned more about Sufi and Buddhist teachings—and as I saw the connections between these world wisdoms and the lessons I learned from my mother—I started to talk more frequently about the deeply holistic, practical, and compassionate understanding that women's experiences and women's spirits bring to the work of social change.

When Rachel came to Colorado for graduate school, she helped us in our work and brought the richness of her own perspective. At times she, her father, and I have conducted workshops with teachers and activists using many of the powerful stories of the VOHP interviews. At other times my daughter and I do retreats together for women, as well as workshops on gratitude and Afro-Atlantic traditions of spirituality and healing.

The activities we choose depend on the amount of time available, and the needs of the folks who come. Specific people might be asked to share a story, others to report on some "good news" they have learned about communities doing creative social action in various parts of the country. We teach Freedom Songs and try to feed people delicious, healthy meals. At some point, Vincent and I will usually talk about some of our own movement experiences and the outstanding people we were honored to join in that blessed work. Sometimes we recite poems and screen films; often I'll teach a bodywork or healing technique. But mostly and especially we tell stories. Whatever the specific theme of the gathering—education for democracy; spiritual resources for social change; ancestors of the social justice struggle; freedom movement history; radical women's history; personal and social healing—it really doesn't matter much. Our focus is to open up a deeper conversation about the resources of spirit and struggle that course through our individual and collective histories. The tools are a way to build community and to get whoever is present to remember and be renewed in what most deeply motivates and inspires them to activism/teaching/ organizing/ministry/etc. Participants bring their experiences, which are evocative and full of interesting questions, and we come with the bits of wisdom we've accumulated over the years—and somehow together, we make something that is useful to everyone.

We try to undergird everything with a spirit of hospitality by making sure there are beautiful flower arrangements and cloths to decorate the space, lots of healthy snacks and, often, a simple altar someplace in the center or at the side of the room arranged with candles, water, plants, and stones. We also try to be sensitive to the weights people carry. In spite of the words that might be coming from their mouths, as they tell their stories or raise their concerns, we look for what is going on underground. If we look carefully, we can see hurts and anxieties and fears in the same places where there are enormous potentials for healing.

Gratitude

In my own counseling work, I use a Japanese practice known as Morita Therapy or Gratitude Therapy. It is a quick way to address deep psychological issues and reduces the need to spend years in treatment. I have found that very few sessions are needed. This model asks clients to reflect on two questions. These can be introduced in a workshop setting, and a brief session devoted to them, but they are most effective when individuals have time to consider their answers carefully.

The first question is "What did my mother do for me?" The second question is "What problems did I cause for my mother?" The exercise requires each individual to answer these questions for three periods in his or her life: from birth through age twelve; from age thirteen through age twenty-one; and from age twenty-two through the present. (The assumption is that we needed more care, attention, and direct guidance in the earlier phases of our life, so childhood and the teen years require their own set of considerations. However, if there is time, adulthood can be subdivided into additional periods for more thorough examination.)

As people contemplate their responses, I note that in our Western patriarchal society, where ideas about psychology are strongly influenced by Freud, mothers are often accused of being the cause of emotional problems in their children, creating a great deal of resentment and anger. If people are having difficulty thinking about what to include in the list of things their mothers did to help them, I might gently suggest: "Who changed my diapers?" "Who fed me when I couldn't feed myself?" "Who took my side when others were against me?" "Who washed and ironed my clothes?" "Who took the blame I heaped on her, uncomplainingly?" So many of these recollections are things we take very much for granted, perhaps thinking they are the natural duty of our mothers and that there is no need to acknowledge their sacrifice in any special way.

Of course, it isn't necessary to do this exercise for mothers only. We can do it for anyone in our lives who has helped us. Mothers are just representative of someone who has usually done a great deal for us that we don't recognize, and that we often don't even remember. Most of us are much more apt to remember the difficulties we feel our mothers caused us, and not those we have caused them.

After ten minutes or so of this exercise, I often suggest that people may want to continue at home, and perhaps even do more specific lists for various stages of our adult life. Inevitably, workshop participants begin to feel some guilt or some sadness as they remember events on their lists. But there are things they can and should do to address this. The point of the remembering is, in fact, to increase our gratitude and our empathy. The shift from forgetfulness to remembering carries us over the bridge of guilt. Many forms of psychoanalysis keep us walking back and forth on the guilt bridge for years without ever crossing it. The point is to get to the other side.

So, one of the most important things we can do to get to the other side is to do "secret service" for our mothers. If our mother is alive, do something that we know will make her happy—send a bouquet of her favorite flowers or help her out financially. In each case, do this anonymously. Sign the flowers, "From someone who loves you very much." If our mothers are no longer living, do the "secret service" for someone else, also anonymously, with our mother in mind.

Another way I have used gratitude in workshops is to ask people to remember out loud the name of someone who encouraged them, who helped them become the person they are today. It might be a relative, a teacher, a friend. Someone who is still living, or someone who has already passed on. The important thing is to remember that person in gratitude. We did a variation on this exercise in 2003, in Jackson, Mississippi, at a Bob Moses Day celebration, a wonderful annual gathering of activists and educators. Vincent and I traveled there with Rachel and two of our Candomblé sisters—Iyalorixá Valnizia de Ayrá and Makota Valdina Pinto—and we met up with Bob and Janet and their family and many other longtime friends who were still on the journey from the movement days.[1]

Bob asked us to lead a conversation circle for anyone who wanted to talk about spirituality and social justice activism. About a hundred people showed up. Vincent and I really wanted people to have a chance to share what was on their hearts, and we were trying to decide how we could arrange a way for everyone to participate in a relatively short time. We always do introductions in our workshop sessions, so this time we asked people around the circle to say their names, tell us where they spent their childhood, and speak gratitude to an ancestor in the struggle for freedom—it could be a blood relative or just someone they knew and/or admired, whose life was important to the work for racial and economic justice in this country, and who should be remembered. I asked everyone to simply express gratitude to the person whose name they called, in whatever way they wanted.

I don't know if it was because we were in Mississippi, ground zero for so many of the hardest battles of the Movement; or if it was because the people who came to the session were men, women, and youth of deep dedication to justice who had been working for years (generations) for freedom for Black and poor people; or if it was because we had our priestess sisters with us from Bahia; but that simple exercise became an extraordinary moment. Some folks remembered well-known leaders of the Movement, especially Mississippi heroes like Fannie Lou Hamer and Amzie Moore. Others recalled people less well known, family members and friends who had taken great risks or made personal sacrifices. One by one, each person stood up and told us to whom they were grateful and why—an aunt who carried groups of family and friends to register to vote, standing up to a local sheriff and a townful of Klan members; an uncle who was killed for refusing to sell a valuable parcel of land for pennies on the dollar; a father who campaigned for the Mississippi Freedom Democratic Party in spite of threats that he and his family would be kicked out of their home; a grandmother who always had strong words of encouragement and blessing; a neighbor who fed children whose parents sometimes didn't have enough in their own house. There were so many beautiful and powerful stories. So many names. The session time ended and we had not yet gotten around the circle, so we went into the dining hall and continued over lunch, people rising and calling names in gratefulness. Remembering and thanking. And that's all we did in that workshop. But it was so powerful and so lovely.

Council Grove

During the early 1990s, Vincent and I participated in several of the annual "Council Grove" gatherings sponsored by the Menninger Institute. We created a workshop there that we called "Remnants." We had been reading Ronald Takaki's book—*A Different Mirror: A History of Multicultural America*—in which the author intertwined the histories and struggles of various ethnic groups in this country.[2] Vincent read some passages aloud, about Irish and

Italians and African Americans and Chinese and Japanese and Jewish people; and as he read, I invited anyone in the room to come up to the front and help me act out and dance the stories. And just about everyone participated. Some people added songs, some people added drumming, and some moved their bodies and danced with me.

One of the stories we shared was that of Jews, during World War II, who were refused admission to the United States and were returned to Europe to their deaths. I was at the center of the room moving slowly, in tense, angular gestures and, at first, only a few people joined me there. Vincent's voice and the whispers of our anguished movements were the only sounds at first. After a while a few others joined us on the floor, a few Jewish brothers and sisters who knew a traditional song of mourning. They began to sing that song while others had instruments they played—some drums, a flute, a shekere; and as the song grew, we who danced moved through the story with the support of the whole workshop. Later, a man told us that the ritual was the first time he had been able to look at that particular historical experience without deep hate and anger. He found something in the ritual that helped him move those emotions out of the center of his heart.

That Holocaust story is similar to what has happened in our time with the Haitian people, being turned away from safety and sent back to suffer and die. In our society, in our world, these things happen to many of us. So we do need exercises of healing—not only to teach the history, but to be released from the history as well. We have to have a way to nurture what is *human* in us, to feed our ability to go on, to continue working for justice in the world. So when I think of "Remnants" I'm thinking *there is always . . . God always leaves us with a way out. Leaves us with a way to hope. Leaves us with a way to recuperate.* If you're so caught up in anger, if you're caught up in hate, it's difficult to heal.

A Remnants Workshop

Using our earlier work as a base, I have been thinking of how to incorporate the "Remnant" quality of spirit—the "Nothing is ever lost" and the "All that remains is love"—into an even broader model of workshop as ritual, gatherings for the healing of our souls and our nation. We have been through so much trauma, so much generational pain, and we are still fighting so many awful injustices built into the structure of our society. We need healing. Our country needs healing. Holding on to angers, to wrongs, becomes a weight on our own bodies, in our own spirits—causing us sickness and passing it on to our inheritors. Forgiveness heals not only our personal agonies but provides a cleansing of the air between us and our so-called enemies and passes on something breathable to our children.

We need to remember the stories—stories of how we have all helped each other: how the Japanese Americans were among the first people to open their churches, temples, and hearts to Muslim Americans after the bombings of September 11, 2001, because they knew what it felt like to be viciously scapegoated. How the Native people of this continent helped so many others who came here, sharing their understandings about everything from democratic governance to foodstuffs and medicine. And how they suffered horribly in spite of their generosity. Harriet wouldn't have made it through those swamps to rescue hundreds of enslaved Black people without their help. They helped *everybody*.

We need time to share our stories. Oh Lord, some of them are so hard, but some of them just shine too. We have to hear both. That's why we love Shakespeare. That's why we love those plays that are reminders of our best and our worst as human beings. We can use the words of people like Rabbi Heschel, like Martin and Coretta, like Florence and Clarence, and Ella Baker and Sue and Howard Thurman, and Anne Braden and Cesar Chavez and Dolores Huerta and others who represent that spirit of justice and forgiveness that connects all of us. The words we share don't have to be from famous people. There are so many examples in our own communities, sometimes in our own families, of people who understand the necessity of this healing. I think about David Chethlahe Paladin who came to our classes at Iliff and talked to us about the importance of forgiveness. Paladin was a gifted artist, a member of the Navajo nation who had been a soldier in World War II and was captured and tortured by the Nazis. He told our students that he didn't heal from the torture until he was able to forgive those men. That's when he finally was able to get well.

We need music from around the world in the workshop too. Native American, Celtic, African and African American music and some good old Southern Folk singing. Bring the fiddles and the harmonicas, the guitars and the drums. Music is just essential. We don't even have to know the meaning of the words all the time, because the tones tell us so much.

The workshops will include music and literature and dance and something like this Gratitude Therapy that I've used. We'll start our work with reasons to be grateful, as opposed to reasons to hold anger, judgment, or mean-spiritedness. I'm going to combine all these traditions—Native American, Korean, Southern Black Folk, Celtic, Maori, and Indigenous Australian and white Southern as well. Folk traditions from around our country and around the world. What they say about love and mercy and how we all belong to this world. What I'm looking to create is a model, a way for people to have an experience of community, of reconciliation, forgiveness, and rest. See, those who need forgiveness will experience that and those who need to forgive will experience *that*.

It will be a model that can be used by many different kinds of people and groups, in an open space, to act out, dance out, poet out, sing out, and tell out the traumas and beauties of our stories. These art forms will give us some ways to see the spirit moving in our work together. People should feel they are in a transformative situation in the workshop, and when they leave, they should be encouraged to go and teach others.

Workshop as Art: George Bass and Rites and Reason Theater

"Mama, you're talking about the workshop as an art form," Rachel tells me. She reminds me of her teacher, George Bass, the magnificent philosopher-playwright who cofounded the Rites and Reason theater company in the African American Studies Department at Brown University. George's plays were intensely multidimensional works. They were theater, they were ritual, and they were communal experiences of myth and healing that extended beyond the stage and even the lobby and out into the streets. In fact, several were specifically designed as ritual street performances.

Vincent and I met George and his wife, Ramona, through our shared work in the Black Arts and Black Studies movements. When Rachel started at Brown in the early 1980s, George was producing a play series called *The Day of No' Mo'* that signified both a meaning of protest in the language of the Black American South ("No Mo' = No More") and the Dogon concept of the essential life force, "Nommo." The plays were performed on street corners around the city of Providence, Rhode Island, as a way to draw attention to violent deaths that had occurred due to police and gang killings. George and his crew brought the full range of theatrical resources to their work—large papier-mâché masks, stilts, music, poetry, and the participation of audiences/bystanders who became part of the ceremony of transformation and release. He really understood the transformative power of theater—as ritual, as medicine, and as a great force for community-building and community critique. Theater as a resource for social change.

The amazing thing about George, and what makes his work a good model for what I envision, is that it was just as important for him to create plays that were rituals of healing and transformation, plays that created new mythologies, or plays that talked about our relationship to spirit and to ancestors, as it was to write plays about the material and political issues affecting African

American communities. In fact, in this way, his work was similar to that of August Wilson—although George's work was more avant-garde in a sense. Both playwrights were conscious of the ritual and mytho-poetic genius in what George called "the Black folk aesthetic." And the connections among spirit, culture, and struggle run strong in the work of both men.

Healing for Our Cities

This "Remnant" workshop model could be used in cities around the country where people are struggling with issues that need some kind of collective understanding—situations in need of a spirit of reconciliation and common good. In those cities, a number of arts groups would be invited (a very deeply and intentionally multicultural mix) to share their work and their wisdom. In Denver, for example, we could ask Cleo Parker Robinson Dance, El Centro Su Teatro, Jewish cantors, Tibetan Buddhist mandala painters, Aztec dancers, African American drill teams, the Spirituals Project, and visual artists, musicians, and storytellers of many backgrounds to come together with participants from all over the city for a week of rites, workshops, and joint performances. The gathering is not simply presentation but a way for people to experience transformation—another way of perceiving and being in the world, even if just for the while.

We would have prayers and songs and blessings at the opening and close of each day from different spiritual and cultural traditions represented in our city. There is such a hungering in our nation for collective gathering, for ritual, for a way to share some real meaning and joy and constructive struggle with other people. We need the opportunities to communicate our mythos as a nation—to express what we don't get to express in our day-to-day lives. Just as human beings are spiritual and religious and material, we are also theatrical, and we are mythical. We have to have some space to manifest that. That's what Carnival and Junkanoo and Crop Over and Second Lines and Powwows and Black marching bands and drill team parades do. They fill a human need.

"Mama, what you're talking about is a way to provide ritual experiences for people, which we desperately need in this country." Rachel is talking to me again. "And there are so many people who know how to do it. People born here, people born in other countries who have come here. Actors, dancers, choreographers, artists, religious communities. We have that wisdom in this country and we have the art."

A gathering of several days or a week would infuse our civic life with creative ideas and an energy of inclusiveness. It would give people the opportunity to work with cultural artists and community activists around a particular theme of civic concern—"Healthy Aging," for example, or "Restorative Justice and Alternatives to Mass Incarceration," "A Living Wage, A Livable City," "The Wisdom of Grandmothers," or "Affordable Housing and Meanings of Home." Some folks might work with painters, or muralists, or sculptors expressing their ideas and responses in visual art. We might have writing workshops focused on the theme. Others could lead dance and music workshops. The full gathering would be a kind of rite of transformation and healing for the city.

Some of this we are already doing—in the "Spirit and Struggle" retreats, in our programs at the Veterans of Hope Project, in the workshops Rachel and I do together, and in the classes Vincent and I have organized at Iliff, Pendle Hill, and elsewhere as opportunities for people to imagine and embody another set of relationships to each other as human beings.

. . .

"I like this idea, Mama." Rachel says to me. "It's fascinating—this meaning and use of ritual. What you're talking about is bringing the gifts of spirit; the gifts of traditional healing from around the world; the gifts of art; all these precious things for the healing of the nation and healing of human relations and even people's individual healing. I think that is gonna get you better, Mama."

It's already getting me better, I tell her. It's already doing it. I am in the midst of my year of the Bunting Fellowship and even as I think about these things and make plans, even as my daughter and I write and meditate on the connections we are finding, I feel myself getting better.

Notes

1. Iyalorixá Valnizia de Ayrá (Valnizia Pereira, known as "Mãe Val") is a high priestess of the Afro-Brazilian religion, Candomblé, and spiritual leader of the Terreiro de Cobre terreiro (temple) community where Rachel is an initiate. Makota Valdina Pinto is a ritual elder in the Tanuri Junçara terreiro community and a noted community historian and brilliant educator. Both women are deeply respected activists and community organizers linking Afro-Brazilian human rights, environmental justice, and the struggle for religious tolerance in their lives as religious leaders and in their work as advocates for social change.

2. Ronald Takaki, *A Different Mirror: A History of Multicultural America* (Boston: Little Brown 1993).

VI · The Pachamama Circle

37 · Pachamama Circle I
Rachel's Dream

My daughter saw the Pachamamas in a dream when I was first sick. It was after I had been diagnosed with diabetes but before we started going to other doctors and hospitals to figure out what was causing all of the complications. Rachel had the dream just at the beginning of her sojourn with me and the pain. She says it was a good thing. She says she needed the clarity it gave her—and even the reproof. It was startling and beautiful, this dream. And it made her a little ashamed, so she didn't tell me about it right away. But a year later, when we were doing the Bunting Fellowship in Cambridge and so much mercy and heaving and magic were circling around us, she shared it with me. And I pulled it close to my heart. And I loved it. I heard echoes of myths and stories I had carried for years, from Mama Freeney and Mama Liza and Grandma Rye, and from things I discovered on my own.

A few days before the dream, the two of us were in a grocery store and my daughter said something to me, sharp and unkind. I turned away in the aisle because it stung. I felt like she had slapped me and we were both trembling.

Then she had the dream. And this is how my daughter told it to me:

There were five Pachamamas. Maybe more. But I remember five Spiritwomen standing in front of me. The women were standing together facing me. They were different heights, but all tall. They were grown women, of full stature, in long, tunic-like dresses. Different colored dresses, some with ribbons flowing from their seams.

There was a Black Pachamama, and an Asian one, and one who looked Indigenous to the Americas. . . . They were all of different "races" and it seemed they each had responsibilities for particular people although overall they shared a collective identity and collective obligations too.

There was also a white Pachamama. This one was yours, Mom. She was a large, sturdy woman, both gentle and serious at the same time. She was protecting you behind her skirts, kind of standing between you and me. She said to me, "What do you know of Mothering?" It was a reprimand. A way of telling me I could not approach you, I could not touch you, if not with gentleness. She would not let anyone harm you.

I heard the dream and I loved it. I told my daughter. I loved the idea of it. Those women protecting the world, guarding each other's children who belong to them all.

As we worked on *Remnants*, the Pachamamas became a powerful recurring motif for us—a source of stories, ritual ideas, and an autobiographical legend in dance that I imagined for Cleo Parker Robinson's dance company. It was as if the presence of the Pachamamas in the dream unearthed for us other rooted memories of the spirit mothers. We saw every life form in the universe reflected in their blessing and continual care—across all generations and across all geographies.

38 · Pachamama Circle II

Sue Bailey Thurman and the Harriets

The quiet ways we developed to protect ourselves, each other, in slavery. The glance, the sent word, the straying . . . Safety construed of open-lacework silence. A circle of energy. A circle of protection in the world.

. . .

In her later years, I would visit Mrs. Sue Bailey Thurman at the town-house in San Francisco where she and her husband had lived together. We were old friends, and after Howard Thurman passed on Vincent and I felt a special concern for Mrs. Thurman. We saw her as often as we could. I always loved those visits with that gentle, brilliant, elegant woman. She had traveled the world and was knowledgeable about many things. She was a writer, a civic organizer, a profound thinker, and, like her husband, she had a deep, abiding interest in mysticism, justice, and peace.[1]

Once, as I was arriving, walking up the hill to her house, I had the sense of something . . . unsafe. You know how you can get a feeling of something not quite right? I felt that. I was nearing the house, so I kept walking toward it, but with my awareness keened to the circumstances around me. By the time I reached my destination, Mrs. Thurman was downstairs waiting for me. Now, normally she didn't meet me downstairs. Normally, she'd wait for me to ring the bell and then she would buzz me in and I'd climb the stairs to the main entrance to the house. But this time, she was downstairs in the foyer and she was opening the door for me. And I could feel she had been sending protection out to me just like I had felt Mama Freeney do once, years ago, as I came up to the door of the house at 41st and Wentworth.

I didn't know exactly what it was I was perceiving as I approached Mrs. Thurman's place, just something not right. A possible danger to me. Anyway, I felt it. And then I felt protected.

When we got upstairs to her living room, we were silent. She and I sat and the two of us went quiet inside ourselves. That's what we would do when we needed to sense the presence of . . . of this circle.

. . .

This circle I'm telling you about . . .

. . .

Howard Thurman has a story about this kind of care in danger. I heard him tell it a few times and a version is printed in his book *The Luminous Darkness*.[2] In the story, Thurman is traveling by railroad and arrives in a small southern town late at night where he is met by a Black man he doesn't know with a message to be cautious. Thurman has disembarked to wait for a connecting train, and the man approaches him unannounced and begins walking alongside him, explaining that there is tension in the area because the sheriff was killed that afternoon and it isn't safe for a Black man to go into town. He advises Thurman to sit in the segregated waiting room, with his suitcase in full view in front of him, so that any white men approaching will see that he is a stranger waiting for a connecting coach and he will be less likely to be harmed. The man doesn't talk long. He has met every train that has arrived during the night and given the warning to Black passengers as they got off.

Thurman told this story from his own experience. But he also told it as an example of what was typical among Black people in that time. It was indicative of the way, if there was danger, someone would be sent to warn you, to protect you. Living in this country in the 1920s and '30s, especially in the South, required a certain sensitivity, an attunement to jeopardy, and an understanding of one's connectedness, as a Black person, to others who shared your vulnerability. That awareness was put at the service of individuals and families as well as the larger community.

The concern was not solely for racist violence, although there was that. It was also, generally, a concern for protection of people who might be in danger. It was something that Black people had to be constantly aware of and so, I think, we developed a certain discernment about it. I think women had a heightened sense of this. And they would send people to look out for those who might be at risk.

This was the kind of perceptiveness Mrs. Thurman carried. My mother had it too. I remember Mama Freeney used to just send us places . . . "Go there," you know. "Go see about Mrs. So-and-So." "Go here." And we didn't ask why, we just went. She would tell us to go check on neighbors or younger nieces and nephews. My niece Jean remembers how Mama Freeney dreamed ways to help people and situations, to know when and what to do. My mother would talk about whom she had seen in a dream, people dead and gone, and what they told her should be done.

. . .

There is a story I have been thinking of that I want to tell about this. There is a group of women, they are women, and they are also spirits. They live all over the world, among all of the world's peoples, and they are connected to each other. But their connection is secret. The women are all African. Because we are all African. They are the daughters of the first mother.

The women carry a knowledge and tradition of protection. A wisdom of transformation. It is not a spoken knowledge. It is not something anyone talks about. It is in the body. Glimpsed from an angle when they are slicing onions or braiding hair or setting the limbs of a poem. Mostly you can see it when they dance. Or when they are sitting, utterly still. It is a gene, an element of their cells that rests in the mitochondria. It vitalizes their bloodline. These women are vessels. And founts. They are a source. The ones who remember what it is to be human in the world. They preserve this wisdom in the art of their lives, cultivating it in stories, in the way they move, in the paintings and pots they sculpt. In the fearlessness of their fighting. They carry this knowledge in their bodies as they go about their tasks and the encounters of their days. And they pass it on. Quietly. Their children, all of their children, have a bit of the inheritance. It is like a seed. But it won't bloom until they, too, are older. And it is the female line that passes the wisdom on.

These women are of every race, and every shade of skin and texture and color of hair. Their bodies are of every size, but all of their spirits are tall. They are physical and they are ethereal. These are the Pachamamas, the protective spirits of the earth, so named by the people of the Andes mountains in the Quechua language. They are the most ancient spirit mothers, sisters to Nanā Buruku and Amaterasu. They are all connected. Wherever they are, they recognize each other.

. . .

You know, my mother told me there were many Harriets. Harriet Tubmans. She told me whispering, as if it were something still to be shrouded, still to be protected—this fact, this sisterhood—so that they could rise again to help us when we need them. My great-grandmother, Grandma Rye, said she had met Harriet; said she knew of other women, too, who stole into the swamps, into the night perils, with one, two, three . . . seven people behind them, following their leading out of slavery.

In my story, these women are all Pachamamas. They are part of that circle of protection. That circle of grace that has been here since the beginning of the world, since the beginning of people. They have promised to take care of each other's children, all over the world. So you cannot tell who will love you by race, who will shelter you just by nation. They are all our mothers and we are all their children.

In slavery-time, some of these women looked white. The caramel tan of their faces, muscled forearms, and exposed feet contrasted with the stark cream color of their legs, of their backs, when the masters lifted their clothes to beat them.

These women, all colors, helped each other. The ones who worked in the big house, sending messages to others in the field: "Tell Minty to go tonight. They gon sell her and her children tomorrow." The ones who worked in the cane, in the cotton, in the smokehouse, dredging out the canals from muck, chopping wood and making bricks alongside the men, found a meeting ground in a hush harbor someplace, steady patting feet and the backs of their babies, moaning in a presence that shored up their hearts for more struggle, more strength.

And these women, in slavery-time, who had been through so much—whipped until they bled; their hands scarred; their faces and breasts scarred because these were the most beautiful parts of their bodies—these women, found their way into the Pachamama circle.

. . .

And there is something they must do, the women in this circle. They have to go to water—to a river, an estuary, to the ocean side if they can reach it. Even just to a deep well if there is no other water around. They have to go to water and dip their cups into the water, dip their pails into the water and drink. There is a root they find nearby. They find a plant whose roots go deep down toward the water. A thick root. Bitter in taste. And they dig this and they share it. And the newest one, the one who is coming into the circle, they put a little of the chewed root at her temple and at the top of her head and they cover her head with a cloth and she sleeps there by the water. And they leave food by the water. What they have, they offer—if it is summer maybe some corn or a plate of greens cooked up with a little salt pork. If it is winter maybe they'll leave cornmeal or make some pone and set it there with stewed beans.

. . .

In slavery-time, the Pachamamas were Harriets. And later they were our Idas and Bessies and they became Sue Bailey Thurman and Elizabeth Catlett Mora and Katherine Dunham and Nina and Billie and Shirley Graham Du-Bois and Ella Baker and Septima Clark. And my mama and grandmama and great-grandmama. They are Cleo Parker Robinson now and Anne Braden and Dolores Huerta and Rachel Noel and Marion King Jackson. We have so many. Women who stand midcurrent in the river. Giving fresh water to the tribes. Showing us how to be well again. They are the warrior-reconcilers. The healer-sorcerers. They are the scientists. Conjurers. The guides.

And they are mothering. They are mothering, Rachel. Drawing their circles of protection and power around us even as we look elsewhere. Teaching about how to be family. How to live like family. How to live with some strength and care in your hands. How to live with some joy in your mouth. How to put your hands gentle on where the wound is and draw out the grief. How to urge some kind of mercy into the shock-stained earth so that good will grow.

. . .

These Pachamamas, let me tell you something about them. Let me tell you something about the way they mother. They stand sometimes a little bit on that side of uncertainty. Just across the edge of where you don't always know what they might do. What they are capable of. I think about Iemanjá—the orixá of salt waters, the sea mother. She is quintessential abundance and maternal energy. Affectionate, generous with her love and her resources—feeding the world from the affluent waters of her womb.

But the ocean is a mighty woman, Rachel. And Iemanjá, when necessary (or as the moment strikes her), can discipline with a swiftness—insistent and devastating. Even wrathful. Imposing her strictures with fierceness and force belying the steady, regular rhythm of her day-to-day waves.

So there is this about the Pachamamas too. The great surge. The mountain. The whirlwind that rises quickly from the solar plexus and rushes wherever it must go, lifting grounded things high into air.

. . .

And this is the circle I'm telling you about. All this is the circle . . .

. . .

There are a lot of things, Rachel, that the family doesn't talk about. Mystic things that occupied Grandma Rye. In her herbs. Her medicines. Her silences. If you listen to the older cousins, to my sisters, without asking them directly, you will hear. Some of the things that Pamp says about how people were afraid of my mother, Mama Freeney—well, that's where Mama Freeney got it from. From Grandma Rye. Also the very quick way that Alma always says our great-grandmother was Christian. As if to head off any possibilities to the contrary.

Some of these things are secret. And some of them will never be spoken. Not from rule or restriction but because they don't live in the language. They live in the body. They live in the gesture and the way the rays of the sun radiate off of the Pachamamas' backs. From their shoulders. Their heads. Their hands. Some of this is not something you talk about. It is in the body like the holy ghost. It is in bone. In blood. In the soft space under the tongue. Resting.

Notes

1. Howard Thurman was a twentieth-century African American mystic theologian, educator, minister, and writer. He was a mentor to Martin Luther King Jr. and other activists/thinkers of the freedom movement and an advocate for a more ecumenical, inclusive Christian tradition. Thurman was the first African American chaplain at Boston University. He and his second wife, Sue Bailey Thurman, were active in national and international efforts at interracial reconciliation and helped found the Church of the Fellowship of All Peoples, the first interracial congregation in San Francicso, California.

2. Howard Thurman, *The Luminous Darkness* (New York: Harper and Row, 1965), 31.

A Choreography of Mothering

This is a Pachamama story in dance. This is my story. A dance to set on Cleo Parker Robinson's company.[1] The dance is a story and the story is a choreography. It is myth and it is truth. This is what happened to me.

. . .

In my story, the Pachamamas attend the birth of a baby girl who is born in a northern city into a family with southern roots. They watch from gentle places in her early life. One of the Pachamamas, dressed as a German nurse, delivers the child in such kindness, into such tenderness, that the baby's mother names her daughter in the nurse's honor.

But the birth is not the beginning. My story begins with death. When my story begins, the girl child is an old woman and the Pachamamas are accompanying her in a dance. They have danced with her all her life. They watched over her as she grew, guided her into the wisdoms of womanhood, comforted her in her sadnesses and trials, spoke to her in dreams, marked the trees of her path, and now they will carry her body to the grave when she breathes her last breath.

The old woman is buried by a river. And after her body is set into the ground, a mythic fishbird rises from the nearby water. The bird has the head of one kind of animal, the scaled body of another, fins and claws, and the long rainbow feathers of the quetzal. The fishbird is medicine; the transformational spirit of life, of exquisite mothering, continuing on.

When the dance begins, the woman is already old. Near dying, though she pulls a thin vigor from the movement of her limbs, from the closeness of the Pachamamas who are dancing with her. They have been her continual company and we can tell from the way they are moving with her, they know her well. They love her. There are many of them. They are like spiritwomen somehow. We must know this from their clothing, from their placement on the stage in relationship to the principal dancer, from their movements.

Then the dance-story goes back. We see the birth, we see the woman as a young girl, and even as she laughs and plays in the streets of her childhood, there are—watching from the porches, the classrooms, the windows—the spiritwomen who are sometimes invisible, sometimes not, nearby. Even her own mother, the one who birthed her, gives the daughter a glance at moments, extends her hands, her arms, in gestures that tell us she, too, is of the circle.

Our dancer eventually marries. We see her dressing up in beautiful clothes. Elegant and tasteful designs. Her movements sensual and strong. Her dance is an invitation to her husband. He comes to the stage and moves as if he doesn't see her. Takes over the stage. Finally, he exits with another woman—younger, with long legs and a short skirt. As soon as the husband and the other woman leave, the Pachamamas come to dance with our protagonist. So that she doesn't cry long. This happens more than once.

When her mood lifts, the Pachamamas retreat to the shadows. And the woman keeps dancing. She keeps dancing. More strongly now. Forcefully. With the movements of whirlwind and hard feet into the floorboards. She falls in a frenzy to the floor. And as she wakes up, she is wearing something different. Another dress. Many things about her are different. Her face is different. Her expression is different. We can see this change in her body. A kind of illumination from inside.

It's important that we see that the dance itself is a redeeming, a healing in the woman's life. Cleo will know this. She will fill out the details of gesture and movement as she is led. Rachel will help as needed. There are motions I have seen in the circle dances of Brazil, of Candomblé; movements of the hands, the wrists, the shoulders, the sliding feet, that remind me of Qigong. Especially the placement of hands. Movements that look like planting and collecting crops, that look like the passages of water. Somehow we will have some circle dances in the story. This is where the woman is joined by the whole group of Pachamamas and they motion her into the circle of mothering, the circle of strength. The memory in the body of how to become a new thing. *"Behold . . . do you not perceive it?"*

. . .

And when she dies, her body is carried to the riverside. And when she is buried and mourned, something rises up out of the water. Something very beautiful. A creature with the spirit of multiple creatures. Something feathered, and skinned, and finned and legged and colorful and magical and lithe and strong.

And we realize that throughout the dance, there have been small things—a red quill tied to the head of one of the Pachamamas with a simple string, a leotard with golden scales along the shoulders worn by another, a snatch of song or scent, a certain movement in the woman's own sinuous body. . . . There have been these things all along from early in the girl child's life that were as hints of what would come at the end. Maybe after one of the circle dances, when the Pachamamas retreat and the woman is alone on stage, she looks in front of her and there is a large colorful plume. Just one, prominent on the stage floor. Or maybe in successive circle dances, more of the Pachamamas wear a feather at their foreheads; feathers of different colors, which, at the end are echoed in the spectacular headdress of the animal-spirit rising out of the current.

As the creature climbs from the river and rises we are struck by its splendidness, by the spectacularity of its colors and its variety of forms; we are moved by the grace and power of its sensuousness. It reminds us of the magnificence, the poetry, the artistry at the heart of life; at the center of who we are as human beings. It reminds us of the connectedness, the startlingly beautiful conjunctions of animal, human, and spirit figures in a contiguous whole. How we are always accompanied, always aided, always joined to the greater source of spirit.

We see in the fishbird moving from the waters, dancing on land, the transformation of the woman's suffering and strength into joy. The Pachamamas have protected and nurtured that joy in the times of trauma. Keeping it alive. They are the tall-spirit women who preserve and defend with a muscular love, an unflinching compassion, and admonishment in the face of mercilessness. Theirs is the knowledge of planting blessings in hard ground. They hold stones and stories under their tongues so that we will have them when we need them. And they teach.

They are—the Pachamamas—our recollection of the universe. They are our memory of what it is to be human. This mothering.

.   .   .

The fundamental condition of the universe is care and love. Everything here is taking care of us. For no fee. An oxygen and carbon dioxide mix breathed constantly into our air by trees and plants and rocks. Breezes to cool us. Sun to warm us. We are charged nothing for this. There is no way to pay. It is given freely. Plants grow and offer their edible parts to us so that we won't starve. (Not us, not animals, not insects . . . so nothing starves.) There is no fee for this. No money involved, except for the commodification by human beings. But the universe, the earth, the sun, does not *charge* us, does not require us to give it money for our survival. The ground holds us as we stand on it, as we walk. Sustains our homes and other structures. We cannot pay the earth any money for this.

This is like the Pachamamas. They bless and protect us because that is who they are in the universe. Because they love us. And because they are our teachers and our mothers. What we are required to do is reciprocate. To return love and care and stewardship to the land. To the water that flows continually, offering us as much as we need. To the air. What we are required to do is to care for each other. Individually and systemically. We, human beings, can create systems of governance and economy that facilitate this mutual caring, or we can create systems that make it more difficult. We choose and we live in the consequences of our choices. The example of our Pachamamas is the example of the universe; is exquisite and spectacular mothering.

Note

1. Cleo Parker Robinson Dance is an innovative multicultural ensemble and the premier modern dance company in the Rocky Mountain West.

There was no vacuum when we came here. When our ancestors came here chained up. Once in a while I get hints of what they came with. When I was reading slave narratives for my work on Ida, I found people who would say, "Now I know this God is a powerful God." They were talking about the God they found in this new place, this Christian God, but even then they were not far from the African Gods. They came here with some powerful Gods. Gods of water. Gods of earth. So, here was another one. That's why I think Grandma Rye loved fishing. Not just to catch fish, but to be near the water Gods. To be near the essential energy of water. And she could be with the essential energy of earth where she got her herbs. And when she would cook, the fire Gods were there to keep her company.

Now, the way I am talking now, I got this kind of thinking from Mom. What I want to say is that Mama Freeney heard those stories from the people before her—from Mama Liza and Papa Jim and Grandma Rye—those stories were ways of talking about the old Gods. Teaching wisdom, building confidence, and telling you there is more to this world than you can see or touch. The stories are a way of talking about spirit things without being labeled an "unbeliever." It really fits the mold of who my mother was. So much of Mama Freeney's spirituality came out in the stories.

And do you know, Efua Sutherland was telling those same stories to her grandchildren when we visited them in Ghana?[1] She'd scrunch up her face and go "Bwrooo!" like that, at the little ones. And they'd run laughing, but frightened, too, away from her. Mama did the same thing. Very same thing. There's a lot in those stories. Caution, moral teachings, and even just the capacity to *feel* the energies around you. To sense things. For Alma, it comes in the scriptures. But the stories, they were a way of teaching African understandings in a transitional mode, moving toward the credo kind of Christianity. But holding on to those mystic meanings. The poetry of the spirit.

Note

1. Efua Sutherland was an influential Ghanaian playwright and children's book author, wife of Bill Sutherland, African American peace activist and pan-Africanist. Rosemarie visited Efua and her family in Accra in 1993.

AfterWords

(Rachel)

41 · *Fugida*
   Poem for Oyá

wind
covering the newly dead with your remnant cloth,
the hush hush of your sanctified, cimarrón name,
your high legs stuttering at the river edge.

       them running meet you there.
       some follow.
       some push ahead.

Oyá   uncaptive wind;
wide-hipped whose
short lance warrior glint
whistles, shears into storm.

the scout. *look for me*
wind.
your sword. your red mouth.
airstream of ribbons lacing your tongue.

guide my fugitive words.

       • • •

water-grown audacity into air.
a fearlessness, the fearlessness of fire. flight.
wordspit spewed like melon seeds spreading creation,
rainfalls and heavy thunder. the outrider. the cyclone
whose banner skirts twist oak and old cypress into baldness.

   . . .

blow clear the quilombo road, Oyá.
their footprints still pressed in a morning clay
longside tracks that feint;
refuge voices from memory hill
timbres of clove and wisteria
high john laughter and ella song
seeping from their long walk clothes.

   . . .

over your shoulder, fugida
turn. hook my gaze.
steady my scripting hand.
your hurricane shimmy in the pine limbs
is the train rolling out.

> *i am two passengers*
> *on your "free or die" railroad.*
> *conduct me. my hidden mouth is*
> *a scythe in cane. is a river*
> *under the ocean.*
> *is my mother's lacework bones*
> *whirled up*
> *gifts and labors*
>
> *words that ride   by moss and starshine*
> *words that run.*

Note

Fugida means "escaped." Oyá is the Yoruba name for the sacred energy of transformation; feminine orixá of storm and movement. Goddess of struggle, of ancestors,
and of empowered utterance. *Cimarrón* is a term for maroons, runaways. A *quilombo*
is a community of fugitive slaves, other refugees, and their descendants. The railroad reference is underground.

42 · Class Visits
Love, White Southerners, and Black Exceptionalism

There is a Southern spirit that is so full of love. If you don't come from the South, you might not know it when you see it. . . . It's such a mixed history, but there is a lot of love in it. Even with the violence, there is love. I want to tell you, without that foundation the South would have destroyed itself a long time ago.

When my mother was alive, one of the pleasures of my teaching career was having her visit my classes. At least once a semester, I would ask Mama to speak to my students from her combined perspective as a scholar of history and participant in social justice movements. Most of my courses were in some way related to African American history, culture, and religion, and Mama was well versed in all of those matters, and many more. But even though I may have asked her to talk about the role of the Black press and the Negro Women's Club movement in the Great Migration in one course, or about women in the civil rights movement in another, or about native white southerners who were antiracism organizers long before the term existed, Mama would always end up talking about love.

At the University of Colorado in Boulder and the Iliff School of Theology in Denver, the vast majority of my students were white. They were young and middle-aged; male and female; and whether they were in the class because they were interested in the subject or just to fulfill a distribution requirement, they were deeply moved whenever Mama came to talk. No matter where she started, Mama always found her way around to reminding them—no, giving evidence, proof, from the widest part of her heart—that all of us are family, all of us are loved, and there is no scarcity on this earth except that conjured by greed and fear.

Inoculate Love

One year, I was teaching a large introductory African American studies class, and Mom came to talk about Ida B. Wells-Barnett and early twentieth-century antilynching activism.[1] She gave an overview of the period known as the "nadir" of African American history—those decades following Reconstruction when it seemed as if, to all intents and purposes, Black people were being pushed back to the edge of slavery. Duly elected officials were illegally deposed; voting rights rescinded or impeded with violence; whole towns of Black people purged or burned out; land stolen; and almost daily, in some town or city of the newly reunited states, a Black man or woman hung from a tree.

Then Mama started talking about Ida. And about Ida's father, Jim Wells, and his mother, Peggy. Jim was born in slavery and his mother had been severely beaten by the plantation mistress who was angry and jealous because of her husband's attraction to the enslaved Black woman. (In fact, Morgan Wells, the white man who "owned" Jim and his mother, was also Jim's father.) But when slavery ended, when the master was dead and the mistress was old and frail, Jim's mother stayed on to take care of the woman who had treated her so badly. Jim wasn't happy with this arrangement. He felt that after everything the mistress had put his mother through, she didn't deserve her former slave's care. It was not an easy choice to understand, my Mama told the students. "But," she said, "Ida's grandmother wasn't the only person who was willing to do this."

Mama said there is a quality of love, a transformative and transforming quality that lies at the base of African American experience; it is not easy to explain and it is sometimes confused with weakness. Although it is not inviolate, it is real. This quality has been nurtured, through generations of enslavement and suffering, perhaps as an inoculation against becoming the worst of what we experienced.

Once, when she and I were talking, Mama remembered something that her Aunt Mary had said to her in the late 1960s. My mother and father had been living in the South for several years and were visiting family in Chicago when they stopped by to see Aunt Mary. Aunt Mary was the oldest of my grandmother's sisters, and she was almost ninety at the time. This was shortly before she died. Newspapers and television stations carried stories daily about the violence and the staunch white resistance to change, and people all over the country were watching intently to see what was happening. Aunt Mary asked Mom to take a note to Martin and Coretta with a small contribution to help the Movement. About the violence, Aunt Mary said that part of the responsibility of Black people in this life, in this world, is to forgive. "You know," she said to my parents, "it's not up to us to judge. We keep doing the work. God judges and we forgive. If we can forgive, then that is reward enough."

. . .

I would say that this perspective is related to a fundamental indigenous wisdom about who we are as human beings, how we are ultimately connected to other people, how we are truly responsible for each other. And like the philosophies of Tibetan Buddhism, Sufi Islam, and the best of the Christian tradition itself, this orientation emphasizes that those who understand are called to live this way even if other people are not yet able.

Aunt Mary's words must have really stuck with Mama, because she remembered that visit and told me about it several times over the years. Mama used to say that white people were her children, that all of us come from an original African mother and that if they sometimes act with violence and arrogance and immaturity, they need mothering so that they can learn to live in the world as family to the rest of us.

This attitude was part of the way Mama saw the world and moved in the world. And it is what I sucked up, in the air around her, from her bones and skin, from walking in her wake and playing in her kitchen. And it is what forms the foundation of the way I myself teach, especially the way I teach my students who are uneasy about their history.

White Southerners in the Movement

Another time, I was teaching a seminar on "the Sixties" and I asked my mother to speak to my students about her experience in the Movement, and especially about some of the native white southerners who were her friends and colleagues in those years. She talked about Clarence and Florence Jordan and Koinonia Farm, the interracial Christian community they founded in post–World War II Georgia. She talked about Will Campbell, a Mississippi-born and bred preacher who went to divinity school up north but returned home to tend to his roots and minister a radical gospel to Klan-based communities. She told the class about Anne and Carl Braden who were fighting segregation and organizing unions in Kentucky in the 1940s and charged with sedition for selling a house to a Black family in a previously all-white neighborhood.

Mama talked about these people with tremendous love and respect. They were white folks who had sacrificed a great deal of security to work on behalf of a transformed nation, a transformed relationship between Blacks and whites, between rich and poor in this country. Indeed, they had come through a hard struggle to transform themselves. They were her comrades and her heroes, just like Ida B. Wells-Barnett was a hero for Mama. And she never missed an opportunity to use their stories to help a younger generation of white youth know that they had deeply committed forebears in the struggle for democracy and justice.

The students were so hungry to hear this. They leaned forward in their desks and listened with their full bodies to news that their racial history included courageous, magnificent folks who stood in solidarity with others who had a vision of a radically different America. Mama said that these people captured and cultivated such a vision of transformation, partly because of the love that they lived with growing up.

A Paradox of Affection: Southern Racism and a Culture of Love

It sounded like a contradiction in a way. (And yet, there is something about love, when it is in fact love, that will not be managed or constrained.) Mama told the class that a loving, racist family is not an incongruity in this country. "The unique history of this nation created a Ku Klux Klan," she said. "It created slavery; and creates the racism we struggle with in our institutions and in our psyches. And yet," she looked around at the students and moved closer to their desks, "there is alongside that history, a culture in the South—among both Black and white—with an enormous capacity for love."

They were really listening now. Some of these students had roots in the South, parents and grandparents with personal memories of the civil rights movement era, and family stories that went further back still. Others came from people who had lived in the Mountain West for generations and had little or no contact with Black people before coming to college. Still others were from the Midwest or California. But all of them had some sense of the racial history of the country. Even if just at an intuitive level—and even those who had arrived with no idea at all received some background in the first weeks of my course. They were interested. As was I.

I had heard my mother speak before groups on many occasions. Both of my parents were excellent public speakers who engaged their audiences with a marvelous combination of solid historical information and a powerful analysis of the facts that emphasized the great potential for change and renewal that is the basis of the human experience. But Mama, even more so than Daddy, had a way of understanding the world that looked injustice squarely in the face, but was always able to locate a redemptive remnant in even the most horrific circumstance. And she wasn't making it up. She just had the capacity, like a master chemist, to isolate that quality of hope and compassion that, for her, existed at the heart of every living thing in the universe.

Mama was walking across the front of the room, and down into the rows. She turned, now and again, to touch a student lightly on the shoulder, or brush their back as she passed. She talked to my students about this southern culture of love and I listened attentively. I was taping this talk, and occasionally I'd get up to check and make sure the recorder was still catching all of her words, or to turn the cassette over to the other side. Mama's warm, conversational style made people comfortable and, I think, willing to listen to words that might go against the conventional wisdom of the mass media, but which nevertheless resonated deeply in their hearts.

This culture of love that Mama spoke about, these traditions of hospitality and caring so common in the South, draw a lot from Black folks who have nurtured a practice of welcome, inclusiveness, and a keen sense of justice through many generations of assault. In fact, the culture became a resource for confronting and transforming the assault. But southern models of inclusiveness and reconciliation also come from whites, many of whom suffered from economic disenfranchisement and marginalization. Some of them, Mama would say, looked beneath white supremacist theologies and found the words and actions of Jesus offering a worthy example for an antiracist life. Some of them, she would say, were raised by Blacks or lived in close proximity to African Americans and came to know and respect our struggles and strains and mercies.

But some of the southern culture of love came as well from "men and women whose belief systems we might have trouble with," Mama said. "People we might call racists. But these people loved and cared for their children. They adored their grandparents. They took good care of their families and tried to live with some sense of integrity." They were people who, at moments, sometimes in the midst of great turmoil, were even able to let their essential humanity push them toward fellowship.

"I don't believe the South would ever have changed if there weren't people there who knew how to love," Mama said. "If your heart is made of steel, maybe you can see young people getting knocked in the head for freedom and your heart won't break. But let me tell you, a lot of those southern white hearts broke."

Anne Braden: The Choking Dress

Anne Braden was one of the great long-distance runners of the freedom movement. She was a white woman, born and raised in the South, who started fighting for racial and economic justice way back in the 1940s, long before there was a mass movement for civil rights. She was trained as a journalist and worked for most of her professional life as a community organizer and editor of activist publications. Anne and her husband, Carl, were often considered "race traitors," that is, white people who stood very firmly against racism and supported the leadership and struggles of African Americans and other people of color. They were also strong advocates of fairness for working people, especially miners, factory workers, and others who suffered from dire poverty in many parts of the South. In the 1950s, because Anne and Carl were so firm in their belief in racial justice, they were called "communists," which was just about the worst political charge that could be levied at a U.S. citizen at that time (kind of like calling somebody a "terrorist" now). But they were both wonderfully committed to creating a truly representative and truly inclusive democracy and, after her husband's death, Anne continued that powerful work for almost forty more years.

In her interview with the Veterans of Hope Project, Anne Braden talks about how she first began to recognize the terrible limitations that racism placed on white people's lives, as well as on Blacks. Anne tells a story of coming into the family kitchen one evening when she was a young teenager and seeing the housekeeper's daughter wearing her cast-off clothes. The two girls were about the same age, but the housekeeper's daughter was heavier and the clothes did not fit her comfortably. Anne's old dresses visibly constricted the other girl. "I'd look at her," Anne remembered, "and I know something happened to me when I looked at her. Of course they couldn't come in our living room or come and sit down and eat, that sort of thing."[2]

Mama told this story to the students in my "Sixties" class and had me read from a section of Anne's autobiography describing the encounter in the kitchen. "She would sit there," Anne wrote, "looking uncomfortable, my old faded dress binding her at the waist and throat. And some way I knew this was not what Jesus meant when he said *clothe the naked*. I recalled that Jesus had also said, *Therefore all things whatsoever ye would that men should do to you, do you even so to them*. And I knew that if I were in her place, if I had no clothes, I would not want the old abandoned dresses of a person who would not even invite me to come into her living room to sit down. And I could not talk to her because I felt ashamed."[3]

For Anne, the discomfort of both the clothes and the encounter was symbolic of the cramping and stultification that racial injustice creates not just for Black people, but for whites as well.

Clarence and Florence Jordan: No Enemies

Within thirty years after the abolition of slavery, most southern states had established a network of prison camps as a way to control and exploit the labor of Black people; these were part of a larger structural attempt to terrorize African Americans into submission. In Georgia, Alabama, Mississippi, Texas, Louisiana, and elsewhere in the region, laws were created against vagrancy and joblessness to ensure a steady pool of prisoners; and Black men were arrested and convicted of crimes in numbers vastly disproportionate to their population. Inmates at the prisons were leased to local businesses (especially agricultural and mining interests) that benefited from what was essentially a new form of slave labor. These practices were very common in the early twentieth century, during Clarence Jordan's boyhood.[4]

Mama talked about the prison camp in Georgia near the town where Clarence Jordan grew up and how he developed a relationship with some of the prisoners, especially a cook who used to give Clarence cracklings (fried pork skins) and cornbread through the fence as the boy passed on his way home from school each day.

The warden at that prison camp was a white man who belonged to the church that Clarence and his family attended. That warden had a beautiful voice and one Sunday he sang "Love Lifted Me" with such emotion that Clarence never forgot it. But that same warden took a sadistic pleasure in torturing the Black men under his watch at the prison camp. He would put them on a stretching board and turn the screws to pull their joints and bones. Clarence heard the screams and recognized the prisoners' voices. He said he also knew who was turning the screws to make them suffer so.

That experience made Clarence question a God who would create this kind of contradiction—a warden who praised Him in church on Sundays and then afflicted men with horrible pain throughout the week. It was also one of the key experiences, early in Clarence's life, that put him on the path of commitment to radical social justice. Mama explained that it would have been almost impossible for Clarence to have been born and raised in Georgia in the 1920s and '30s and not have had some Klan roots in his family.

But at the same time, Clarence had received a foundation of compassion from his parents and from his faith, and he had experienced fellowship and friendship with the prisoners. These things compelled Clarence to reexamine the rote theology with which he had been raised and encouraged him to struggle up to an attitude, much like that of the Dalai Lama, "that he had no enemies. Everyone was his brother and sister. No matter who they were and no matter what they did."

"That's how Clarence lived his life," Mama said. And for some of his white friends and family, his mutual fellowship with whites and Blacks was radical enough that they thought he should leave the state. But Clarence's example was a reminder that the tradition of fellowship, of justice-seeking and reconciliation in the South was not a foreign import. Surely it was a struggle, even a great danger, to try to live out such a commitment before the movement days in Georgia, but it was a homegrown compulsion in many ways.

And there was something in Clarence's compulsion that reminded my mother of her own family, especially her father, my grandfather, Daddy Freeney. Daddy Freeney, too, was a brilliant farmer, a dependable neighbor and friend, who invented techniques for grafting fruit that he shared with others. "They even sounded alike," Mama said. Those gentle, gravelly southern tones and the stories that taught and entertained. They were born in the same state, not terribly far from each other, my grandfather and Clarence Jordan. "Whenever I would hear Clarence talk, it reminded me of my Daddy," Mama would say. I think that was part of why she loved him so.

My parents spent a lot of time at Koinonia. For a while, it was a kind of sister community to the Mennonite House project they had established for movement volunteers in Atlanta. Several times a year, everybody from Mennonite House would pile into a couple of cars and caravan down to Americus to plant trees or help with the pecan harvest or hold retreats and meetings on the farm. When I was born, Mom asked Clarence Jordan to be my godfather and he said yes.

Koinonia Farm was an experiment in radical Christian community-building established in the 1940s in Americus, Georgia, by Clarence and Florence Jordan and their friends Martin and Mabel England. At the time, strict social, economic, and political arrangements governed relationships between whites and blacks—generally to the advantage of whites and the detriment of African Americans. Anyone who attempted to alter those arrangements was threatened with many kinds of harm. Slowly, as Koinonia's commitments to racial and economic justice became known throughout the area, they began to suffer increasingly harsh retribution from local whites.

Mama told my students the story of the Klan members who had terrorized the Koinonia community for many years, shooting up their homes, setting fire to their roadside fruit and vegetable stands and boycotting their products so effectively that Clarence had to go more than one hundred miles away to find a bank that would loan them any money.[5] After Clarence died, the men who had so harassed the community came, as a group, and told Florence they were sorry for all the violence they had done. Clarence had helped many of them improve their land and had brought new farming techniques to the region that benefited everybody in the area. He had been a good neighbor, trying to live by the example of fellowship and community from the Gospels. It was 1969 and times were changing. The Movement had been active in the area since the beginning of the Albany campaigns in 1961 and even some of the hardest-hearted white supremacists were beginning to wonder about the things they had been raised to believe. They asked Florence for forgiveness and prayer. So she prayed with them. And she forgave them.

For Mama, this was an example of the necessity of "never giving up on anyone." She told the class that the Dalai Lama teaches that there is no human being who does not have the capacity to change. "You have to know that all of us have the same heart, all of us. And there is a southern spirit that is so full of love," Mama said.

"If you don't come from the South, you might not know it when you see it. But I can tell you stories of white people who saved Black people's lives and I can tell you about Black people who saved white people's lives. And then there are some people who are white who are Black—I mean, they look white but they're really Black. It's such a mixed history, but there is a lot of love in it. Even with the violence, there is love. I want to tell you, without that foundation the South would have destroyed itself a long time ago."

Will Campbell

Then my mother told my class about Will Campbell. "I think he went to Harvard or someplace like that and got a PhD in theology. But he was a Mississippi country boy, so he didn't let Harvard go to his head.[6] He came back home and had a little church and he started preaching this *loving your neighbor* and *loving everybody* stuff and got in a little trouble.[7] So he moved to Tennessee, that's where he is now. And he started a magazine—called *Katallegete*—that published for a long time in the sixties and seventies. It was full of articles about people like Clarence Jordan and the kind of witness they were trying to live out. For me," Mama said, "Will is a typical white southern man."[8]

There is an interview with Will Campbell, published in the *Christian Century*, three years after Mom passed, where he talks about his love of country music and country musicians, the weakness of genuine religious conviction in our time, the inexcusability of the Iraq war, and the relative value of voting. He also tells the interviewer about his family and the grounding they gave him for the work he did in his life, for the kind of man he became. Will was born in the 1920s and raised in a close community of relatives in rural East Fork, Mississippi. He said his father and grandfather, both of whom were also southern born and bred, "knew that racism was wrong" and even in those years when violence of so many kinds (physical, social, economic, psychic) was endemic against African Americans, they reprimanded the children of their households for disrespecting Black people.

Will was at his grandfather's house one Sunday after church, with a group of "yearling boys" (what the family called the growing young males in their midst), when the children saw a Black man coming down the road. Will tells the story: "We started taunting him and calling out the n-word. Grandpa called us over. He called everybody 'Hon'—didn't matter who they were—and we didn't have those Freudian hang-ups in those days. He said, 'Hon, that man is a colored man. Not a nigger. There aren't any niggers, and I don't want to hear you calling anybody that.'"[9] His grandfather's words, and his elders' examples, made a lasting impression on Will and became part of the impetus for his professional and personal choices later in life.

Anne Braden too was a "typical southern white woman" to my mother— an outstanding journalist and organizer who, despite tremendous persecution, and into her nineties, worked for interracial justice and equality. Mama said the Movement benefited from the wisdom, commitment, and groundedness of people like Will and Clarence and Florence and Anne. "These are the kind of folks who have given our country a foundation in hope. These are people who are saving our nation, helping our nation to become the best it can be for all of us."

. . .

By now, the students were fascinated. Some of them, I could tell, weren't so sure about Clarence and the "having no enemies" part, and others were clearly not accustomed to hearing this kind of history, not quite sure what to make of it, but something rang true with them and they were listening closely. Mama stood at the front of the room and told them, "It's so important to tell the stories of these people, people like this." She was leaning against the teacher's desk, balancing with one hand and raising the other into a sharp wave for emphasis. "So important. I hope some of you will go on and do your PhDs on the lives of these people, because our country really needs to know them. These men and women have built the foundation of hope in our country. And many of you have people like this in your own families. I'm sure you do. We all do. I'm sure that in your families you have people who are just magnificently compassionate and loving."

She looked around with a wry smile. "Well, now, we have *all kinds* of folks in our families, don't we?" There were a few knowing chuckles from the students. "But if you think about it," Mama continued, "I'm sure you can think of *someone*—maybe a sibling or a grandparent or a cousin. Maybe your mother or father, or an uncle or aunt—someone who you have seen take care of people. You've seen them go out of their way to look out for family. They've taken care of *you*. So just think about them. We really need to develop a sense of gratitude to our families. A gratitude to our immediate ones—starting with our mothers and fathers and grandparents. The people who made a space for us in the world, and helped us fill it."

Then, as if she were thinking ahead for the response of those who may have had neglectful or traumatic childhoods, Mama said something else. She said that our nation's history is full of contradictions and our personal histories are full of contradictions. Every human being has things we are proud of and things we are ashamed of. Even the most shameful abuser has something in him or her that is capable of transformation. Something that holds out hope for change. Regardless of what that person has done. "I'm talking about myself now," Mama said. Regardless of what the person has done, he or she does not want to be set so far apart from the rest of humanity as to be left without hope.

"Are They Still Klan Members?"

A young woman in the class asked a question about the Klansmen who had come to Florence Jordan seeking her forgiveness for the meanness and violence they had done toward the Koinonia community. "If they were still Klan members, were they really changed?" the student wanted to know.

Mama approached an answer to the question from an oblique direction, as she often did. She ended up sharing a perspective I doubt any of us anticipated. "How should I put this?" she started. "All of us want to be liked. We all want to be accepted. I don't want to walk into a room and have people not want me." She made a comparison to sororities and fraternities, asking students to think about how it feels to be excluded from a group when, in your heart, you want to be included. "Now maybe you don't care about those things," she said, "but some people do. And they will do almost anything to be a member of those organizations. Including hurting or scorning someone else. Fraternities and sororities are a minor thing, but take that small example and try to place yourself in a southern tradition where the custom is that you can be friendly to Black folk but Black folk are never to get out of their place. And if you help them to get out of their place, you're in trouble. You're in deep, deep trouble."

But in our history, a lot of white people did just this, Mama told the students. During slavery there were white people who were killed for aiding Blacks to escape. "There are a lot of white bodies at the bottom of the Ohio River because they gave their lives for people who were enslaved. And when other white people found out what was going on, they killed them. We need more of this history in our schools. Much more," Mama said. "Because you get the attitude that all white people hate Black people. And it makes you ashamed to be white. Which is ridiculous. You should not be ashamed to be a human being."

Mama said that guilt, by itself, doesn't serve much purpose. It just makes people angry. And then we start projecting our guilt and anger onto others. Yes, there are things we've done that we should be ashamed of. But the way to address guilt and shame is to work on someone else's behalf. *Go do something for somebody.* Help someone else. Make sure someone has what they need. Do something without expectation of reward. And express gratefulness. To your parents, to anyone who has helped you. Gratefulness is the solution to shame. "Thank the people who sacrificed so you could be sitting here; thank your parents, your grandparents, the generations of people who made your life possible. And help someone."

Mama told my students that what Clarence and Anne and Will and others did to deal with some of the guilt or shame they may have felt about white racism was to take responsibility for creating an alternative.

Furthermore, Mama said, it didn't bother her "one bit" if the men who came to Florence were still Klan members or not. "They're no better, but they're no worse than I am. They're no worse than I am. In the sight of God, in the face of reality, *who knows all the meanness that I've done; that I've hidden? Who knows about it? Nobody. I keep it hidden.* I am the only one who knows. Me and God." Mom said Clarence and Florence understood that, too, and didn't judge the men.

"The fact that those men came to Florence and asked forgiveness already implies a tremendous leap. And they may call themselves Klan members, but I don't believe they are, in their hearts. If you can come, in front of all your friends, and ask Florence Jordan to forgive you for the meanness you've done, well, you're alright now as far as I'm concerned. You're alright. Who am I to judge? Who am I . . . to judge? That's Not My Affair."

African American Exceptionalism: What Black Folks Have to Teach

For Mama, there was something transformative, instructive, beautiful, and profoundly healing in the Black experience. Something that could serve as a mnemonic device for other peoples. To help them remember the power and joy in their own roots. But she also knew that Black people could be just as selfish and silly as anybody else sometimes. We're all human. She didn't believe in African American exceptionalism. Rather, she did . . . and she didn't.

The Black North American experience was the history she knew best and the example she drew from most readily, but she would tell you in a minute that other people had profound wisdom to share out of their own lives and traditions.

She and I were talking one day about Septima Clark and Ella Baker and Ruby Sales—about how they each went through terribly hard times, so much hell, so much disappointment. And survived it. "There is something about going through hell that *can* give you a vision," my Mama said. "It's not guaranteed. And we have to look not only at the experience itself, but at *how* to go through it with sanity and compassion." One of the keys, in Mama's view, was honoring and understanding your roots. For the women she had just mentioned, "no matter how much education, experience, acclaim they might have gotten—they all went back to their roots." She meant they stayed connected to the sources that strengthened them, the family sources, the ancestral sources, the cultural and community traditions.

She said that Howard and Sue Thurman understood this too—the power of roots. "All of our roots are connected, you see. Everybody in this country has interconnected lines of blood and culture. And everybody's roots need to be integrated into our lives. We have to experience other people's roots. That's how we'll recognize the connections."

With all of the history she knew, and all the history she had lived, Mama still said it was "foolish" to think that Black folks have a special position from which to judge because of what we and our ancestors have been through in this world. She told the students. "If I go around judging white people from that position, I'm in as much trouble as Anne Braden was talking about. I'm the one sitting in that chair with the tight collar choking my *own* neck."

How many people of other races are responsible for my being here today? People I don't even know about. Teachers who sacrificed time and energy for me. Men and women who shared resources that benefited me in ways I know nothing about—like the man who donated money Clarence used to buy the Koinonia land. I never knew that man. Koinonia was such a beautiful and blessed retreat for me. I have nothing to do but say, *I'm grateful.* I'm grateful for our history and our struggle as Black people. So much wisdom, so much intellectual and artistic creativity arises from that struggle. The compassion. I am grateful for it. But that struggle doesn't mean I'm better than somebody because I'm Black. And that struggle doesn't give me a right to be mean and unforgiving. It gives me something I need to share. It gives me an understanding of what it is to go through some of the world's worst trauma—to know that people *can* and *do* go through these things—and *survive.* To know that we can bring magnificent light out of shrouded places. And it's not just Black people who can do it. Many other peoples as well—can and have and will yet.

All of us, she said, need to be grateful to all the people who have helped us. If we can't thank them personally, do something on behalf of someone else.

. . .

Another student commented to Mama that my class was unusual in its emphasis on what human beings can positively change. Mama thanked the student for the comment then she talked about the extraordinary creativity in our country, and how we may not think of it much because it isn't often in the news. She said watching TV news could make you think the world is an evil, terrible place and that there is nothing any of us could do to make it better. But she said, "None of us can survive living in negativity for long. You have to be around people who make you feel good. At least that's the way I am; when I get together with my friends, we have a good time." She asked the students to think about the experimentation that could be encouraged in environmental science, in healing, in education and architecture, if we were willing as a nation to cultivate *all* of our voices and talents and not just those of a privileged few. If we were willing to fund projects that benefited the society as a whole and not just a few people with a lot of money. The absence of money or whiteness is in no sense an absence of genius. In fact, there is often more genius where people have had to be astoundingly creative about navigating the many barriers to their well-being.

An Exercise in Compassion

Toward the end of her talk, my mother gave my students a homework assignment. An exercise to do on their own. "Think of someone who does not look like you, someone you don't know and perhaps have preconceived notions about. Or someone you have strong disagreements with. Get a picture of that person, or someone who represents such a person in your mind, and put it someplace where you can see it before you go to sleep at night."

"I do this," Mama told the class. "I will look at that picture, perhaps a Klan member, and say, *You are my brother. You are my father. You are my son. God be with you and bless you.* Or if you are Buddhist, chant on the person's behalf. And go to sleep with those thoughts and those prayers on your mind. You'll be amazed at the transformation—in us."

Through the stories she shared with the students, Mama was comparing the perspectives of people in the Movement to Buddhist philosophies of compassion. She said the Movement, from early on, focused on freedom and justice, not simply "rights." "Rights" is an insufficient concept. What movement folks did with their activism, with their commitments, was push larger and deeper into our connectedness. They were not focused on individual rights but on how to make our nation a better place for everybody. "That's a different worldview," Mama said. "They said: *Your well-being is related to my happiness; is, in fact, my goal.*" This was the same perspective she heard from the Dalai Lama and other Tibetan Buddhist teachers in Dharamsala, India.

Speaking directly to one of my students and asking his name, Mama said, "Andrew, what makes you happy is my goal. *My* goal. What makes *you* safe. Are you safe? Are you secure?" She said this was the attitude of the people whose stories she was sharing. She said it was not an unusual attitude in the world, but we don't talk about it enough. It is not celebrated enough.

Then she told the students, "Your life and your health is due to someone else's sacrifices and love. People like your family members who made their goal your well-being. People who sacrificed for you."

Anything we do to benefit another person is a way of passing on the kindness we received. We are all connected. Mama said, what kindness we do to anyone reverberates back to those whose kindness benefited us. "Read the Dalai Lama," she told the students. "And when you wake up each morning, be thankful to your teachers, your friends, your family; be thankful to people you don't even know who may have done something to help you."

We're All Connected: None of Us Is Better Than Anybody Else, and None of Us Is Worse

The class was drawing to an end. The students had listened carefully for more than an hour. Some had asked questions, but most of them were, it seemed, soaking in the gentle intensity of the graceful, velvet brown woman standing in front of them. No one seemed anxious to leave. Mama asked if there were any other questions and there was silence for a moment or two. Then, a young woman sitting near a window raised her hand and asked if Mom wanted things to change in our country. "Do you believe things can actually change?" the student wondered.

"Oh yes," Mama said to her. "Change will happen. Change is one of the constants of the universe and yes it is going to happen. What we need to do is contribute as much positiveness as we can to that change." Mama looked around at the rest of the room, "Change happens all the time. We are different people every day. We may look the same, but we're not. Changes are occurring in our bodies every day. None of us is the same person we were yesterday. And we're certainly not the same person we were seven years ago."

Mama talked about the vibration that is living energy in the universe, the vitality that is in constant movement and in constant presence in all living beings. The subtle-essential connection among all things, the life force:

Whether we call it prana or axé or chi, it is in every living thing in the universe. Even things that appear lifeless, like rocks and buildings. Everything in the world shares in this energy, contributes to it, benefits from it, is sustained by it. This energy connects us; it is in all of us and it passes into and around all life from other life. Whether we are conscious of it or not, we're in constant interaction with the rest of the universe. That is simply the way the universe is made. We call it community. That's what Clarence Jordan would call it. Living in community. It's the way the universe is made.

And nothing we do as human beings can destroy that energy in the world. We may be able to harm individual people, but we cannot destroy the life force. It encompasses us and is beyond us.

So the Klan brother is really a brother. And it's important for you to realize that. This Klan man that you'll be meditating and praying with—he'll feel the energy. And so will you, and so will I. And at some point you will be able to hug him. If not physically, then through the energy of your prayers and compassion for him.

And . . . how should I say it? Okay, my own belief system is coming out now. Let me just go ahead and say it. I believe we have all lived through different lives. And if that is so, then I was a Klan member at one time. Or something similar, you understand? I was a murderer at one time. I could have been someone who was hanged or I could have been the executioner.

We're only given a short time on this earth, in this life. At this point, it really doesn't make any difference which one I was. We've all been both. And the important thing is to take some wisdom from that experience, from my ancestors, from your ancestors, from all of our ancestors together, and try to live a life that benefits and supports and encourages other people. The reason we have this crazy, mixed-up history in this country is so that we can learn from it. Not avoid it. Not be guilty about it. Okay, we may need to be a little ashamed. But let the shame go into doing something on behalf of somebody else. None of us is better than anybody else. And none of us is worse.

And furthermore, meanness is fear. If you know anything about psychology, you know that people who show meanness are afraid. Now, we do have to protect folks. If somebody is afraid and they decide to hit someone in the head, we want to try to keep them from doing that. But we recognize that they are afraid. And the fear is covered up with bravado, "I can beat anybody. I'm tough." But we know it's not true.

The main thing is to be grateful. Call your parents and tell them how much you appreciate what they've done for you. Or anybody else who has helped you to become the beautiful, loving, and intelligent person you are. Thank someone. Thank your ancestors. That will make us rise to the occasion.

Notes

1. In the late nineteenth and early twentieth centuries, Wells-Barnett, an editor and publisher, was a major voice for the rights of African Americans and women. She became the principal investigator and denouncer of the practice of lynching in the United States. She wrote, organized, lobbied, and spoke eloquently and passionately against racist violence and suffered greatly for doing so.

2. "Anne Braden: Organizing the Other America," Veterans of Hope Project Pamphlet Series 2, no. 2 (2004): 5.

3. Anne Braden, *The Wall Between* (New York: Monthly Review Press, 1958), 23.

4. For information about the history of the convict lease system, see Douglas A. Blackmon, *Slavery by Another Name: The Reenslavement of Black Americans from the Civil War to World War II* (New York: Doubleday, 2008); and Robert Perkinson, *Texas Tough: The Rise of America's Prison Empire* (New York: Metropolitan Books, 2010). See also Michelle Alexander, *The New Jim Crow: Mass Incarceration in the Age*

of Color Blindness (New York: New Press, 2010) for an exploration of the ways in which the contemporary justice system criminalizes blackness.

5. A Black-owned bank in Atlanta was one of the few Clarence found that was willing to advance credit to Koinonia.

6. It was Yale Divinity School. He graduated in 1952.

7. After finishing at Yale, Campbell pastored in a little town in Louisiana for a short time, then moved to the University of Mississippi where he became director of religious life for the college for two years. He was asked to leave that position because of his support for integration. Campbell then became the southern field director of the National Council of Churches, Division of Racial and Cultural Relations, a position from which he was able to openly support the efforts of the freedom movement. His office was based in Nashville.

8. *Katallegete* (Greek for "Be Reconciled") was the journal of the Committee of Southern Churchmen.

9. From Amy Frykolm, "Bootleg Preacher: An Interview with Will Campbell," *Christian Century*, November 27, 2007, 9–10.

It was soon one morning
Death come creeping in my room
Soon one morning
Death come creeping in my room, God Almighty
It was soon one morning
Death come creeping in my room,
Oh my Lord, Oh my Lord, What shall I do to be saved?

Hush children hush
I heard my Lord call
Hush, Hush
Well I heard my Lord call, God Almighty
Well, hush, hush
I heard my Lord call,
Oh my Lord, Oh my Lord, What shall I do to be saved?

I'm gonna stand right here
Wait till Jesus come
Stand right here
I'm gonna wait till Jesus come, God Almighty
I'm gonna stand right here
Wait till Jesus come
Oh my Lord, Oh my Lord, What shall I do to be saved?
—TRADITIONAL

When Mom died I was devastated. I didn't know just how much at first. At first, it was actually a relief. For two or three days. She wasn't in that horrific, unrelenting pain. She wasn't so bloated that drops of water seeped from the parched, overstretched pores of her skin. She wasn't unconscious in a hospital room with tubes and wires everywhere and EMT workers were not hollering at me and Daddy to "stand back!" I wasn't waking in dark morning hours, stark straight up in bed, hearing her call me across dreams and sleep and the distance from my parents' home to my apartment, and knowing instinctively I had to get to her as quickly as possible, right away. I wasn't searching desperately for something other than steroids to reduce the swelling and trying to convince doctors that Mama's reaction was to the insulin itself (they finally agreed it was a strange and unusual case; but by then she was hours from gone).

For weeks before she died, Mama had been trying to talk to me. With the slant skim of her eye. Her quiet bones stretching to my shoulder. Her weight shifting. Open-winged.

The auguries came constant now: *Something out of your hands. Not your decision to make.* The I Ching alerting again and again the inevitable. *Slow down and stay close; be easeful and accepting as possible. This . . . is . . . something . . . else.* I couldn't hear it. And I trudged on too heavily—daily lining up doctors and therapists and masseurs and prayer warriors and anybody else I could think of who might save my mama.

Mama was dying and I didn't want to know. Had been through seven years of illness and miracles and all I knew of my mother was her astounding capacity to draw the healing up out of her body by dint of her will and whatever that private-quiet-thing was she did with God inside herself. That's all. I had seen her live through so many alarms, I just figured we'd make it through this one too.

Mama couldn't walk so she slept on the couch with everything she needed close by. Me and Daddy slept on the floor and took turns getting up through the night. It was always night. Even in the daytime. The air low and shallow. A foreign air—nothing I recognized. No language I spoke. Mama wanted us close. For company. To hold her and sing sometimes. We stayed in that room, in vigil, until death crossed the hall, a naked, pale, and heavy ghost. "Don't say it," Mama whispered and put her finger to her mouth when I asked if she saw it too. People came. I was bereft early and pulled back in fear and disconsolation. Daddy didn't miss a beat, took hold of Mama's hand. Stayed there.

Death is a shroud. A heavy stone. A mercy.

In the days immediately following, I sometimes felt it was an adventure. Something else my mother had given me, freely, generously—like a blouse she wore once, dazzled the world in, then passed along to me before I could even open my salivating mouth to ask for it. Always the pioneer, going before me to make sure the route, the place, was safe. Why not now, go first and send me back word? *"Mama, tell me what's it like over there. Come on, let's make us some tea. Let's sit in the kitchen. Tell me."*

After a while, what luster I conjured from my grief peeled loose and I ran into bricks and walls and fell into sarcophagal trenches.

Mama's arms somehow reached me even there. Invisible but certain. Pulling me up off the floor. Patting me to sleep at night, her hands on my back like a baby. Her baby. She got me through it. And the parts she couldn't do herself she sent help. And she put a little more fire, a little more iron, a little more solid earth, a little more hard wave, a little more sweet honey in my limbs. A little wind to move death . . .

(Rosemarie)

Grandma Rye and those old Africans put something in the ground. When they got here, they stepped off of those boats, chained up and weary. They looked around at this new land and they could see the heartbreak and suffering that were waiting for them and their generations. They saw these traumas waiting for us here. And they knew we were going to need something strong. Some medicine. Some spirit medicine to carry us through these storms.

So they made things. I can't tell you exactly what it was. Some of that they kept secret. But they made things out of what they came with—their spit, the water from their eyes, the hair on their heads, stones they hid under their tongues the whole journey long. They made things with the songs and the screams that rode them over that Atlantic Ocean in the holds of those leaking ships. And blood. They gave us their blood. Those old Africans blew on the ground, put their breath on this soil. Set their hands on this land and gave it some holiness to hold for us for when we would soon need to dig it up. They made prayers from their hands and put sounds on the air. Calling.

And when they got to those farms, those plantations, those houses in the ports where they slept in the basements and attics, where they slept in the barns. When they got to those places where they worked and where the leather stung them where it fell on their shoulders, on their backs, even the blood that streamed off of their bodies was libation. Sanctifying.

And that blood, that breath, the prayers did something to the land here. Put a mercy in the land that took root. Blessed it, really. Blessed the air, the water, all this fertile soil that is the Southland's big black belly. So that, generations later, those of us descended from them would walk across the roads and fields and woods and creeks and touch the blessing they put there for us. Grandma Rye and those old Africans.

There is some kind of strength here, people. There is some kind of strength that our ancestors saw and made and sent down into the bloodline for their children coming up behind. And it is a strength everybody who lives here, everybody who descends from anybody who ever lived here, can touch. Because it rides in the soles of the feet you walk on the ground with.

All the southwest Georgia people, C. B. and Slater and Marion; Bernice and Otis and Sherrod; and Clarence and Jimmy Carter too—all were blessed by Grandma Rye's current. The breath she blew on the land. Sanctifying. The call. She put a compassion in that land like seed. All that is what came up in the Albany Movement—those seeds of song and sweeping, those years of building in quiet and behind laughter. What those Africans planted got rooted deep down in that Georgia soil and rose.

I wasn't born there. But it didn't matter. That holiness Grandma Rye blew on the earth laid in wait for me. Rushed me like a magnet soon as I touched down, surrounded me like nieces and nephews hugging my legs, my waist, hanging on to my arms. Then, too, it had traveled the railroads and highways to Chicago so I had its taste in my mouth, was carrying it like mitochondrial cells, even before I ever thought of going down home.

Prathia Hall's father had a vision. He spoke it in his pulpit, back in the forties when she was a girl. "I saw India *rising*. I saw Africa *rising*!" The dream-sign was the wind of colored nations gathering strength. Anticolonial resistance. Another world coming. Grandma Rye's wind and those old Africans. And the Native folks before them. Blowing into Albany and Montgomery and Greenwood and Selma and Tallahassee and Macon and Knoxville and Little Rock and all the hundreds of little and big towns around this country where our movement stood up. It was the call. The holiness wind.

I heard it.

THE HARRIS SISTERS FAMILY TREE

This family tree information is reconstructed from family stories, obituaries, funereal data, and census information. Birth dates (especially of the older generations) are generally taken from census records and, as such, are approximate. Death dates are not known for all.

Mariah (Grandma Rye), 1829–1934, is Rosemarie's great-grandmother on her mother's side. Mariah married **Robert Grant.**

Their children are

Willoughby (aka William) Grant

Eliza Grant

Hester Grant

Mariah had another, older, daughter named **Ella** who was the child of a white man, probably the slave master. Mariah and Robert also helped raise Ella's daughter **Middie Cato.**

Lydia Harris, b. 1818, is Rosemarie's great-grandmother (or grandmother, we're not sure which) on her father's side. Lydia is the mother or grandmother of Papa Jim, Rosemarie's grandfather. We don't know the name of her children's father.

Lydia's children (or grandchildren) are:

Jim Harris

Cater Harris

Jane Harris

Cornelia Harris

Thomas Harris

Eliza Grant (Mama Liza), b. 1862, was married to **Jim Harris (Papa Jim)** b. 1850. They are Rosemarie's maternal grandparents.

Their children are

Mary Elizabeth Harris

Elizabeth (Itty) Harris

Tom Harris

Ella Lee Harris (Mama Freeney, Rosemarie's mother)

McFall Harris

Mamie Harris

Alberta (Bird) Harris

Hettie Mae Harris

Mary (Aunt Mary) Harris (1878–1967) married **William Daniels.**

Their children are

Wiley Daniels

Willie B. Daniels

Pansy (Pamp) Daniels Smith

Dorothy (Dot) Daniels Parker Gray

Joseph (Joe) Daniels

Percy Daniels

Isaac Daniels

Elizabeth (Aunt Itty) Harris, b. 1883, married **Coleman Anderson.**

Their children are

Cora Anderson

Mary Anderson

Annie Anderson

Pearl Anderson Daniels Dixon

Ella Lee Anderson

Ella Lee Harris (Mama Freeney) (1888–1991) married **Dock Freeney (Daddy Freeney)** (1886–1976). Ella Lee and Dock are Rosemarie's parents.

Their children are

James Monroe (Son) Freeney (1911–93)

Charles Dock (Bud) Freeney (1915–42)

Alma Georgia Freeney Campbell (1918–2007)

Mildred Elizabeth Freeney Dozier (1919–2013)

Thelma Sue Freeney Verrett (b. 1922)

Thomas Harold Freeney (1924–87)

Alberta Catherine Freeney (1925–80)

Norma Gloria Freeney (1928–2002)

Rosemarie Florence Freeney Harding (1930–2004)

Mamie (Aunt Mamie) Harris, b. 1890, married **Julius Smith**, b. 1885.
Their children are
Ann L. (Sister) Smith Morris
Myra Bea Smith Carter
Julia Helen Smith Buggs

Hettie (Aunt Het) Harris, b. 1895, married **Clarence Arthur Jackson**, b. 1896.
Their children are
Clarence Jackson Jr.
Juanita Olivia Jackson
Lionel Barrymore Jackson

Alberta (Aunt Bird) Harris, b. 1896, married **Sylvania Johnson**.
Aunt Bird's children are
Willa Mae (Sissy) Johnson
Evelyn (Charlie) Johnson

Mama Liza and Papa Jim's sons, Tom and McFall Harris, left Georgia as young men sometime after 1910 and never returned. Family stories suggest that they may have traveled as far as the Panama Canal, Mexico, and the Philippines. They kept in touch with their sisters by letter for a while, but over time the younger generations lost contact with them.

FREEDOM MOVEMENT COLLEAGUES
AND SPIRITUAL TEACHERS

An alphabetical listing by first name or title of coworkers and mentors Rosemarie notes in the text. Inclusive dates are recorded for those individuals who are no longer living.

Abdulalim Abdullah Shabazz (Lonnie Cross: 1927–2014)—a nationally recognized math professor and mentor of African American students, Shabazz was head of the math department at Atlanta University in the early 1960s.

Alice Walker—Pulitzer Prize–winning novelist, poet, and essayist whose "womanist" understanding of the lives and culture of African American women gave important theoretical grounding to this text.

Amzie Moore (1911–82)—entrepreneur, World War II veteran, and pioneering activist/strategist in the Mississippi Freedom Movement; mentor to Bob Moses.

Andrew and Jean Young (Jean: 1933–94)—close companions of Martin and Coretta King and friends of Rosemarie and Vincent in the Atlanta days. Andy served in the leadership cadre of SCLC and later became mayor of Atlanta, a congressman, and U.S. ambassador to the United Nations. Jean was an internationally recognized educator and advocate for child welfare.

Anne Braden (1924–2006)—one of the unsung group of white southerners who were deeply committed to the African American freedom movement in the 1950s and '60s. Cofounder of the Southern Conference Education Fund, Braden was a committed activist for labor rights and racial justice.

Bawa Muhaiyaddeen (d. 1986)—Sufi sheikh from Sri Lanka who established a spiritual community in Philadelphia in the 1970s. Rosemarie was introduced to the Bawa Muhaiyaddeen Fellowship by Zoharah Simmons and studied the teacher's writings with special attention.

Bernice Johnson Reagon—cultural historian, activist, and song leader, Bernice was a founding member of the SNCC Freedom Singers and later organized and led the Harambee Singers and Sweet Honey in the Rock; she met Rosemarie and Vincent in the Albany Movement and lived for a time in the same house as the Hardings at the corner of Ashby and Fair streets in Atlanta.

Bertha Gober—student activist with SNCC and the Albany Movement; she was a powerful song leader and composer in the SNCC Freedom Singers.

Bob and Janet Moses—both former SNCC activists. Bob was the principal organizer-leader of the Mississippi Freedom Movement of the 1960s and currently directs the nationally recognized Algebra Project, which he founded in the 1980s; Janet recently retired as a pediatrician.

C. B. King (1923–88)—prominent Albany lawyer who defended many leaders of desegregation efforts in southwest Georgia; befriended Rosemarie and Vincent during the Albany Movement.

C. T. Vivian—an ordained minister, Vivian worked with the Nashville Student Movement and SCLC in pivotal campaigns; cofounded the Center for Democratic Renewal with Anne Braden and continues to serve as racial justice and human rights activist.

Charles Dock Freeney Jr. (1937–99)—Rosemarie's nephew, son of her brother Bud; a chef, poet, and tenor song leader who was an aide to Septima Clark at SCLC during the freedom movement, archivist with the Martin Luther King Center for Nonviolent Social Action, and librarian in the Chicago Public Libraries and at Woodruff Library of Atlanta University.

Charles H. Long—preeminent African American historian of religion whose work has influenced several generations of scholars; one of Rachel's graduate professors and mentors.

Charles Sherrod—key organizer in SNCC and director of Southwest Georgia projects for the organization; with his wife, Shirley, he founded a cooperative farming project, New Communities, and the couple continues to work on issues of social and racial justice.

Clarence and Florence Jordan (Clarence: 1912–69; Florence: d. 1987)—cofounders of Koinonia Partners, a small farming collective in southwest Georgia, created in 1942 with the intention of demonstrating Christian reconciliation, discipleship, and interracial fellowship in the context of the U.S. South.

Cleo Parker Robinson—dancer, choreographer, community organizer, and founder of Cleo Parker Robinson Dance (based in Denver), one of the premier modern dance companies in the country.

Cordell Reagon (1943–96)—activist in the Albany Movement, Cordell was one of the founders of the SNCC Freedom Singers.

Daisaku Ikeda—leader of Soka Gakkai International (SGI), a global Buddhist organization based in the tradition of Nichiren Buddhism.

David Chethlahe Paladin (1926–84)—painter, World War II veteran, and member of the Navajo nation who visited Rosemarie and Vincent's classes to talk about the role of art and forgiveness in healing.

Dhyani Ywahoo—founder and leader of the Sunray Meditation Society and chief of the Aniyunwiwa band of the Tsalagi/Cherokee people.

Diane Nash—a widely respected leader and strategist of the Nashville Student Movement and SNCC; Nash was deeply committed to the transformative power of nonviolent direct action.

Dorothy Cotton—educator, facilitator, and activist; Cotton served as education director for SCLC for most of the 1960s.

Dorothy Swisshelm—a psychiatric social worker who joined the Koinonia community in Americus, Georgia, in the late 1950s.

Eddy Van der Hilst—Surinamese linguist and scholar of Afro-Surinamese culture and religion; met Rosemarie, Vincent, and Rachel in 1992 at an ecumenical gathering in New Mexico.

Edgar Metzler—head of the Mennonite Central Committee (MCC) Peace Section in the early 1960s when Rosemarie and Vincent were representatives of the Mennonite Church to the Southern Freedom Movement.

Efua Sutherland (1924–96)—Ghanaian playwright, pan-Africanist, director, and children's book author; was married for a time to antiwar activist Bill Sutherland, through whom Rosemarie met Efua.

Elizabeth Catlett Mora (1915–2012)—acclaimed sculptor and printmaker whose work particularly celebrated the strength and power of African American women.

Ella Baker (1903–86)—civil and human rights activist who had a profound influence on the founding of SNCC and the development of youth leadership within the freedom movement; a lifelong community organizer, Baker was an important inspiration for Rosemarie, who conducted extensive oral interviews with Baker in the late 1970s.

Enid Cox—social worker, educator, and community activist; Rosemarie's professor at the University of Denver School of Social Work.

Fannie Lou Hamer (1917–77)—former sharecropper and widely respected grassroots activist in the Southern Freedom Movement; one of the founders of the Mississippi Freedom Democratic Party. After receiving a severe beating in Winona, Mississippi, Mrs. Hamer stayed at Mennonite House a while to recover.

Fu-kiau Bunseki (1934–2013)—Congolese philosopher, writer, ritual healer, and archivist whom Rosemarie met through their mutual friend, Makota Valdina Pinto. Dr. Fu-kiau visited with Rachel and Rosemarie when they lived in Cambridge.

George H. Bass (1938–90)—playwright, philosopher, and educator; taught for many years at Brown University where he cofounded the Rites and Reason Theater. He and his wife Ramona were friends of Rosemarie and Vincent. George was also Rachel's professor.

Gloria Anzaldua (1942–2004)—Chicana feminist scholar and writer whose works addressed many intersections of social justice struggle and personal/collective identity.

Grace Lee Boggs (1915–2015)—longtime community activist in Detroit, Michigan; she and her late husband, Jimmy Boggs (1919–93), influenced several generations of radical community activism. The Boggs and Hardings were good friends and comrades.

Gwendolyn Zoharah Simmons—friend of Rosemarie and Vincent from the Atlanta days; leader of SNCC project in Laurel, Mississippi, in 1964. Zoharah introduced Rosemarie to Bawa Muhaiyaddeen and his spiritual community in Philadelphia in the late 1970s.

H. Rap Brown (Jamil Abdullah Al-Amin)—was successor to Stokely Carmichael (Kwame Ture) as chairman of SNCC; converted to Islam in prison and became an imam and community leader in Atlanta after his release. Currently serving life in prison based on a questionable conviction.

Harriet Tubman (1820–1913)—legendary conductor of the Underground Railroad who led hundreds of enslaved people to freedom and served as a scout, planner, and nurse for the Union Army in the Civil War.

Howard Thurman (1899–1981)—African American writer, mystic, and theologian. He was the first black chaplain at Boston University and was a mentor to Martin Luther King Jr.; Thurman was cofounder of the Church of the Fellowship of All Peoples, San Francisco's first interracial congregation.

Howard Zinn (1922–2010)—renowned Americanist historian and outspoken social justice activist. Former chair of the Department of History and Social Sciences at Spelman College who became an adviser to SNCC during the movement.

Ida B. Wells-Barnett (1862–1931)—the major antilynching activist of the late nineteenth and early twentieth centuries, Wells-Barnett was an editor and publisher who lobbied incessantly for an end to racist violence. In the late 1970s, Rosemarie researched and wrote a master's thesis on the pioneering advocate.

James Bevel (1936–2008)—student organizer in the Nashville Student Movement and later an important strategist with SNCC and SCLC.

John and June Yungblut—Quaker friends of Rosemarie and Vincent; they founded Quaker House in the 1950s, an Atlanta-based peace and social justice project.

Jonathan Daniels (1939–65)—Episcopalian seminarian killed in Hayneville, Alabama, for his participation in the Southern Freedom Movement.

Julia Esquivel—Guatemalan poet who was exiled during the years of military dictatorship because of her work as a human rights activist; she was one of the early interviewees of the Veterans of Hope Project.

Julius Lester—prolific author, educator, musician, and photographer; Julius Lester was head of photography for SNCC in the late 1960s.

Katherine Dunham (1909–2006)—anthropologist, educator, writer, dancer, choreographer, and social justice activist, Dunham led one of the earliest and most successful African American modern dance companies.

Keith Block—internist and founder of the Block Medical Center; Keith's specialist colleagues in the Chicago area successfully diagnosed and began treating Rosemarie's illness.

Kofi (Herman) Bailey (1931–81)—African American artist who created posters, cards, paintings, and other artwork for freedom movement organizations. Kofi lived in Atlanta in the 1960s and was a good friend of the Freeney-Harding household.

Lama Zopa Rinpoche—Tibetan Buddhist monk, teacher, and spiritual director of the Foundation for the Preservation of the Mahayana Tradition; one of the major teachers of Tibetan Buddhism in the West. Rosemarie studied with Lama Zopa in the United States and India.

Lucille Clifton (1936–2010)—African American poet, essayist, and children's book author.

Mãe Val (Iyalorixá Valnizia de Ayrá; Valnizia Pereira)—chief priestess of the Terreiro do Cobre Candomblé community in Salvador, Bahia, Brazil; Rachel's *mãe de santo*.

Makota Valdina Pinto—Makota Ngunzu (elder in charge of ritual initiation) of the Tanuri Junçara Candomblé terreiro in Salvador, Bahia, Brazil. Racial and environmental justice advocate and grassroots community historian.

Mamie Till-Mobley (1921–2003)—mother of Emmett Till, the African American youth whose martyred death in Mississippi in 1955 helped launch the civil rights movement.

Martin and Coretta King (Martin: 1929–68; Coretta: 1927–2006)—the eminent leaders of the Southern Freedom Movement; neighbors, friends, and colleagues of Rosemarie and Vincent during the early 1960s.

Mary Bixler—a volunteer who lived and worked at Mennonite House in the early 1960s.

Marion and Slater King (Marion: 1932–2007; Slater: 1927–69)—local leaders in the Albany Movement who became close friends of Rosemarie and Vincent; Slater was also a real estate broker and entrepreneur; his wife, Marion, became a lawyer and conflict resolution specialist.

Maurilio Gonzalez—santero who was also a caretaker at Grandma's Rose Garden Inn in Berkeley, California, in the mid-1990s, when Rosemarie stayed there during her Feldenkrais trainings.

Michael Eric Dyson—scholar, minister, and public intellectual who writes and lectures widely on issues of racial and social justice.

Michio Kushi—a pioneering teacher of macrobiotic diet and philosophy in the West; cofounder with Aveline Kushi of the Kushi Institute in Massachusetts where Rosemarie studied macrobiotic nutrition.

Mwalimu Imara—Episcopal priest and pastoral counselor; Imara assisted Elisabeth Kübler-Ross in the early development of her death and dying seminars.

Ndugu T'Ofori Atta (1924–2012)—Pan-Africanist Christian educator, theologian, and AME Zion minister whose approach was deeply influenced by his commitment to nonviolence and love of diasporan ritual and cultural traditions.

Nelson and Joyce Johnson—lifelong labor and human rights activists who founded the Beloved Community Center in Greensboro, North Carolina; they established the country's first "Truth and Reconciliation Commission" as a way to address and heal the profound violence of the 1979 massacre that occurred in the city.

Paramahansa Yogananda (1893–1952)—internationally renowned Indian yogi and spiritual teacher; Rosemarie was introduced to Yogananda's Self-Realization Fellowship by Bob and Janet Moses in the early 1980s and for many years studied the teachings and meditation techniques.

Prathia Hall (1940–2002)—SNCC activist, educator, and womanist theologian; Rosemarie met Prathia in the Albany Movement.

Rabbi Abraham Joshua Heschel (1907–72)—renowned Jewish philosopher and theologian whose teachings on peace, social justice, and interreligious understanding resonated deeply with Rosemarie.

Rachel B. Noel (1918–2008)—educator, political activist, and spiritual elder in the Denver community; she was the first African American woman elected to public office in Colorado and was a dear friend to Rosemarie and Vincent.

Ralph Featherstone (1939–70)—SNCC activist who, with his coworker William "Che" Payne, was killed by a car bomb possibly meant for H. Rap Brown.

Ronald Arky—endocrinologist and professor of medicine at Harvard Medical School. Dr. Arky was Rosemarie's physician during the year she lived in Cambridge, Massachusetts, and was tremendously kind.

Ronald Takaki (1939–2009)—scholar of the multicultural history of the United States whose books Rosemarie and Vincent used in workshops on themes of racial reconciliation, democracy, and healing.

Ruby Doris Smith (1942–67)—dedicated racial justice activist and first female executive secretary of SNCC; she died of a rare blood disease.

Ruby Sales—human rights advocate, writer, and social critic who was a member of SNCC in Alabama; founder and director of the SpiritHouse Project that trains young activists in social justice organizing and public policy work.

Sammy Younge Jr. (1944–66)—Tuskegee Institute student and activist in the Southern Freedom Movement who was murdered by a gas station attendant for using a white's-only bathroom.

Septima Clark (1898–1987)—community activist and educator who directed the literacy and citizenship education workshops program at the Highlander Folk School and later continued that work through the Citizenship Schools of the Southern Christian Leadership Conference; Clark lived at Mennonite House with the Hardings in the early 1960s.

Shirley Graham DuBois (1896–1977)—writer, activist, and advocate for racial and social justice, Graham DuBois was also the widow of activist-scholar W. E. B. DuBois; she visited with Rosemarie and Vincent in Atlanta.

Sister Souljah (Lisa Williamson)—author, recording artist, and hip-hop community activist who worked with the United Church of Christ Commission for Racial Justice and organized the National African Youth-Student Alliance. She participated in the first "Spirit and Struggle" retreat organized by the Hardings.

Sonia Sanchez—poet, playwright, educator, and advocate for racial and gender justice and human rights; Sanchez and her sons lived briefly with the Hardings when they first moved to Philadelphia in the 1970s and remained close to the family.

Staughton and Alice Lynd—longtime friends of Rosemarie and Vincent who are labor and peace activists. Staughton taught at Spelman College and was director of the SNCC Freedom Schools during Mississippi Summer, 1964.

Sue Bailey Thurman (1904–96)—journalist, editor, librarian and organizer of African American women's associations, Sue Bailey Thurman was a lifelong advocate for racial reconciliation and international understanding; second wife of theologian Howard Thurman. The Thurmans and the Hardings were good friends.

Thomas Banyacya (1909–99)—a spiritual leader from the Hopi nation who was selected by his elders to communicate and interpret the traditional prophecies to the wider world. The Hardings met him in the early 1980s when they moved west and traveled to New Mexico.

Thupten Kunsang—a Tibetan monk from the Sermey Monastery in Karnataka, India; Rosemarie met him in Dharamsala and they informally adopted each other as mother and son.

Tom Feelings (1933–2003)—award-winning artist, illustrator, educator, and community activist whose work explored and celebrated the tenacity and beauty of African and African American culture and history.

Victoria Jackson Gray Adams (1926–2006)—Southern Freedom Movement veteran who helped found the Council of Federated Organizations and the Mississippi Freedom Democratic Party, and challenged the seating of the all-white Mississippi delegation at the 1964 Atlantic City Democratic Party convention.

Vincent G. Harding (1931–2014)—Historian, activist and educator. Rosemarie's husband and partner in more than forty years of movement work, teaching, writing, and community-building—including the establishment of Mennonite House and the Veterans of Hope Project. Jonathan and Rachel's father.

Wazir (Willie) Peacock (1937–2016)—freedom movement veteran who was active in SNCC in Mississippi in the early and mid-1960s; he later moved to California and became a natural-healing practitioner and massage therapist.

Will Campbell (1924–2013)—a southern-born white Baptist minister who became a staunch supporter of the freedom movement. He was southern field director of the National Council of Churches, directed the Committee of Southern Churchmen, and published the magazine *Katallegete*.

William "Che" Payne—SNCC activist who was killed in 1970 with Ralph Featherstone by a car bomb apparently meant for H. Rap Brown.

ACKNOWLEDGMENTS

The good of this book is a collective good. I have many people to thank for their help with this project. Poet Marion Bethel, editor Brooke Warner, and two anonymous readers gave significant time and attention to the text. Their multiple readings and recommendations benefitted the work considerably. Friends and family over more than ten years showed me tremendous encouragement and support. I am grateful to the women of the 1997–98 Bunting Institute cohort of fellows—especially Indira Ganesan, Carol Ockman, and again, Marion Bethel. Renny Harrigan, who was the Institute's associate director, did much to enable my presence with my mother in that pivotal year in Cambridge. Paul and Lois King shared photographs and stories while Linda Mizell and Roger Clendening; Ruby Sales and Cheryl Blankenship; Deb Sanchez (in memoriam); Daniel and Marcia Minter; Linda Somers; Lorelei Williams; Isabel Cristina Ferreira dos Reis; Cristina Brayner; Kathy Garcia O'Brien; Al Zook, Kerry Kurt, Shirley Strong, Arleth Monteiro, and Nate Williams all listened to ideas and chapters and helped me recognize that I was on the right road.

I thank Sterling Stuckey, Stacy M. Floyd-Thomas, Joanna Shenk, Toni Cook (in memoriam), Kate Ott, and Rose Marie Berger for providing opportunities for me to tell some of my mother's story along the way to this book—with special gratitude to Melanie Harris and Alice Walker. I'm indebted to my editors Miriam Angress and Jessica Ryan who appreciated the narrative, valued its unusual format, and gently guided the book through the publication process at Duke University Press. I'm also grateful for the generosity of Donna Martinez and my colleagues in the Department of Ethnic Studies at the University of Colorado, Denver.

Members of the extended Harris-Freeney clan readily shared memories, pictures, and love. Without them the book would have been much poorer. I thank especially Auntie Mildred Dozier, Auntie Alma Campbell, Cousin Charles Freeney, Cousin Pansy Daniels, and Cousin Joe Daniels (all of whom are on the other side now), and my mother's remaining living sibling—my Aunt Sue Verrett. My cousin Gloria Smith moved to Denver to direct the Veterans of Hope Project and to ensure that I would finish *Remnants*. Gloria and her sister, Jean Campbell, who were raised with their Aunt Rose, were consistent sounding boards and shared my excitement at every discovery of new information about my mother's life and the history of the family. This book is for all of the Harris-Freeney and Broome people, in honor of the elders and especially for the generation of my younger cousins, so that you will know some of the history that belongs to you and so that you will learn more stories and pass them on to the children who come after you. I thank my brother, Jonathan, for the benefit of his insights, the relief of his humor, and for his high opinion of his sister's work.

I also thank my Iyalorixá, Valnizia de Ayrá; Makota Valdina Pinto; and Marilene Pulfira de Jesus Cruz, three women among my many elders in Candomblé who have guided me with special care and whose wisdom, I hope, is in some measure evident in the spirit of these pages.

On May 19, 2014, in the University of Pennsylvania Hospital in Philadelphia, my father died. He was eighty-two years old and I was not ready. The time we had for the words we needed to say to one another was foreshortened but Daddy would not stop squeezing our hands, calling and praising our family ancestors, thanking us for the joy of waking from surgery to our faces, and singing the old hymns in a final, stunning, bedside communion with my brother and me a few days before he passed. *We have strong ancestors!* Mama Jean told me they came for him, the strong ones. "They standing all around your Daddy." And we, on this side of the river, felt the oddness of the time, but we were still not ready. This book was finished and on its way to production when Daddy died. And while I had shared sections of the text with my father over the years, and depended on his memory to verify details of the early years of his life with my mother, he did not know I had finally found a publisher for *Remnants*.

My father was my first model as a writer. He taught me scholarship and gave me as much of his incisive love for language as I could absorb. Daddy could intuit the homelands of strangers he met on the street from their last names or their accented English. And he absolutely loved writing. My father's essays were painstaking and lyrically potent and, in college, I found myself writing papers in which his voice was like a guide to my own—sturdy training wheels for my wobbly, early two-wheeler texts. He was my first reference. Generous with his knowledge and supportive of me in so many ways, I honor my father's spirit and I thank him for singing with me and for remembering.

Finally, I am grateful to my orixás and to my mother's eternal guidance and blessings. *Thank you, Mama.*

RACHEL ELIZABETH HARDING
DENVER, COLORADO
AUGUST 2014

INDEX

Mennonite House (Atlanta, Georgia), xiii, xxii, 120, 127–138, 140; co-leadership of with Vincent Harding, 128–131, 138; as community center, 128; kinship with Koinonia, 18, 148; relationships with neighbors, 131–132; as retreat and healing space, 120, 130, 133–134

Mennonites/Mennonite Church, xii–xiii, 2, 16, 56, 128, 140–141, 157; African Americans among, xiii, 157

Merton, Thomas, xii

Metzler, Edgar, 131

Middle Passage, 11

Middleton, Catherine (Aunt Bey), 72

Mississippi, 43, 118, 141, 220–221, 249

mitochondria, 233, 269

Mizell, Linda, 215

Montgomery (Alabama), 147, 269

Moore, Amzie, 222

Moses, Bob, 118, 165, 167, 171, 188, 209, 220

Moses, Janet, 220

mother-daughter relationship: Rosemarie and Rachel, xix, 206, 207, 215, 224–226

mothering, xvi, 196, 230, 235, 238, 240; as activism, ix; against Freud, 219; as indigenous wisdom, xi, xiv; circle of, 239

Movement, the. *See* Southern Freedom Movement

Muckalee Creek, 15

Murray, Lilla Freeney (Aunt Sut), 72

Muslim Americans, scapegoated, 223

mysticism, xiv, xx–xxii, 62; African-based, xv, 241; Black southern, xviii; family traditions of, 13, 236, 241; silence and, 13–14; social justice activism and, 168

Naikan/Morita Therapy, x; specific techniques of, 219–220

Nana Burukû (orixá), 234

Naropa Institute, seeing Dalai Lama at, 192–193

Nash, Diane, 171

Nation of Islam, 132–133

National Baptist Church, 72

National Geographic (magazine), article on Underground Railroad for, 11

Native Americans, 12, 94, 165, 269; as ancestors, 18; Cherokee, 73; Choctaw, 73; help given to Harriet Tubman, 223;

Hopi, xiv; indigenous wisdom of, 215; Navajo, 223

natural environment, Rosemarie's connection to, 63–65

Negro Women's Club movement, 247

Nicaragua, 173, 175

Noel, Rachel, 235

nommo, 224

nonviolence, 2, 56, 140–141, 151; danger of romanticizing, 160; as a spiritual value, 157–159; tool for building inclusivity, 169

nursing, family tradition of, 121; Rosemarie's interest in, 2, 96, 98, 104

Oakland (California), 206

Ockman, Carol, 215

orixás, xviii, xxiv, 110, 213

Ortega, Daniel, 175

Oyá (orixá), xxii, 213

Pachamamas (Spirit mothers), xxii, 113, 233–240; Rachel's dream of, 229–230

Paladin, David Chethlahe, 223

Parada, Esther, 215

Paramahansa Yogananda, xii, 171

passing (for white), 139

Payne, Che, 175

Peacock, Wazir (Willie), 171

Pereira, Valnizia (Valnizia de Ayrá), 220, 226n1

Pinto, Makota Valdina, xiii, 214, 220

Poulan (Georgia), 117

powwows, 225

preservatives, in food, 93

prison camps, 253

Qigong, 238

Quaker House, 131

Quakers, xii, 134

racial justice, xxiii, 128, 157, 162n1, 211, 252

Radcliff, Miss (Rosemarie's teacher), 78

Reagon, Bernice Johnson, xx, xxii, 118, 163, 269; on alchemy of movement singing, 122–123; singing for Aunt Hettie, 164; singing in mass meetings, 155, 162n2; on transformative power of congregational singing, 170–171